D0898754

In Search of Guidance

In Search of Guidance

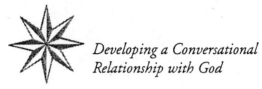

*Developing a Conversational
Relationship with God*

DALLAS WILLARD

Wipf and Stock Publishers
150 West Broadway • Eugene OR 97401

396330110

To Jane Lakes Willard
sweet lady,
good soldier,
faithful companion on the way

Dylan Thomas: *Poems of Dylan Thomas*. Copyright © 1939 by New Directions
Publishing Corporation. Reprinted by permission of New Directions Publishing
Corporation.
For Bible source citations see next page.

In Search of Guidance: *Developing a Conversational Relationship with God*
By Dallas Willard

Copyright© 1993 by Dallas Willard.

ISBN: 1-57910-028-7

Printed by *Wipf and Stock Publishers*
150 West Broadway • Eugene OR 97401

Contents

Preface   ix

1. A "Paradox" Concerning Divine Guidance   1

2. Guidelines to Guidance   20

3. Never Alone   34

4. Our Communicating Cosmos   59

5. The Still Small Voice and Its Rivals   87

6. The Word of God and the Rule of God   122

7. Redemption Through the Word of God   153

8. Recognizing the Voice of God   178

9. Guidance and Beyond: A Life More Than Guidance   208

Epilogue: The Way of the Burning Heart   234

Index   241

✳ *Preface*

Among the loneliest of moments is the time of *decision*. There the weight of our future life clamps down on our hearts. Whatever comes will now be our responsibility, "our fault." Good things we have set our hearts on become real only as we choose them. But those things, or those as yet undreamed of, may also be irretrievably lost if our choice is misguided. We may find ourselves saddled with failures and dreadful consequences that must be carried for life.

And soon there follows the time of second thoughts—and third and fourth. Did I do the good and wise thing? Is it what God wanted? Is it even what I wanted? Can I live with the consequences? Will others think I am a fool? Is God still with me? Will he be with me even if it becomes clear I made the wrong choice?

While we are young, desire, impulse, and personal associations may blithely carry us through choices that would paralyze us ten years later. In the bloom of youth, we just do "what we *have* to do" or whatever "turns us on." How simple it is! Often we are not even conscious of choosing.

But after collecting a few disasters, learning that actions are forever, that opportunities seldom return, and that consequences are relentless, we hungrily cry: "Thy will be done on earth as it is in heaven!" More than any general concern for "world affairs" to conform to his will, our prayer expresses the burning need for God to be a constant guiding presence in our individual lives.

This book is written for those who already believe that there is a personal God, present throughout our world and deeply concerned about what becomes of us. It does not attempt to prove that there is such a God, though what it says may help open-minded people find him for themselves.

The main point is that God has created us for intimate friendship with himself, both now and forever. This is the Christian viewpoint, as is made clear throughout the Bible and especially in such passages as Exodus 29:43–46 and 33:11, Psalm 23, Isaiah 41:8, John 15:14, and Hebrews 13:5–6.

As with close personal relationships in general, we may count on God to speak to each of us when and as it is appropriate. What this means and how it works is the task of the following pages to make clear.

Needless to say, many prejudgments and misconceptions about God, the individual soul, and their relationship must be removed if we are to be successful. Please don't be impatient with the work to be done. As you read this book you will be dealing with matters of tremendous significance for good and evil in your own life and for your ability to help others.

We all live at the mercy of our ideas. This is never truer than for our ideas about God. Those who operate on wrong information will very likely never come to know the reality of God's presence in the decisions that shape their lives. They will miss the divine companionship for which their souls were made. The model for divine guidance we will be looking to is communication and guidance at its best among human beings at their best. "Their best" will be understood by reference to Jesus Christ and his followers: to Christ in his church and to the Scriptures and the history of which he is the Crown Jewel.

Although we must always keep a close eye on the actual course of human life, we must not try to judge what is possible for us as human beings merely from what we see, or think we see, in day-to-day existence. Our possibilities are to be fully revealed only from the mind of our Maker.

Archbishop William Temple has wisely written:

We do not know what Matter is when we look at Matter alone; only when Spirit dwells in Matter and uses it as a tool do we learn the capacities of Matter. The sensitiveness of eye and ear, the delicacy of the artist's touch, are achievements which we could never anticipate from the study of the lifeless. So, too, we do not know what Humanity really is, or of what achievements it is capable, until Divinity indwells in it. If we are to form a right conception of God we must look at Christ. The question is not "Is Christ Divine?" but, "What is God like?" And the answer to that is "Christ." So, too, we must not form a conception of Humanity and either ask if Christ is Human or insist on reducing Him to the limits of our conception; we must ask, "What is Humanity?" and look at Christ to find the answer. We only know what Matter is when Spirit dwells in it; we only know what Man is when God dwells in him.[1]

So our strategy will be to take the highest and best type of communication and guidance we know of from human affairs. We then place these in the even brighter light of the person and teaching of Jesus Christ. In this way we arrive at our model, or "ideal picture," of what divine guidance is meant to be.

To take this picture seriously is to exclude all tricks, mechanical formulas, and gimmickry for "finding out what God wants me to do." Indeed, the intent here is to make it clear that the subject of divine guidance cannot be successfully treated by thinking only in terms of *what God wants us to do* if that automatically excludes, as is usually assumed, *what we want to do* and even *what we want God to do.* God's guidance is but one dimension of a richly interactive relationship. It cannot be reduced to a device we use to make sure we are always right.

It may seem strange, but being in the will of God is very far removed from just doing what God wants us to do. It is so far removed, in fact, that we can be solidly in the will of God, and know that we are, without knowing God's preference with regard to various details of our lives. We can be in his will in doing certain things without his having any preference that we do *them,* as opposed to certain other possibilities.

When our children were small, they often were completely in my will as they played happily in the backyard, though I had no preference that they be doing the particular things they were doing there or even that they be in the backyard instead of in their rooms or having a snack in the kitchen. Generally speaking, we are in God's will whenever we are leading the kind of life he wants for us, which leaves a lot of room for initiative on our part.

Of course, we cannot fail to do what he directs us to do and still be in his will. And, quite apart from any specific directions he may give us, there are many ways of living and being that clearly are not in his will. The "ten commandments" given to Moses are so deep and powerful on such matters that if humanity followed them, daily life would be transformed beyond recognition and large segments of the publishing industry would collapse. Take a daily newspaper or weekly newsmagazine and eliminate from it every report that presupposes a breaking of one of the ten commandments. See how much you have left.

But the serious inquirer after divine guidance still must never forget that we could even do all the particular things God wants and commands us to do and still not be the person he would have us to be. It is always true that "the letter kills, but the spirit gives life." An obsession merely with *doing* all he commands may itself rule out our *being* the kind of person he is and calls us to be. I have witnessed many sad cases of this.

Jesus told a parable to make clear what God treasures in those who would serve him: "Will any one of you," he asked, "who has a servant plowing or keeping sheep, say to him when he has come in from the field, 'Come at once and sit down at table'? Will he not rather say to him, 'Prepare supper for me, and gird yourself and serve me, till I eat and drink; and afterward you shall eat and drink'? Does he thank the servant because he then does what was commanded? So you also, when you have done all that is commanded you, say, 'We are unworthy servants; we have only done what was our duty'" (Lk 17:7–10, RSV; compare Mt 5:20). The watchword of the worthy servant is not obedience, but love, from which obedience naturally flows.

Much of what you will read here is mere elaboration on this parable. Of course, I hope to be of some service to those who continue to think only in terms of doing what they are commanded. But for all the good that is in that attitude, it remains the attitude of the "unprofitable servant." And it severely limits spiritual growth, when measured against the possibilities of a life of free-hearted collaboration with Jesus and his friends in the Kingdom of the Heavens.

Moreover, it is only as we are firmly gripped by a true picture of a life of divine guidance on the Way with Jesus and are moving by experience deeper and deeper into its reality that we shall be able strongly but calmly to resist the mistakes and abuses of religious authority. From the local congregation to the highest levels of national and international influence, people and groups claim that they have been divinely guided to direct us in what we are to do. This direction is often benign and correct, both in intention and outcome. But not always.

An appropriate response to misuse of religious authority will be available to those who have an understanding of how individualized divine guidance, on the one hand, and individual or corporate authority, on the other, meld together in Jesus' community of transforming love. We need large numbers of people, distributed throughout our various populations, who without arrogance are competent and confident in their own practice of his life.[2]

Such people would concretely redefine a Christian *spirituality* for our times. They would show us an individual and corporate human existence freely and intelligently *lived* from a face-to-face conversational relationship with God. That is the biblical ideal for human life.

The pages that follow deal with divine guidance as it bears on a *life* in the will of God: on the question of who God wants us to be as well as, where appropriate, on the question of what he wants us to do. What he wants us to do is very important, and we must be careful to learn how to know it and do it. But such knowledge is never enough by itself to allow us to understand and enter that radiant life before the shining face of God, which is offered to us in the grace of the gospel: a life pleasing to him, in view of which he can say, "This is my beloved child, in whom I am well pleased."

Several people have worked with me on this material. Above all, Raymond Neal has devoted much mental and physical labor to this project over the years and thoughtfully and critically typed the entire book into his computer. Beth Weber's thoughtful editorial work has made this a much better book, as has that of Evelyn Mercer Ward and Mimi Kusch.

The material was drawn into its original form because of an invitation from Pastor Gary Smith, now of blessed memory, to present it in an evening series at Woodland Hills Presbyterian Church.

More than any others, I suspect, the congregants at Valley Vista Christian Community in Van Nuys, California, with their pastor, Dr. Larry Burtoft, have really tried to put these ideas to the test. I am grateful to them for their loving fellowship and encouragement.

Notes

1. William Temple, "The Divinity of Christ," in *Foundations,* ed. H. B. Streeter (London: Macmillan, 1920), 258–59.
2. I do not in this book deal with the topic of corporate guidance. One of the most helpful writings known to me on this subject is secton 2 of Danny E. Morris's *Yearning to Know God's Will* (Grand Rapids, MI: Zondervan, 1991). See also the excellent chapter 12 of Richard Foster's *Celebration of Discipline,* Rev. ed. (San Francisco: Harper & Row, 1988.)

In Search of Guidance

I · A *"Paradox"* Concerning Divine Guidance

There is not in the world a kind of life more sweet and delightful than that of a continual conversation with God. Those only can comprehend it who practice and experience it; yet I do not advise you to do it from that motive. It is not pleasure which we ought to seek in this exercise; but let us do it from a principle of love, and because God would have us.

BROTHER LAWRENCE[1]

God Speaks to Me?

Sunday dinner was finished, but we lingered around the table, savoring the good food and reflecting on the morning's service at church. The congregation at which I then served as a very young and very green assistant pastor was excited about its plans for a new sanctuary to replace its old building, much loved but long outgrown and overused.

The morning message had focused on plans for a new building. Our pastor spoke of his vision for the increased ministry of the church. He indicated how strongly he felt God's guidance in the direction the congregation was going and testified that God had *spoken* to him about things that should be done.

My wife's grandmother, Mrs. Lucy Latimer ("Mema" to us all), seemed deep in thought as we continued to chatter along. Finally, she quietly said, "I wonder why God never speaks to me like that."

This simple comment, coming from the heart of a woman of unshakable faith and complete devotion, forever changed my attitude toward glib talk about God speaking to us or about divine guidance. Through her words, in a way I came to recognize only later, *God* spoke to me.

I was given a vivid realization that was never to leave me of the extent to which such talk places many sincere Christians "on the outside looking in." Not that their experience is lacking. But they do not understand the language. And this lack of understanding leaves them feeling confused and deficient and may lead them to play a game they don't really understand, which rightly makes them very uncomfortable. This situation undermines their confidence that they are fully acceptable to God.

Mema, in fact, had a richly interactive life with God, as we all knew. But because of inadequate teaching, she had not been able to relate her experience of God's presence in her life—of which she was completely certain—to the idea of God speaking with her. This left her at a loss for how to deal with the conversational side of her friendship with God.

To that point in my own experience, I had simply assumed that if you were really Christian, God spoke to you as a matter of course, and that you knew it. I was sure that he spoke individually and specifically about what he wanted each believer to do and that he also taught and made real on an individual basis the general truths all must believe in order to enter life with him.

The Moving of God

Later, I came to realize that this confidence came from a series of revival meetings in which I was immersed as a young man in high school. During those meetings I became accustomed to interacting with a characteristic type of thought and impulse, which was to me the moving of God on my mind and heart. It was an experience clearly marked out for me and one that guided my actions, though I held no theory or doctrine about it.

Then, as I subsequently grew into the Christian ministry, I learned to wait on "the Word of God" to come to me. In the most primary of senses, the Word of God is simply *God speaking*. I also learned to expect his speaking to come through me to others. Experience taught me to identify a remarkable difference between when it was "just me" talking, or even "just me" quoting and discussing Scripture, and when a certain "something more" was taking place. Jeremiah's comparisons of God's Word to wheat over against the chaff, and to a fire, or a hammer that crushes rock, all came to describe something with which I was very familiar (Jer 23:28–29).

Through their writings, such great Christians of the past as John Calvin[2] and William Law[3] had the ministry of Eli to me. (See the story in 1 Sm 3:8–9.) These writings gave me further insight into what was happening in my experiences and why it was happening. They helped me identify and respond to experiences of God speaking, just as Eli helped Samuel.

They also gave me assurance that the same Spirit who delivered the Scriptures unto "holy men of old" speaks today in the hearts of those who gather around the written Word to minister and to be ministered unto. And they also warned me that *only if* the Spirit spoke in my heart could I avoid being just another more-or-less clever "letter-learned scribe" trying to nourish the souls of my hearers out of the contents of my own brains, giving them only what *I* was able to work up though my own search in the Bible or elsewhere.

But it was not easy for me to see that our most sacred experiences often blind us. The very light that makes it possible for us to see may also dazzle our eyes to the clearest of sights or make it impossible to see what lies in shadow. Caught up in my own experiences of God's voice, I really did not understand its workings at all. I only knew its reality and thoughtlessly assumed that it was a functioning, intelligible fact in every believer's life.

So I was for a long while unable to appreciate the huge problems that the very idea of God's speaking to us created for some of the most faithful adherents of the church, not to mention those entirely outside of it.

When someone seemed to have difficulty with divine guidance, I simply passed it off as a sign of weakness of faith or even of rebellion. Yet I could not entirely avoid awareness that the most faithful and devout of Christians often can make no sense of a "divine guidance" that comes in forms other than the necessities imposed on us by circumstances.

I saw such individuals driven to turn all "guidance" into blind force and treat "God's will" as nothing but fate. And I was distressed at how often people identified some brutal event as God's will, even when it clearly came from a decision made by human beings. They then easily moved on to the faith-destroying, even blasphemous, idea that everything that happens in this world is caused by God.

The Ongoing Conversation

Today I continue to believe that people are meant to live in an intermittent but ongoing conversation with God. When it is rightly understood, I believe that this can be proven in experience. The visits of God with Adam and Eve in the garden, Enoch's walks with God, the face-to-face conversations between Moses and Jehovah, as these are referred to in the Bible, are commonly regarded as highly exceptional moments in the religious history of humankind.

Aside from their obvious historical significance, these events are not meant to be exceptional at all. Rather, they are examples of what normal human life was intended by God to be: the carnate habitation of a spiritual God, God indwelling his people through personal fellowship. We live—really live—only by the constant speaking of God in our souls and thus "by every word which proceeds out of the mouth of God."

During the months engaged in the writing of this book, I have made a special point of drawing others out in conversation concerning their experiences with divine guidance. When a spirit of acceptance is established, and it is clear that the topic is to be dealt with seriously, then the stories begin to flow. And as understanding and confidence grow, other cases come to mind that are seen to be, or to contain, a "word" from God to the individual. Many might be surprised to discover what a high percentage of serious Christians, or even non-Christians, can tell of specific experiences in which they are sure God spoke to them.

Of course talking *to* God is an almost universal practice. The words "Talking to God: An Intimate Look at the Way We Pray" appeared on the cover of *Newsweek* for January 6, 1992. The main article is devoted to recent sociological studies of the practice of prayer in the United States.

The results? "This week . . . more of us will pray than will go to work, or exercise, or have sexual relations. . . . 78 percent of all Americans pray at least once a week; more than half (57 percent) report praying at least once a day. . . . Even among the 13 percent of Americans who are atheists or agnositics, nearly one in five still prays daily" (p. 39).

As these studies also found, it is widely recognized that a major part of prayer is listening to God and "letting God direct me." And such direction is widely claimed. But those who experience a directing word from God rarely speak about it. Often they have never spoken of it at all, even to their closest friends.

The UFO Syndrome

And is it not with good reason that we hesitate to speak about experiences we yet feel compelled to regard as God speaking to us? Similarly, those who think they have sighted UFOs, or those who have had the after-death experiences much discussed in recent years, soon learn to keep their mouths shut. They know that they may single themselves out for unwanted attention if they are not very careful.

Perhaps they will be regarded as crazy. And since *those* experiences really are strange and very hard to interpret, they genuinely fear being misguided. They do not wish to "go public" with something that might just be a mistake on their part. They also fear being thought of as arrogant, as taking themselves to be "someone special" or, to borrow language the Apostle Paul used about his experiences, as being "exalted above measure through the abundance of the revelations" (2 Cor 12:7).

Similar doubts and hesitations justifiably trouble those who feel they are spoken to by God. "Why is it," comedienne Lily Tomlin asks, "that when we speak to God we are said to be praying, but when God speaks to us we are said to be schizophrenic?"

Such a response, from us or others, is especially likely today just because of the lack of specific teaching or pastoral guidance available in such matters. Indeed, like the Sadducees of old, many churches discourage the very thought that God *would* speak to the individual. And some leaders obviously prefer that he speak only to them and not to their flock. After all, it is well known that people become prone to all sorts of errors and become quite unmanageable once "God starts talking to them."

Guidance Is There for Our Leaders

Faced with such inner fears and such a lack of teaching—or even with explicit denial or discouragement—disciples of Christ today may be somewhat encouraged by another message that emanates from their surroundings. For they are also constantly confronted with suggestions or implications that ideally we should be engaged in communications with God, just like our leaders.

Certainly our Christian leaders do commonly indicate that God has spoken to them. And precisely *because* they are our leaders, there is a strong suggestion that we should strive to be like them. Here are a few cases selected almost at random:

The internationally known Methodist evangelist and faith healer Oral Roberts informed his audiences some time ago that he had had a seven-hour talk with Jesus through which, "in that calm voice I have heard so many times before," he received instructions for a fundraising plan that would lead to a discovery of a cure for cancer.[4]

David Wilkerson, highly successful and well-known author and minister, records that in the summer of 1973 he had a "vision of five tragic calamities coming upon the earth. I saw no blinding lights, I heard no audible voices, nor did I hear from an angel. While I was in prayer late one night, these visions of world calamities came over me with such impact that I could do nothing but kneel, transfixed, and take it all in."[5]

In a television interview on January 31, 1983, Dr. Ken Taylor, who produced the widely used version of the Scriptures known as *The Living Bible,* told how he had been concerned about children having a Bible that they could easily understand. According to his statement, one afternoon "God revealed" to him "the idea of a thought-for-thought translation instead of word-for-word." This idea worked so well that such versions have now been published in many languages around the world.

Joyce Landorf, a popular Christian writer and speaker, tells in one of her books about a conflict with one of her daughters who was engaged in an unhappy love relationship. For four years the struggle continued. Then, "in November of that fourth year, I told the Lord that Thanksgiving would be the day we would all talk to Laurie. We, as her immediate family, would tell her she had to break off this devastating relationship. We would not stand by and watch her go over a cliff and destroy herself any longer. I asked the Lord for the right words. Instead of giving me the appropriate remarks, He commanded sternly, 'Be quiet.'

"I told Him I didn't think He knew how long this had gone on or how serious the whole thing had become, and asked again what He wanted me to say. Once more, the Lord said, 'I want you to be quiet.'"

But she wasn't quiet. She disobeyed the Lord's instruction and it led to a severe alienation between her daughter Laurie and the rest of the family. Laurie walked out. Mrs. Landorf records that then "clearly I heard the Lord say, 'I *told* you to be quiet.'"[6]

Very commonly it is in times of great inward distress that we hear the voice of God directed specifically to us. In the 1640s George Fox, founder of the Friends, or the Quaker movement, wandered the fields and byways of the English countryside, seeking someone who could show him the way to peace with God. But he finally became convinced that "there was none among them all that could speak to my condition. And when all my hopes in them and in all men were gone, so that I had nothing outwardly to help me, nor could I tell what to do; then, oh! then I heard a voice which said, 'There is one, even Jesus Christ, that can speak to thy condition'; and when I heard it, my heart did leap for joy. Then the Lord did let me see why there was none upon the earth that could speak to my condition, namely, that I might give Him all the glory."[7]

In Book VIII of his *Confessions,* St. Augustine, who lived from 354 to A.D. 430, tells how in a similarly distraught condition he "heard from a neighbouring house a voice, as of boy or girl, I know not, chanting, and oft repeating, 'Take up and read. Take up and read.'" He could remember no child's game with these words. "So, checking the torrent of my tears, I arose; interpreting it to be no other than a command from God, to open the book, and read the first chapter I should find." Thus he came upon Romans 13.13—14. His condition was immediately transformed, as was Fox's centuries later, and one of the greatest and most influential of all Christians entered the Kingdom of the Heavens.

A weekly publication from a large local church tells us that the pastor "has been given a bold vision by our Lord." The vision is that every person in the entire geographical area where the church is located should be called to Christ in a one-year period by a telephone call from some person in the church. This is not described as a bright idea that struck the pastor, but as a vision communicated to him by God. And of course that makes all the difference in the world in its meaning for the congregation the pastor leads.

I cite these cases here not because they are exceptional, but precisely because *they are so common.* There is a practically endless supply of such stories. They vary in detail as we move from one denominational tradition to another. But they are to some degree present in all Christian communions except those that have moved beyond theological liberalism into simple humanism. (I should add that I frequently find in the most liberal of groups many people to whom "talking with God" is an ordinary event.)

But then we should expect nothing else, given the words of the scriptural record and the heritage of the Christian Church. As Christians we stand in a millennia-long tradition of humans being addressed by God. The ancient Israelites heard the voice of their God speaking to them out of the midst of fire (Dt 4:33). A regular place of communion and conversational interchange between the high priest and God was established in the "mercy seat" over the ark of God (Ex 25:22; see also Lk 1:11–21).

But the individual with faith among the Israelites also cried out expectantly to be taught by God: "Teach me to do thy will; for thou art my God: thy spirit is good; lead me into the land of uprightness" (Ps 143:10). The experience of Israel led the prophet Isaiah, who also had firsthand experience in conversing with God (Is 6), to describe conditions of the faithful in which "then shalt thou call, and the Lord shall answer; thou shalt cry, and he shall say, 'Here I am.'. . . And the Lord shall guide thee continually" (Is 58:9, 11).

"Abiding" Includes Conversing

On the evening before his crucifixion, Jesus assured his little band of followers that, although he was leaving them, he would continue to "manifest" himself to all who loved him. Judas, who was also called Thaddeus (not Iscariot), then asked just the right question: *How* would this "manifesting" take place? Jesus' reply was that he and his Father "will come unto them, and make our abode with them" (Jn 14:23).

Now we can be sure that this "abiding" of the Son and the Father in the faithful heart involves more than conscious communication or conversation. But it surely does involve such communication, in a manner and a measure our Lord deems appropriate. It is simply beyond belief that two *persons* so intimately related, as indicated by Jesus in his answer to Thaddeus, would not speak with each other. The Spirit that inhabits us is not dumb, restricting himself to an occasional nudge, a brilliant image, or a case of goose bumps.

Such simple reasonings add a further weight to the examples set by well-known Christians, confirming us in the thought that ideally we should be engaged in personal communion with God. And we might well ask: How can there be *personal* relationships, a personal walk, with God—or with any other person—without individualized communication?

Sometimes today it seems that our personal relationship with God is treated as no more than a mere "arrangement" or "understanding" between Jesus and his Father *about* us. Our "personal relationship" then only means that believers have their own unique "accounts" in heaven that allow them to draw on the merits of Christ to pay their sin bills. Or possibly it means that God's general providence for his creation is adequate to provide for each person.

But who does not think that there should be much more to a personal relationship than this? A mere benefactor, however powerful, kind, and thoughtful, is not the same thing as a *friend*. "But I have called you friends" (Jn 15:15). And: "Look, I am with you every moment, even to the end of the age!" (Mt 28:20; compare Heb 13:5–6).

One-to-One with God

In the last analysis, nothing is more central to the practical life of the Christian than confidence in God's individual dealings with each person on a one-to-one basis. The individual care of the shepherd for his sheep, of the father or mother for the child, and of the lover for the beloved are all biblical images that have passed into the fundamental consciousness of Western humanity.

These images pervasively and essentially mark Western art and general culture as well as religion. Not only conservative and liberal Christians, high-church and Pentecostal, but also Christian and Jew, and even Jew and Muslim, come together in saying: "The Lord is *my* shepherd; *I* shall not want. *He* maketh *me* to lie down in green pastures: *he* leadeth *me* beside the still waters" (Ps 23:1–2, italics added).

The biblical record always presents relationships between God and the believer as more like friendships or familial ties than mere arrangements by one person for the needs of another. If we pass before our minds that startling array of biblical personalities from Adam to the apostles Paul and John, we behold the millennia-long saga of God himself invading human personality and history on a one-to-one basis. There is nothing "general" or secondhand about the divine encounters with Abraham, Moses, Isaiah, Nehemiah, Mary, or Peter.

The saga continues up to our own day in the lives of those recognized as leaders in the spiritual life. When, reviewing the ages, we consider a Saint Augustine, a Saint Francis of Assisi, a Martin Luther, a George Fox, a John Wesley, a C. H. Spurgeon, a D. L. Moody, a Frank Laubach, an A. W. Tozer, or a Henri Nouwen, we see in each case a person for whom personal communion *and* communication with God are regarded both as life-changing episodes *and* as daily bread.

Untold thousands of humble Christians whose names will never appear in print, who will never preach a sermon, never lead a crusade, could equally well testify to exactly the same kinds of encounters with God as are manifested in the "great ones" in the Way.

Robert C. McFarlane is a well-known businessman in the "South Bay" area of Los Angeles. He moved to California from Oklahoma in 1970, and within just a few days of his arrival—due to a disastrous misunderstanding with a very close, lifelong friend—he fell heir to an insurance agency. He did not want it, but he had to make it succeed in order to save his investment in it.

By the spring of 1973 he was in the third straight year of constant strain and stress in the operation of the business. He had recently been converted under the ministry of the Rolling Hills Covenant Church in Southern California, in answer to the prayers of his wife, Betty, and her many Christian friends.

But one day that spring the continual facing of defeat, the daylight and dark hours of effort, the frustration at every turn, and the hardened memories of the cause of his financial difficulties came on him with special force. Robert drove toward his office, facing yet another day of futility and failure but knowing he had to accomplish the absolute necessities to keep the business afloat.

Suddenly he was filled with a frantic urge to turn left onto the Harbor Freeway—and just disappear. To this day he honestly feels he was going to make that turn. How far he would have gone is, of course, unknown. But be that as it may, into the midst of his inner turmoil there came a command: "PULL OVER TO THE CURB." As he relates it, it was as if the words were written on the windshield. After pulling over, there came to him, as from someone in the car with him, these words: "My Son had strains that you will never know, and when he had those strains he turned to me, and that's what *you* should do."

After hearing these words Robert sat at the wheel for a long time, sobbing aloud. He then drove on to his Long Beach office. During that day, of the twenty-two major problems—whether they concerned company disagreements, agency clients deciding to remain with the agency, payments by clients of sizable late premiums, or whatever—all of any significance were substantially resolved by the day's end.

Wilhelm Hermann, a great theologian of the late nineteenth century, goes so far as to mark the Christian out in terms of a personal communion with God. "We hold a man to be really a Christian when we believe we have ample evidence that God has revealed Himself to him in Jesus Christ, and that now the man's inner life is taking on a new character through his communion with the God who is thus manifest."[8]

More recently, the English philosopher and theologian John Baillie wrote: "Our knowledge of God rests on the revelation of His personal presence. . . . Of such a presence it must be true that to those who have never been confronted with it argument is useless, while to those who have, it is superfluous."[9]

The faith in a God who speaks personally to the soul is nowhere recorded more plainly than in the hymns of the church, from all ages, sung week by week as we congregate and day by day as Christians go about their individual ways at work, at home, at play: "Saviour, Like a Shepherd Lead Us," "All the Way My Savior Leads Me," "Lead On, O King Eternal," "Where He Leads Me," "Lead Kindly Light," "He Leadeth Me," "Holy Spirit, Faithful Guide," "Jesus Saviour, Pilot Me," "If Thou But Suffer God to Guide Thee," " Guide Me, O Thou Great Jehovah," "Jesus, Still Lead On."

This brief list hardly begins to mention all of the hymns devoted to personal divine guidance and the conversational communion of the soul with God.

He walks with me, and He talks with me,
And He tells me I am His own,
And the joy we share as we tarry there,
None other has ever known.[10]

The Paradox

In the light of all the foregoing, it is not an exaggeration to speak of a *paradox* in the contemporary experience and understanding of divine guidance.

On the one hand, we have massive testimony to, and widespread faith in, God's personal, as opposed to merely providential and blindly controlling, guidance. Such guidance is not only recorded in Scripture and emblazoned on the history of the church, but also lies at the heart of our worship services, of our individualized relationships with God, and actually serves as the basis of authority for our teachers and leaders.

Only very rarely will one find someone who professes to teach and lead the flock of God on the basis of his or her education, natural talents, and denominational connections alone. Authority in spiritual leadership derives from a life in the Spirit, from the minister's personal encounter and ongoing relationship with God.

But on the other hand, we also find a pervasive and often painful uncertainty concerning how divine guidance works and what its place is in the church and in the Christian's life. Even those who firmly believe that they have been addressed or directly spoken to by God may be at a loss to know what is happening or what to do about it.

Poor flustered Gideon of the biblical story said to the Lord, who in some fashion stood before him, "Do something to prove that you are the one who is speaking to me!" (see Jgs 6:17).

Even if we have begged for a word from God, we may have so little clarity on what it should be like when it comes, and so little competence in dealing with it, that the communication will only add to our confusion. I believe that this is one reason why such a "word" may be withheld from us by God when it otherwise would be entirely appropriate and helpful.

The need for understanding is clearly very great. We are all too familiar with the painful confusion of individuals—once again, frequently those who are the most sincere and devout—in their efforts to determine God's will for them. We see them make dreadful errors following a whim or chance event that, because of their desperation, they *will* to be a sign from God. We see them sink into despair, skepticism, even cynicism, often continuing their religious routine, which is now utterly mechanical and dead. They "know" on the basis of what has happened to them that for all practical purposes they are simply on their own.

And we also are all too familiar, if we only read the newspapers, with the tragic domination of groups by those who lay claim to a special sign or word from God. The Jim Joneses and other religious dictators are in unceasing supply and show up in surprising forms and places. Often they are not effectively resisted precisely because the other members of the group have no clear idea, tested and proven in experience, of how such a "word from God" really works. They are vulnerable to madness in the name of God.

Toward a Solution

I believe we cannot, as disciples of Jesus Christ, abandon faith in the availability of God's personal and intelligible guidance for our minds and our lives. To abandon this is to abandon the reality of a personal relationship with God. This we cannot do. Our hearts and minds, as well as the realities of the Christian tradition, stand against it.

The "paradox" of divine guidance must, then, be resolved and removed by *providing the believer with a clear understanding and a confident practical orientation toward God's way of guiding us and communicating with us.* That is the aim of the chapters that follow. But before we can even make a beginning on this task, there are three *general* problem areas that must be briefly addressed.

First, what we know about guidance and the divine-human encounter from the Bible, church history, and the lives of the great ones in the Way, shows that *God's communications come to us in many forms.* This multifaceted communication is appropriate to the complexity of human personality and cultural history, as well as to the fact that God in redemption must reach out to a humanity that is in a fallen and weakened condition.

We accept this fact from the outset and then carefully look at these many forms to see which ones are most suited to the kind of relationship God intends to have with his people. If we give primacy to forms of communication God does not on the whole prefer in relation to his children, we will be hindered in our understanding and in our cooperation with his guidance, perhaps even totally frustrating it. One of the main tasks of the chapters that follow is to prevent this from happening.

Second, *we may be seeking guidance for the wrong motives.* We all, in some measure, share in the general human anxiety about the future. By nature we live in the future, constantly hurled into it whether we like it or not. Knowing what we will meet there is a condition of our being prepared to deal with it. Or so it would seem from the human point of view. Francis Bacon's saying that knowledge is power is never more vividly realized than in our concern about our own future. So we ceaselessly inquire about events to come.

The great businesses and the halls of government are filled today with experts and technocrats, our modern-day magicians and soothsayers. A new discipline of "futurology" has recently emerged within the universities. The age-old trades of palm reading and fortune-telling still flourish.[11]

Within the Christian community, teaching on the will of God and how to know it continues to be one of the most popular subjects. Russ Johnston draws on his own wide experience to remark:

> A certain church I know has elective Sunday School classes for their adults. Every three months they choose a new topic to study. The pastor tells me that if they can have someone teach on knowing God's will, they can run that class over and over, and still people sign up for it in droves.
>
> I've spoken at many conferences where part of the afternoons are set aside for workshops on various topics. If you make one of the workshops "Knowing the Will of God," half the people sign up for it even if there are twenty other choices.[12]

But is there not at work here a self-defeating motive—one that causes people to take these classes and workshops over and over without coming to peace about their place in the will of God? My own observations suggest that many people seek the will of God as a manipulative device for securing their own safety, comfort, and righteousness.

Even for those who busy themselves to know the will of God, however, it is still true that "whosoever will save his life shall lose it" (Mt 16:25). Extreme preoccupation with knowing the will of God "for me" may only indicate, contrary to what is often thought, an over-concern with myself, not a Christlike interest in the well-being of others or the glory of God.

Frederick B. Meyer writes: "So long as there is some thought of personal advantage, some idea of acquiring the praise and commendation of men, some aim of self-aggrandizement, it will be simply impossible to find out God's purpose concerning us."[13] Nothing will go right in the search for guidance if this false motivation is its foundation. God simply won't cooperate. In the chapters to follow we must make clear a different type of motivation for knowing God's guidance and listening to his voice.

Third, a truly overwhelming problem blocks understanding of divine guidance when *we misconceive the very nature of our heavenly Father and of his intent for us* as his redeemed children and friends. From this then comes a further misunderstanding of what the church, his redemptive community, is to be like and especially of how authority works in the Kingdom of the Heavens.

God certainly is not a jolly good fellow, nor is he our "buddy." But then neither are we intended by him to be robots wired into his instrument panel, puppets on his string, or slaves dancing at the end of the whiplash of his command. Such ideas must not serve as the basis for our view of divine guidance.

As E. Stanley Jones trenchantly observed:

Obviously God must guide us in a way that will develop spontaneity in us. The development of character, rather than direction in this, that, and the other matter, must be the primary purpose of the Father. He will guide us, but He won't override us. That fact should make us use with caution the method of sitting down with a pencil and a blank sheet of paper to write down the instructions dictated by God for the day. Suppose a parent would dictate to the child minutely everything he is to do during the day. The child would be stunted under that regime. The parent must guide in such a manner, and to the degree, that autonomous character, capable of making right decisions for itself, is produced. God does the same.[14]

A Conversational Relationship

The ideal for divine guidance is finally determined by who God is, what kind of beings we are, and what a personal relationship between us and God should be like. Failure of competence in dealing with divine guidance has its deepest root in a failure to understand, accept, and grow into a conversational relationship with God: the sort of relationship suited to friends who are mature personalities in a shared enterprise, no matter how different they may be in other respects.

It is within such a relationship that our Lord surely intends us to have, and to readily recognize, his voice speaking in our hearts as occasion demands. I believe that he has made ample provision for this in order to fulfill his mission as the Good Shepherd, which is to bring us life and life more abundantly. The abundance of life comes in following him, and "the sheep follow him, for they know his voice" (Jn 10:4).

We now begin to deal with these problem areas that confront our search for divine guidance by looking at some general but essential preliminary guidelines to guidance.

SOME TOPICS FOR REFLECTION

1. Could you be sure that God has *not* spoken to you? What events in your past life *could* have been a message from God? Reflect on the details of some such events.

2. What is the "paradox" about divine guidance discussed in this chapter? Do you find the tension it sets up present in the lives of religious people around you?

3. What might be the drawbacks of having a "conversational relationship" with God? What kinds of people would you expect to be somewhat less than enthusiastic about living in such a relationship?

4. Can you make any sense at all of an intimate personal relationship in which there are no specific communications?

5. Should a leader who claims to have been spoken to by God ever be questioned about this? How might one intelligently go about such questioning in a spirit of love?

6. Everything considered, would you really like to be spoken to by God?

Notes

1. Brother Lawrence, *The Practice of the Presence of God* (Westwood, NJ: Fleming H. Revell, 1958), 46.
2. John Calvin, *Institutes of the Christian Religion*, trans. Henry Beveridge (Grand Rapids, MI: William B. Eerdmans, 1975), bk. 1, chap. 7.
3. William Law, *The Power of the Spirit* (Fort Washington, PA: Christian Literature Crusade, 1971), chap. 5.
4. *Christianity Today*, February 18, 1983, news section, p. 29.
5. David Wilkerson, *The Vision* (Old Tappan, NJ: Fleming H. Revell, 1974), 11.
6. Joyce Landorf, *Change Points* (Old Tappan, NJ: Fleming H. Revell, 1981), 156–57.
7. George Fox, *The Journal of George Fox* (London: J. M. Dent & Sons, Ltd., 1948), 8–9.
8. Wilhelm Hermann, *The Communion of the Christian with God*, 3rd English ed. (London: Williams & Norgate, 1909), 14.
9. John Baillie, *Our Knowledge of God* (New York: Scribners, 1959), 132.
10. C. Austin Miles, "In the Garden," in *The Broadman Hymnal* (Nashville, TN: The Broadman Press, 1940), #356.
11. J. A. Sargent, "Astrology's Rising Star," *Christianity Today*, February 4, 1983, pp. 37–39.
12. Russ Johnston, *How to Know the Will of God* (Colorado Springs: Navpress, 1971), 5.

13. Frederick B. Meyer, *The Secret of Guidance* (Chicago: Moody Press, n.d.), 12.

14. E. Stanley Jones, *Victorious Living,* for Sunday of Week 41, (Nashville, TN: Abingdon Press, 1938), 281.

2 Guidelines to Guidance

He brought me to the banqueting house, and his banner over me was love. . . . Eat, O friends, and drink: drink deeply, O lovers!

SONG 2:4, 5:1, RSV

Those possessed of genuine love have God's life in them and are well acquainted with Him. Those who are not have no knowledge of Him, for God is Love.

I JN 4:7−8

The Perfectly Guided Wife

You may have seen the movie *The Stepford Wives*. It is the story of a couple, probably in their early or mid-thirties, who move into the upper-middle-class community of Stepford, where the men are mostly workers in high-tech industries and businesses and the women are homemakers.

The wife soon notices that most of the other "Stepford wives" uniformly exhibit very strange behavior patterns. They are continuously ecstatic over sewing, cleaning their houses, manicuring their lawns, and baking cookies. When they get together they mainly trade recipes or coo over their clean floors and their latest triumphs in making their husbands lives more comfortable. They never fight or are unpleasant with anyone, especially not with their husbands, and they have no opinions or interests that reach beyond their family, home, and club.

There are a few wives who remain on the feisty, individualistic side, but they usually leave for a "vacation" with their husbands and, on returning, are as focused on cookies and clean floors as the rest.

When this happens to the best friend of the most recent Stepford wife—who was already very suspicious about what was going on—she becomes desperate and stabs her old friend with a knife to see if she will bleed. She doesn't! She merely repeats pathetic little maneuvers around her kitchen, mouthing the same inane niceties over and over, while her frightened friend backs away and runs out the door.

By this time, however, her own robot replacement is almost ready. In the end we see her (or it) with the placid robot look on her face, ready to wear frilly blouses and aprons, make cookies, grow ecstatic over clean floors, and be sweet, *sweet,* SWEET—the totally guided wife!

Leaving its social agenda aside, the message of *The Stepford Wives* is obvious and important. But it is a message that is too often forgotten. In close personal relationships, conformity to another's wishes is not desirable, be it ever so perfect, if it is mindless, purchased at the expense of freedom, and destructive of personality. This is a point that must be firmly grasped as we come to think about God's relationships to his human creation and about what his love for us means.

Specifically, in our attempts to understand how God guides us, we must above all hold to the fact that guidance is to be sought *only as a part of a certain kind of life:* a life of loving fellowship with the King and his other subjects within the Kingdom of the Heavens.

We must never forget that God's guidance for us, however we experience it in our initial encounter, is intended to develop into an intelligent, freely cooperative relationship between mature persons who love each other with the richness of genuine *agape* love. We must therefore make our primary goal not just to have the guidance of God, but to be such mature persons in such a loving relationship to him. Only so will guidance itself come right. This is our first general guideline for guidance.

Love: a Way of "Being With"

When we love someone, we of course want to do what they wish, but not just because we wish to avoid trouble or gain favor. Cooperation is a way of being with them, of sharing their life and their person. The gushing pleasure of the small child who is "helping mama" comes from the expansion of his little self through immersion in the life of a larger self to which he is lovingly abandoned. *With* mother he does "big things" he could not undertake on his own. But he would not even be interested in doing them apart from her or her interest, attention, and affection.

The sense of larger power and larger life that comes to adults when they enjoy requited love is also a valid perception of the expansion of self and enlargement of world through identification with another that comes when, in the manner appropriate to the people involved, two become one.

When the two are one, the beloved who also loves does not want to be in the position of forever ordering the lover-beloved about: "Do this for me! Do that for me!" The less of such talk there is, the better, as everyone knows. All of us would like to be understood in a manner that makes such directiveness completely unnecessary.

To be always telling the other what to do is simply not compatible with that union of souls—that sweet repose upon, that conscious delight and rest in another—that is the highest act and most exalted condition possible between people.

And this is true with God also, who is a person loving and beloved. Our highest calling and opportunity in life is to love him with all our being. And he has loved us so much that his only Son was freely allowed to die in order to bring salvation to us.

God as Taskmaster

Far too commonly, no doubt, we think of God as did the man in the parable of the talents, who regarded his lord as "a hard man," was accordingly afraid of him, and proudly, in his blindness, gave him back exactly what "belonged" to him (Mt 25:14–30).

Such a one cannot "enter into the joy of his lord" because, misconceiving of their relationship as he did, he could not enter into his lord's mind and life nor open his own life to his lord. He actually abused his lord by taking him to be interested only in "getting what was coming to him," while the lord for his part was really interested in sharing his life and goods with others.

In the same way, we immeasurably demean God by casting him in the role of the cosmic boss, foreman, autocrat, whose chief joy in relation to humans is ordering them around, taking pleasure in seeing them jump to his commands, while painstakingly noting down any departures from his wishes.

I have no doubt at all that a record *is* kept. It is written automatically in the texture of our souls, our bodies, and the surrounding universe and can be read by him when desired. Its keeping requires no special effort on his part. But the Heavenly Father's ideal for his family is clearly something very different from the relation of a boss to subordinates. It was expressed by Jesus in his prayer: "That they may all be one; even as thou, Father, art in me, and I in thee, that they also may be in us" (Jn 17:21, RSV). The intended relation is one of *being in* us. We are to be friends (2 Chr 20:7; Jn 15:13–15) and fellow workers (1 Cor 3:9) with God.

The role of taskmaster, pleased *or* angry, is one that God accepts only on man's mean and ungenerous appointment. He thus often condescends to us because our consciousness (clouded as it is by our experiences in a fallen world with "superiors," whether they be parents, bosses, kings, or those who stand over us in manipulative "love") cannot rise any higher. And the rule then is, as always: "As is your faith, so be it unto you" (see Mt 8:13). No doubt it is better that we have *some* relation to God than no relation at all!

But when we come in search of divine guidance, we must be sure to come in such a way that we do justice to the revelation of God in Christ. Guidance, as we have noted, is an almost universal human preoccupation. It is hard to cleanse our minds of those motives, images, and conceptualizations that would brutalize the very God whom we hope to approach.

From primitive ritual to the "Bible roulette"—picking verses at random for guidance—frequently practiced by present-day believers, we see both the desperate urgency and superstitious character of human efforts to get a word from God on what is going to happen and what we should do about it. If necessary, an effort is made to *force* it from him or someone else. Like King Saul of old, many of us have our own versions of a "witch of Endor" (1 Sm 28).

Here as elsewhere we must take with utmost seriousness Jesus' words: "No one knows the Father except the Son and those to whom the Son chooses to reveal him" (Mt 11:27, JB). And this means, above all else, that the conscious seeking of divine guidance is safe and sensible only within that life of experiential union with God in his Kingdom that Jesus Christ brought to light. He revealed it in his own person and passes it on in his continuing incarnation, the church.

Divine guidance cannot be ours as a reliable and intelligible fact of life except when seen as one aspect of God's presence with us, of his life in us. Only our *communion* with God provides the appropriate context of *communications* between us and him. And within those communications, *guidance* will be given in a manner suitable to our particular lives and circumstances. It will fit into our life together with him in his earthly and heavenly family. To repeat, this is our first preliminary insight to guide us in our search for divine guidance.

Merely Human?

And when the people saw what Paul had done, they shouted out
. . . "The gods are come down to us in the likeness of men,"
. . . and would have done sacrifice. . . . But Barnabas and Paul ran
in among the people, saying, "Sirs, why do ye these things? We also
are men of like passions with you". (Acts 14:11–15)

A second truth that is preliminary to any successful attempt to understand divine guidance concerns the relationship of *our* experience to the contents of the Bible and, by extension, to the lives of the saints and heroes of the faith throughout the ages.

The scene just given through a quotation from the book of Acts portrays the common human response to those who are living in such a close relationship with God that special manifestations of the divine presence stand out in their lives. We immediately think, "They just aren't human!" By which we mean that their experience, including their experience of God, is not like ours and that perhaps they are even a special *kind* of person, so that our experience of God never could be like theirs.

It is hard to believe that someone clearly manifesting a transcendent life could still be human. One of the most serious and severe doctrinal struggles in the early church was over whether Jesus was authentically human. A primary function of the doctrine of the virgin birth, when first introduced, was to secure the fact that Jesus really did have a human body, since he was literally born of a woman. His body came forth from a womb.[1] Still earlier, in "the days of His flesh," when his humanity was quite visible through his literal bodily presence and processes, his closest friends and associates apparently could not see his divinity. Philip, as the end drew near, said, "Lord, show us the Father and that will be enough." Jesus could only reply, "Have I been so long time with you, and you still have not recognized me, Philip? He that has seen me has seen the Father" (Jn 14:8–9).

He was human, yet divine; divine, yet human. This precarious balance is required to do justice to the realities of Jesus' redemptive presence in history. It is fairly easy to state, but only the gracious inward assistance of God will enable us to base our lives on it.

The problem of uniting the life of God with the life of humanity continued to bother the early believers. In this respect, Elijah was cited by James, the Lord's brother, as a well-known case that could help them understand their own experience and its possibilities.

The story of Elijah's terror before Jezebel, of his running for his life, of his dissolving into a mass of righteous self-pity (1 Kgs 19) shows clearly that he really was human. He was, after all, "a man subject to like passions as we are" (Jas 5:17), regardless of his fantastic feats in the power of God.

The humanity of Moses, David, and Elijah and of Paul, Peter, and Jesus Christ himself, of all that wonderful company of riotously human women and men whose experience is recorded in the Bible and in the history of the church, teaches us a very important lesson: *our humanity will not by itself prevent us from knowing and interacting with God as they did.*

How to Believe the Bible Stories

Conversely, if we are really to understand the Bible record itself, we must enter into our study of it on the assumption that the experiences recorded there were basically of the same type as ours would be if we were there. Those who lived through them felt them very much as we would if we were in their place. Unless this feeling of identification comes home to us, the things that happened to the people in the Bible will remain unreal to us.

We will not be able to *believe* the Bible, or find its contents to be *really* so, because it will have no experiential substance for us. It will mean nothing "concrete," and our blindness will shut the door on those tender overtures of God that now in our own times invite our souls to individual communion with him (Rv 3:20). We will be left without the God-provided scriptural keys for interpreting our own encounters with him and will, like Balaam, be unable to recognize the angel standing directly in our pathway (Nm 22).

We must tell Elijah's story from the inside, realizing how it would have been for us to be in his place. Just imagine yourself rising before a joint session of Congress, or standing before the president and nationwide television in the White House Rose Garden. Imagine announcing that it would not rain until *you* said so. Think of disappearing amid incredulous snickers, possibly escorted away by police, and then of being dismissed as a harmless crackpot.

Think of becoming one of the FBI's ten "most wanted," or of your picture going up on "wanted" posters, of being regarded as endangering national security. Then you reappear, and before a worldwide television audience, you call down fire from heaven, gun down the false leaders of the country, and ride down Madison Avenue to a ticker-tape parade!

While enjoying a rally in your honor in Yankee Stadium or the Rose Bowl, word comes that the most powerful man in the country has vowed to kill you within twenty-four hours. How do you feel then? Then what do you do? If you are human, you probably do just what Elijah did.

Failure to read the Bible in this way accounts for two common problems in Christian groups that hold the Bible central to their faith. One is that it becomes simply a book of doctrine, of abstract truth *about* God, which one can endlessly search without encountering God himself or hearing his voice.

This same attitude led the religious authorities of Jesus' own day to use the Scriptures for the very purpose of avoiding him. They fervently searched the Scriptures, yet Jesus said of them, "Ye have not his word abiding in you!" (Jn 5:38).

A. W. Tozer has pointedly remarked, in this connection:

> It is altogether possible to be instructed in the rudiments of the faith and still have no real understanding of the whole thing. And it is possible to go on to become expert in Bible doctrine and not have spiritual illumination, with the result that a veil remains over the mind, preventing it from apprehending the truth in its spiritual essence.[2]

The other problem that arises when we do not understand the experience of biblical characters in terms of our own lives is that we simply stop reading the Bible altogether. Or else we take it "in regular doses," choking it down like medicine because someone told us that it would be good for us, though we really do not find it to be so.

The open secret of many "Bible believing" churches is that only a very small percentage of their members study the Bible with even the degree of interest, intelligence, or joy they bring to bear on their newspaper or *Time* magazine. In my opinion, based on considerable experience, this is primarily because they do not and are not taught how to understand the experience of biblical characters *in terms of their own experience.*

Perhaps they are even warned *not* to so understand it. But that we are to understand the Bible in terms of our own experience is exactly what the Bible itself is teaching when it says that Paul, Barnabas, and Elijah were "subject to like passions as we are" and that Jesus was touched with the feeling of our infirmities because he himself "was in all points tempted like as we are" (Heb 4:15). It means that their experience was substantially like our own.

If we are to understand divine guidance for ourselves and on an individual basis, we must, above all else, observe how the word of God came to those people described in the Scriptures. How was it that they experienced God's communication? We must prayerfully but boldly use our God-given imaginations to fill out the reality of the events in terms of what it would be like if *we were* Moses standing by the bush (Ex 3:2), little Samuel lying in his darkened room (1 Sm 3:3–7), Elisha under inspiration from the minstrel (2 Kgs 3:15), Ananias receiving his vision about Paul (Acts 9:11), or Peter on his rooftop (Acts 10:10).

We must pray for the faith and for the experiences that would enable us to believe that *such things could happen to us.* Only so will we be able to recognize them, to accept them, and *dwell in* them when they come. This is our second general guideline to guidance.

Humble Arrogance: Who, Me, Lord?

> Notwithstanding in this rejoice not, that the spirits are subject unto you; but rather rejoice, because your names are written in the Heavens. (Lk 10:20)

The script of Richard Attenborough's *Gandhi* has a section in which the young Indian lawyer and a white clergyman are walking together on the boardwalk, contrary to South African law at the time. They are accosted by some brutish looking young white men who seem about to harm them. But the mother of the ringleader calls from an upstairs window and commands him to go about his business. As they walk on, the clergyman exclaims over their good luck. But Gandhi comments,

"I thought you were a man of God." The clergyman replies, "I am, but I don't believe he plans his day around me!"

The audience laughs, of course. A cute point indeed! But beneath it lies an attitude and a set of beliefs that may make it impossible for us to take seriously the possibility of divine guidance. And if we do not take it seriously, then of course we shall not be able to enter into it.

To the statement made above, that we must think of ourselves as capable of having the same kinds of experiences as Elijah or Paul, many will spontaneously reply: "But who am I to put myself in the place of these great ones? Who am I even to suppose that God might guide *me* or speak to *me*, much less that my experience should be like that of a Moses or Elisha?"

Such a reaction poses as one that does honor to the greatness of God. In fact, it contradicts what God taught about himself in the Bible and in the person of Christ. *His greatness is precisely what allows him to "plan his day" around me or any and everyone else, as he chooses.*

Within the scriptural record, those spoken to by God, such as Moses or Gideon, often tried to plead unworthiness or inadequacy. Although such responses are in a sense fitting, they are also beside the point. They are irrelevant, as God makes perfectly clear in the stories concerned.

Similarly, we might find it hard to believe that the president of the United States or some other human dignitary had called to talk to us. We think, on the one hand, that we are not *that* important and, on the other hand, that such a communication might seem to *make* us important. Similar thoughts may be stirred up at the suggestion of God talking to us. But they are irrelevant to his purposes in dealing with us. Moreover, they contain tragic misconceptions with the power to shut us off from the individualized guidance of God.

In the first place, *we are that important.* We were important enough for God to give his Son's life for us and to choose to inhabit us as a living temple. Obviously, then, we are important enough for him to guide us and speak to us where that is appropriate.

And in the second place, *his speaking to us does not in itself MAKE us important.* Like the ancient people of Israel, it simply gives us greater opportunity to be and to do good and greater responsibility for the care and guidance of others. Divine-human conversation is one aspect of that multifaceted personal interaction for which man was created in the first place. Through it the sweet society of God's own Trinitarian personality is extended toward the maximum goodness and glory possible in the created universe.

But if we allow God's conversational walk with us (or anything else, for that matter) to make us think we are someone great, guidance will pretty certainly be withdrawn. Under the Kingdom of the Heavens, those who exalt themselves will be abased, as Jesus taught, and pride is the condition that comes right before a fall.

In seeking and receiving divine guidance, therefore, we must at the same time seek and receive the grace of humility. God will gladly give it to us if, trusting and waiting on him to act, we refrain from *pretending* we are what we know we are not, from *presuming* a favorable position for ourselves in any respect, and from *pushing* or trying to override the will of others in our context. (This is a fail-safe recipe for humility. Try it for one month. Money-back guarantee if it doesn't work!)

Moses may well be the all-time record holder for lengthy conversations with God. If there were such a category in the *Guinness Book of World Records,* he would certainly head the list. But he was also one of the least presumptuous human beings who ever walked the earth: "Now the man Moses was very meek, more than all men that were on the face of the earth" (Nm 12:3, RSV). There certainly was a connection between his meekness and his close working and talking relationship with God. Psalm 25:9 states: "The meek will he guide in judgment: and the meek will he teach his way."

The Strength of True Meekness

In his book *George Mueller of Bristol,* A. T. Pierson comments on this verse in a way that both elaborates the present point and will prove highly useful for our later discussions:

Here is a double emphasis upon *meekness* as a condition of such guidance and teaching. *Meekness is a real preference for God's will.* Where this holy habit of mind exists, the whole being becomes so open to impression that, without any *outward* sign or token, there is an *inward* recognition and choice of the will of God. God guides, not by a visible sign, but by *swaying the judgment.* To wait before Him, weighing candidly in the scales every consideration for or against a proposed course, and in readiness to see which way the preponderance lies, is a frame of mind and heart in which one is fitted to be guided; and God touches the scales and makes the balance to sway as He will. *But our hands must be off the scales,* otherwise we need expect no interposition of His in our favor.[3]

And this brings us to the third preliminary truth that we must keep constantly before us in our search of divine guidance: When God speaks to us, *it does not prove that we are righteous or even right.* It does not even prove that we have *understood* correctly what he said. The infallibility of the messenger and the message does not guarantee the infallibility of our reception. Humility is always in order.

This is an especially important point to make because the appeal to "God told me" or "the Lord led me" is commonly used to prove that I am right, or that *you* should follow *me,* or that I should get my way. No such claim is automatically justified.

But this is such a common misunderstanding of divine guidance that some may say, "What is the use of it then? Why should God speak to me, or I listen, if it will not give me unquestionable authority and absolutely ensure that I am on the right track?"

The chapters that follow can hopefully lead us to discover a fully satisfactory response to this question. We shall, in due order, have to examine the entire issue of authority and "being right" in relation to divine guidance. But what we must never lose sight of in our efforts to comprehend what guidance is and how it works is that God's purposes in guidance are not merely to secure and support us in our various roles or to make sure that we are right.

Indeed, being right is one of the hardest burdens humans beings have to bear, and few succeed in bearing up under it gracefully. There is a little placard I have seen that reads: "Lord, when we are wrong, make us willing to change, and when we are right make us easy to live with!" A very wise prayer.

Paul the apostle warned us that knowledge puffs up, while love builds up, and that no one knows anything as well as he ought to know it (1 Cor 8:1–2). The guidance we seek in the Way of Christ is only one part of a life of humility, power, faith, and hopeful love, whose final overall character is *life with God* in the embrace of "the everlasting arms" (Dt 33:27).

Our next chapter must give us a clearer picture of what the experience of that life is like, of how it is that we are to be *with God.*

SOME TOPICS FOR REFLECTION

1. Why does *The Stepford Wives* model of human relationships seem attractive to some people? What are its strengths and weaknesses?

2. Does the picture of love as a way of "being with" fit with what you have experienced in your life? Think of all the types of relationships in which love plays a role.

3. "One of God's main tasks is to see to it that no one gets away with anything." Discuss.

4. What is the relationship between communion, communication, and guidance in human affairs? For example, between a mother and daughter, or between friends? To what extent would this relationship carry over or *not* carry over to God and his children?

5. Do you see inherent conflicts between being spoken to by God and meekness or humility? What things does one need to understand in order to resolve these conflicts?

6. Can you identify the three general "guidelines to guidance" presented in this chapter?

Notes

1. The Council of Chalcedon (A.D. 451) makes this use of the idea of Virgin Birth: "That Christ was really divine and really human; in his divinity co-eternal, and in all points similar to the Father; in his humanity, son of the Virgin Mary, *born like all others,* and like unto us men in all things except sin." (Quoted, with italics added, from "Monophysites," in J. McClintock and J. Strong, eds., *Cyclopaedia of Biblical, Theological and Ecclesiastical Literature* [New York: Harper & Row, 1894], 509.)
2. A. W. Tozer, *The Root of the Righteous* (Harrisburg, PA: Christian Publications, 1955), 34.
3. A. T. Pierson, *George Mueller of Bristol and His Witness to a Prayer-Hearing God* (New York: Baker and Taylor, 1899), 185–86.

3   *Never Alone*

And the Lord God said, It is not good that the
man should be alone.

GN 2:18

Behold, a virgin will be with child and bear a son,
and she will call his name "Immanuel," that is,
"God with us."

IS 7:14

And, lo, I am with you always, even unto the end
of the world. Amen.

MT 28:20

A little group from the college I attended as a young man used to
hold religious services on Thursday evenings for the inmates at a
county workhouse located about thirty miles east of Chattanooga,
Tennessee. The people imprisoned there were not hardened crimi-
nals but quite ordinary men who were serving short sentences of several months to a year for minor offenses. Isolation from their friends
and families caused them to suffer acutely.

They seemed for the most part really to look forward to our weekly
visits, but I suspect it was more for the singing than anything else. In
our group was a young lady named Norma Carrier, who was a beautiful Christian as well as a fine musician. She would play the accordion,

and the men would enthusiastically join in the songs and hymns. There was one song in particular they rarely if ever failed to request:

> I've seen the lightning flashing,
> I've heard the thunder roll;
> I've felt sin's breakers dashing,
> Trying to conquer my soul.
> I've heard the voice of Jesus,
> Telling me still to fight on.
> He promised never to leave me,
> Never to leave me alone.

Then they would swing into the chorus with all the pathos of desperate men contemplating their last hope on earth:

> No, never alone; no, never alone!
> He promised never to leave me,
> Never to leave me alone.

I once found myself in London with several days on my hands while waiting for a charter flight back to the United States. A great deal of my time was spent in Westminster Cathedral in meditation and prayer. Not Westminster *Abbey.* In the abbey one senses the great past: the majestic history of the English people and of God's dealings with them. In the cathedral, by contrast, which is several blocks up from the abbey toward Victoria Station, there is a divine presence beyond all national histories. Something about the vast, obscure interior of that building impresses me with the nearness of God.

In front of the cathedral is a square with benches and some tables, and off to one side, a religious bookstore and a McDonald's—golden McArches and all. Here street people of London come to sleep safely in the morning sun if it is shining and to glean scraps of haute cuisine left by those who dine with McDonald.

I recall watching one woman in particular on a number of occasions as she slept, with children and pigeons flocking around her. She was blonde, a little heavyset, and about middle-aged. Although she showed the marks of street life, she looked very much like many a housewife at the center of a happy family. And I thought: "Whose daughter is she?

Whose sister, or mother, or neighbor, or classmate? And here she is, alone, alone, alone!"

A similar feeling, but even more profound, came over me when our first child was born. I painfully realized that this incredibly beautiful little creature we had brought into the world was utterly separate from me and that there was nothing *I* could do that would shelter him from his aloneness before time, brutal events, the meanness of other human beings, his own wrong choices, the decay of his own body, and, finally, death.

It simply is not within human capacity to care effectively for others in the depths of their life and being, or even to be *with* them in finality, no matter how much we may care about them. If we could only *really* be with them that would almost be enough, we think. But we cannot, at least in a way that would satisfy us. For all of us the words of the old song are true: "You must go there by yourself."

And that would be the last word on the subject, but for God. He *is* able to penetrate and intertwine himself within the fibers of the human self in such a way that those who are enveloped in his loving companionship will never be alone.

This is the meaning of the great affirmations at the end of Romans, chapter 8: "Who shall separate us from the love of Christ? shall tribulation, or distress, or persecution, or famine, or nakedness, or peril, or sword? . . . Nay, in all these things we are more than conquerors through him that loved us. For I am persuaded, that neither death, nor life, nor angels, nor principalities, nor powers, nor things present, nor things to come, nor height, nor depth, nor any other creature, shall be able to separate us from the love of God, which is in Christ Jesus our Lord" (vv. 35, 37–39).

Even our anguish over those dear to us can be completely put to rest when we see them enter this presence from which nothing can separate. The final and complete blessing and ultimate good, the *summum bonum* of mankind, comes to those with lives absorbed in the Way of Christ. That is life in the presence of God. The completely adequate word of faith in all our sorrows and all our joys is "Immanuel, God with us!" Thus we sing:

Where'er Thou art may we remain;
Where'er Thou goest may we go;
With Thee, O Lord, no grief is pain,
Away from Thee all joy is woe.

Oh, may we in each holy tide,
Each solemn season, dwell with Thee!
Content if only by Thy side
In life or death we still may be.[1]

"In thy presence," the psalmist says, "is fullness of joy; at thy right hand there are pleasures forever more" (16:11). Even in the valley of the shadow of death there is nothing to fear. Why? Because "thou art with me" (23:4).

And on the other hand, the fact that God alone can by his presence take away our aloneness explains why the ultimate suffering and punishment is to be separated from the presence of God. The psalmist cries out in terror, "Cast me not away from thy presence; and take not thy holy spirit from me" (51:11).

Hell itself essentially consists in irreparable separation from God. It is made even more unbearable by the never-ceasing realization that this was not his choice for us but that our preferred course of life led us there. We each turned to our own way and wandered off the cosmic cliff.

The Giver and His Gifts

It is of course true that the person and presence of God with us is sought, in part, for its external effects. In many of this world's religions, the favor of the gods is mainly, or totally, sought simply because of the advantage it brings. The psalmist, once again, describes the presence of God as a place to hide from the pride of man (31:20; and see 32:7, 27:5). After refusing to enrich and fortify himself with plunder from his victory over the kings (Gn 14:22–24), Abraham, father of the faithful, is given a vision of God saying to him, "Fear not, . . . I am thy shield, and thy exceeding great reward" (Gn 15:1).

When Jehovah was angered by the sins of the Israelites in their journey to Canaan and seemed about to desert them, Moses prevailed on him by saying: "For how then can it be known that I have found favor in Thy sight, I and Thy people? Is it not by Thy going with us, so that we, I and Thy people, may be distinguished from all the other people who are upon the face of the earth?" (Ex 33:16, NASB).

Yet the control of our circumstances by means of the presence of God is not, finally, what we rest in as disciples of Jesus. We are instructed to "be content with such things as you have: for he has said, 'I will never leave you nor forsake you.' So that we may boldly say, The Lord is my helper, and I will not fear what man shall do unto me" (Heb 13:5–6). The promise here is *not,* however, that God will never allow any evil to come to us, but that no matter what befalls us, we are *still* beyond harm because he is still with us and because his presence is utterly enough by itself.

Our contentment lies not in his *presents* but in the *presence* of the One whose presents they are. In all our trials we are more than conquerors, because nothing "shall be able to separate us from the love of God which is in Christ Jesus our Lord."

Good Thomas à Kempis speaks for the ages when he represents Jesus as saying to him: "A wise lover regards not so much the gift of Him who loves, as the love of Him who gives. He esteems affection rather than valuables, and sets all gifts below the Beloved. A noble-minded lover rests not in the gift, but in Me above every gift."[2]

The sustenance of the Presence Beloved has, through the ages, incidentally made the sickbed sweet and the graveside triumphant, transformed broken hearts and relations, brought glory to drudgery, poverty, and old age, and has turned the martyr's stake or noose into a place of coronation.

And when we come to our final home, as Saint Augustine has written, "There we shall rest and see, see and love, love and praise. This is what shall be in the end without end."[3] It is this for which the human soul was made. It is our temporal and eternal calling, "Man's chief end is to glorify God and enjoy Him forever."[4]

But now loneliness is loose on the landscape, haunts the penthouse and the rectory, the executive suite and the governor's mansion as well as the barren apartment, the assembly line, the cocktail lounge, and the city streets. It is, as Mother Teresa of Calcutta has said, the leprosy of the modern world. The popular song of some years back deplored the fate of Eleanor Rigby and exclaimed, "All the lonely people! Where do they all come from?"

There is a simple and correct answer to this question. The lonely people live apart from God. They have "no hope, and are without God in the world" (Eph 2:12). Their many other alienations are rooted in their alienation from God.

But is it possible to make clear what life with God is like, that life wherein one is *never alone?* Can we at least explain it in terms that would enable the honest and open-minded person to approach the possibility of entering into it? We shall attempt to do this by discussing various forms that God's presence with us may take.

We will be looking at concrete ways of understanding our "with" relationship to God that forever excludes isolation and loneliness. The following words from Scripture provide some intriguing suggestions:

> And ye shall be unto me a kingdom of priest, and an holy nation. (Ex 19:6)

> Unto him that loved us, and washed us from our sins in his own blood, and has made us kings and priests unto God and his Father; to him be glory and dominion for ever and ever. (Rv 1:5–6)

The basic idea here is that God calls us to direct and fully self-conscious or personal relationship with him (as priests) in which we share responsibility with him (as kings) in the exercise of his dominion.

But exactly what does this involve, and how do we experience it? We shall describe a number of phases.

"Blind" Faith

First of all, what we may call "blind faith" is a valid, though very minimal, way of God being with us. In this state we find ourselves really believing in God and believing that he is with us. Perhaps we believe because of past experiences, or because we have faith in the faith of others, or even because of abstract reasonings that tell us he simply *must* be here. But our conviction—almost a will that it *shall* be so— is the only way that he is present in our lives. There is no *awareness* of him being here with us at all and no evidence of his action in or around us. Still we believe. Still we are faith-full.

The phrase "dark night of the soul" has for centuries been used in deeper discussions of the spiritual life. It is a season in which we walk by blind faith alone. St. John of the Cross describes it as a condition "souls begin to enter when God draws them forth from the state of beginners . . . and begins to set them in the state of proficients."[5] It serves an essential function in bringing the children of God to maturity, and especially in advancing them to the point where they no longer serve God because of the "kicks" they get out of it.

Hence this kind of faith stands out very clearly and is thought to be "dark" precisely because of its strong contrast with those other times when God is tangibly encountered as "our refuge and strength, a very present help in trouble" (Ps 46:1).

Richard Foster describes a time in which, pulled by God out of a busy and successful life as a teacher and writer, he lived for eighteen months with a silent God. "I waited in Silence. And God was silent, too. I joined in the psalmist's query, 'How long will you hide your face from me?' (Ps 13:1, NIV). The answer: nothing. Absolutely nothing! There were no sudden revelations. No penetrating insights. Not even gentle assurances. Nothing."[6] Then, when God's intended work had been accomplished in his soul, the Divine Voice returned to his experience.

Although this kind of faith is not to be despised—far from it— the human heart can never be content to treat God's being "with us" merely as a matter of blind faith, with nothing else to go on. Abstract reasoning from the doctrine of God's omnipresence, or mental assent to the dogma that God *must* be with the believer, or faith in the faith of others, or even remembrance of past experiences of God cannot be an adequate basis for our spiritual growth.

Those who understand his presence in these ways only must be encouraged to believe that there is much more for them to know and receive. Otherwise they will never enter into their capacities as kings and priests, never "reign in life by one, Jesus Christ" (Rom 5:17).

Sensing God's Presence

Perhaps the first step beyond mere faith that God must be here is an indeterminate but often very powerful sense or feeling or impression of God's presence. Much like our experience of the *voice* of God, as we shall see later, considerable experience is required to recognize accurately and assess the meanings of such impressions. Yet a sense of God's presence frequently finds its verification in the judgment of the worshiping community and serves as a basis for intelligent appraisal and cooperation by and between individual members of the group. Different people simultaneously sense that certain things are to be done: that God is here and is moving in *that* direction.

This sensing of God's presence is a well-known phenomenon. Experienced ministers and laymen frequently unerringly synchronize their activities in a meeting or other form of service through their "sense" of God's presence and of his intent for the particular occasion. This sense is something they come to expect and rely on.

Those, on the other hand, who sense God's presence while alone in prayer, service, mediation, or study find easy communication with multitudes of others who have had similar or even, it often seems, identical experiences. These individuals talk a common language based on the sameness of their individual experiences.

Such a sense of the presence of another person also occurs, as we know, at a purely "secular" level, where the "other" is a human being. We may have the distinct impression that someone is looking at us or listening to us and later learn that in fact a certain person *was* looking intently at us or listening to us at that time. This is not an uncommon occurrence.

There are those who are able to get the attention of others (across a large auditorium, for example) merely by intently staring at the back of their heads. Some "smart" weapons of warfare are able to detect when they are being "watched" by radar, and perhaps we are not altogether unlike them. Some people seem more sensitive than others to such things, just as some have better eyesight or more acute hearing than others.

It seems clear that the conscious concentration of one person on another frequently evokes a reciprocal awareness in the one who is focused on. Since this is true among human beings, we should not be surprised that God's attention to us should result in a reciprocal awareness of his presence.

Sometimes, of course, the sense of "God with us" becomes much more determinate. My oldest brother, J. I. Willard, served for over thirty years as a pastor under the great blessing of God. But his entry into the ministry came through long and intense struggles with personal and financial issues.

One evening he faced a major decision to be made the next day that would commit him for years into the future. He prayed long into the night, falling asleep around 1:30. But at 2:00 A.M., he relates, "That room lit up with the glory of God. I saw a figure. I did not see a face, but I recognized it to be the person of Christ. I felt a hand on my shoulder, and I heard a voice which said, 'Feed my sheep.'"

The presence of God almost overwhelmed his consciousness, as it has with many others who have been given such experiences, and it also transformed various aspects of his personality. He suddenly was living in the study of the Bible, memorizing much of it without trying to, even though his days were spent at hard physical labor. He had been painfully addicted to tobacco all of his adult life. Desire for it was removed without his asking. According to him, the "aroma" of that room full of the presence of God has stayed with him ever since. Many others would testify to this presence in his life.

The God Who Acts

The sense of God's presence is sometimes accompanied in Christian experience by extraordinary events or powerful effects not easily attributable, if at all, to merely "natural" causes. This range of effects is a third form taken by God's presence with us, and a sense of presence is by no means essential to it. One of the functions of the "dark night of the soul" referred to earlier is to train us to act in reliance on God and to cooperate with his working when we *feel* as though we are acting alone.

To be able to so act is absolutely necessary if we are to live as freely dependent agents in harmony with the workings of God's Kingdom. Beyond the maturation of our own souls as co-laborers with God, the crucial thing in our service with his Kingdom is the work done. The mark of the working of God's Spirit with us is always the *incommensurability* of effects with our merely human powers. The outcome is beyond natural powers to accomplish. Such humanly unaccountable effects fit into, and even certify, the principles and purposes of the rule of God in human history, as manifested in the works of Christ and the Scriptures generally.

After many years of highly successful ministry, Dwight Lyman Moody had an experience of which he himself said:

> I cannot describe it, I seldom refer to it, it is almost too sacred an experience to name. . . . I can only say God revealed Himself to me, and I had such an experience of His love that I had to ask Him to stay His hand. I went to preaching again. The sermons were not different; I did not present any new truths; and yet hundreds were converted. I would not now be placed back where I was before that blessed experience if you should give me all the world; it would be as small dust in the balance.[7]

In his day, Moody was a constant source of wonder precisely because the effects of "his" ministry were so totally incommensurable, even incongruent, with his obvious personal qualities. He was a man of very ordinary appearance, unordained by any ecclesiastical group, and quite uncultured and uneducated—even uncouth and crude to many.

At the height of Moody's effectiveness, in 1874–75, Dr. R. W. Dale, one of the leading nonconformist clergymen in England, observed his work for three or four days in Birmingham. He wished to discover the secret of Moody's power. After his observations were completed, he told Moody that the work was most plainly the work of God, for he could see no relation between him personally and what he was accomplishing. A smaller person might well have been offended at this, but Moody only laughed and replied that he would be very sorry if things were otherwise.[8]

We recall the biblical story of how Abraham fathered Isaac, the son of promise and spirit, on Sarah, *contrary* to nature. It was through the energy of the spirit, altogether beyond him and her. But at an earlier point in time, Abraham and Hagar were quite competent to beget Ishmael through the mere energies of their bodies (Gal 4:22–28). Life with effects beyond the natural always depends on intimate interactions between us and God, who is therefore present.

When Paul and Barnabas went forth on their first missionary journey (Acts 13–14), they moved at every turn in a power that was far beyond themselves. The result was an astonishing series of events, establishing communities of believers in Christ throughout central Asia Minor. When they returned to their home in Syrian Antioch they brought the community of believers together and matter-of-factly "rehearsed all that God had done *with them,* and how *he* had opened the door of faith unto the Gentiles" (Acts 14:27, italics added).

There was no doubt of God's presence with them, because it was he who energized their activities with a power beyond themselves. The fulfillment of Jesus' words concerning the divine helper—"He dwells with you, and shall be in you" (Jn 14:17)—was to them the most obvious fact of their lives. "He that raised up Christ from the dead" also quickened their mortal bodies by his Spirit, which dwelt within them (Rom 8:11; also Eph 1:19–20).

Is That All?

I make it my business to persevere in His Holy presence, wherein I keep myself by a simple attention, and a general fond regard to God, which I may call an ACTUAL PRESENCE of God; or, to speak better, an habitual, silent, and secret conversation of the soul with God, which often causes me joys and raptures inwardly, and sometimes also outwardly, so great that I am forced to use means to moderate them and prevent their appearance to others. (Brother Lawrence) [9]

We have thus far considered three forms or aspects of God's presence with us: (1) when he indeed is close to us but we are not aware of him or his effects, having only "blind" faith or abstract reasoning to turn us toward him; (2) when he is sensed or there is a strong impression of his presence; and (3) when he acts in conjunction with our actions to change our surroundings in ways beyond our own powers.

Many who would agree thus far might wish to accept what has been said as a complete account of the forms of God's presence "with us." But I believe that to stop now would be to omit what is most important in the ongoing relationship between human beings and God and to rob the idea of the *priesthood* and the *royalty* of the believer of its substance. It would leave our interaction with God too close to the level of vague feelings, the Ouija board, and even superstitious conjecture.

How can we be friends of God if this is all there is to it? How is the rich *conceptual content* and knowledge found in the Bible to be understood as something communicated to us in revelation if the three forms of presence thus far discussed are the totality of the human interaction with God? Why, if God be personal, would he not also *talk* with us?

So we must add to the above that God is also with us in a conversational relationship: that he *speaks* with us individually as it is appropriate—as is usual between persons who know one another, care about one another, and are engaged in common enterprises.

Such a conversational manner of presence is suited to that personal relationship with God that is so often spoken of in the community of believers. It is this relationship that turns Paul's statement "As many as are led by the Spirit of God are the children of God" (see Rom 8:14) into a framework for personal development, as distinct from incitement to play the robot or be a mere reader of vague impressions and signs.

Two Types of Guidance

There are, as is generally understood, two types of "guidance" commonly found in human experience. One is the *mechanical* variety that occurs when we drive an automobile or in the remote electronic control of a model airplane or space probe. *We guide something when, by conscious effort and means, we bring it to proceed in a certain way preferred by us.* The simplest and clearest cases of this type of guidance fall within the area of mechanical guidance.

But there is also personal guidance. Here too we wish to bring events to proceed in a certain way. But now we are dealing with *people.* They have a mind with which to consider matters on their own and a *will* concerning what is to be done. The ideal, then, for personal guidance is to bring things to the desired outcome but, at the same time, to give the mind being guided its fullest scope and the will its uncoerced play.

Thus the outcome really is the work of the guided individual, not merely of the one who is guiding. These individuals' uniqueness counts before God and must not be overridden. It remains their life, after all, because we have "guided" them only through their own understanding, deliberation, and decision.

For this purpose we must *communicate* with those to be guided. Only this communication will provide a mode of personal interaction that permits us to impact those guided in a way that makes a difference and yet leaves them the mental and spiritual space to retain their integrity as free personalities, to live as our friends, and to govern their own lives.

God generally deals with his nonhuman or nonpersonal creation as one guides an automobile: by a causal influence mediated through the general system of physical reality he has ordained in his creation. Job is asked whether he, like God, "can lead forth a constellation in its season, and guide the Bear with her satellites" (Jb 38:32, NASB). The answer is clear.

But God's personal creatures, whether angelic or human, are guided by *communication* of his intentions and thoughts. They are addressed by him. We are admonished in Psalm 32:9: "Do not be as the horse or as the mule which have no understanding, whose harness includes bit and bridle to keep them in check." We are to be led by, guided by, reasonable, intelligible communication, not by blind impulse, force, or sensation.

Guidance by Words

Such a communication may occur in one of two ways. First, *through what we will recognize as a voice,* or as *words* addressed to, or even through, us. If one takes away this type of communication, the biblical experience of God's presence is wiped out. The primary manner of communication from God to humankind is the Word of God, or God speaking. The Bible itself is God's Speaking preserved in written form. God spoke directly to Moses, to Ezekiel, to Paul, and to many others. Through them he spoke indirectly to the people of Israel, to the church, and now, in the Bible, to world history.

In Acts 9:10–16, for example, we have the story of a man named Ananias. The events in this story immediately follow the time in which Paul was struck down as the risen Christ addressed him on the road to Damascus. Paul went into seclusion in Damascus and was fasting and in prayer for three days. Apparently, about the end of that period of time, the Lord appeared to his fellow believer Ananias, of the same city, and told him that he should go and speak to Paul (then Saul). Thus Paul was put in touch with and ministered to by the believers in Damascus.

What we see here is not a matter of abstract argumentation, of strong impressions, or of naturally unaccountable events. The same is true for Peter's experience on the rooftop in Joppa (Acts 10) before being called to preach the gospel in the house of Cornelius, the Roman.

According to the records we have, such things happened to Paul over and over. He was about to go into Bithynia on his second missionary journey, but somehow, as we are told in Acts 16:6–9, the Holy Spirit would not let him go. Then, as he waited at Troy, he had a dream that he should, instead of staying in his home territory in Asia Minor, take a radically new direction and enter into Europe. In the dream, a man of Macedonia called him to "come over and help us."

These purposeful and conscious communications by words seem to have been quite normal experiences for the early Christians. If we look at the advice on how the meetings of the church were supposed to proceed, as given in 1 Corinthians 14, we see that it is assumed that numerous people in the congregation will have some kind of communication from God that they will be sharing with the others in the group. "What is the outcome then, brethren? When you assemble, each one has a psalm, has a teaching, has a revelation, has a tongue, has an interpretation" (14:26, NASB).

The ancient prophecy of Joel was fulfilled in the early church: "Your sons and daughters shall prophesy, and your young men shall see visions, and your old men shall dream dreams" (Acts 2:17, NASB; Jl 2:28–32). The wish of Moses, "that all the Lord's people were prophets, and that the Lord would put his spirit upon them" (Nm 11:29), is then substantially granted in the Church of Jesus Christ functioning as intended by its Lord.

Guidance by Shared Activity

But there is yet another way in which intentions and thoughts of God are communicated to those who are "with him." One way involves a much more active role on the part of the recipient and is very common to those who are most mature in his family or Kingdom. In this way we come to understand what God wants us to understand through immersion in his work with him. We understand what he is doing so well that we know what he is thinking and intending to do.

I believe that this is a great part of the condition described by Paul the apostle as *having the mind of Christ:* "He who is spiritual appraises all things, yet he himself is appraised of by no man. For who has known the mind of the Lord, that he should instruct Him? But we have the mind of Christ" (1 Cor 2:15–16, NASB).

In Psalm 32 there is an interesting statement in relation to this way of being with God. The psalmist says (in the King James version), "I will instruct thee and teach thee in the way which thou shalt go: I will guide thee with mine eye" (v. 8). Newer versions generally say: "I will guide you with my eye upon you."

There are two very clear and distinct types of experiences in which one person is guided by the eye of another. First, there are very few husbands, wives, or children who have not on occasion been forcibly guided by being looked *at* by their mate or parent. The fatherly or motherly eye on the child speaks silent volumes of profound instruction at a moment's notice.

But there is yet another and even more important way in which we are guided by the eye of another. This is when we are working or playing closely with them and know the intents and thoughts of their mind *by our awareness of what they are focused on.* Someone can effectively work with me only if they can see what I am doing and not have to be told what I am thinking and what they should do to be of help. The model employee, for example, is not someone who stands waiting, no matter how solicitously, for someone to tell them what to do. Everyone breathes easier when the new person on the job no longer has to be told.

There is a similar distinction to be drawn with respect to levels of friendship. In *The Transforming Friendship,* Leslie Weatherhead describes a kind of friendship interaction that is cognitive but occurs *beyond* words. He asks:

> If my friend's mother in a distant town falls ill and he urgently desires to visit her, which would reveal deeper friendship—my lending him my motor-bike in response to his request for it, or my taking it to his door for him as soon as I heard of the need, without waiting to be asked? In the first case there has to be a request made with a voice. But in the second the fact of the friendship creates in me a longing to help. The first illustrates the communion between two persons on what we might call the level of the seen; but the second illustrates the communion, at a deeper level, of two persons on what we may call the level of the unseen.[10]

In many cases our need to wonder about, or be told, what God wants in a certain situation is nothing short of a clear indication of how little we are engaged in his work.

On one sabbath Jesus came upon a man with a withered hand in the synagogue (Mk 3:1–5). He called him forth and asked the good people gathered about whether or not one should do good on the sabbath (heal the man) or do evil (leave him in distress). The whole condition of these people was loudly and eloquently declared by their silence. They did not know what to do! "They held their peace."

After he had healed the man, however, they thought it right to lay plans to kill Jesus. This was only another fruit of the same heart that could wonder whether or not the man should be healed. But Jesus knew what God wanted done in this case because he knew the mind of God generally. On another occasion in which Jesus was denounced for healing on the sabbath, he calmly replied, "My Father worketh hitherto, and I work" (Jn 5:17).

So our union with God—his presence "with us," in which our aloneness is banished and the meaning and full purpose of human existence is realized—*consists chiefly in a conversational relationship between God and the individual soul who is consistently and deeply engaged as his friend and co-laborer in the affairs of the Kingdom of the Heavens.*

I want to emphasize that there is a important place for "blind" faith in God's presence, as described above, as well as for the feeling or sense that "He is here," and for the display of supernatural effects of his presence. But no amount of these experiences can take the place of intelligible communication through word and shared activity.

When all of these types of presence are in place, it is then that the royal priesthood of the believer (Ex 19:6) is realized as it should be. It is then that having a personal relationship with God becomes a concrete and commonsense reality rather than a nervous whistling in the spiritual dark.

God indeed does guide us in many ways, by special acts of intervention in our lives, as well as by general providential ordering of the world. But his direct communication with us, by word and by shared activity, is the most important part of his guidance. This is because *it calls forth to full development that in us which is most in his image and constitutive of our individuality: our understanding, our values, and our will.*

Human personality in the Christian viewpoint is an incarnate system of mental and physical acts designed to be inhabited by God. We are to be the temple of God, but one that actively understands and co-operates with God's purposes and is inhabited through a willing, clear-eyed identification of ourselves with Jesus Christ, enabled by God himself.

It is Christ *in us* that is our hope of glory (Col 1:27). A strange and tortured description by Paul attempts to capture this paradoxical reality: "I am crucified with Christ: nevertheless I live; yet not I, but Christ liveth in me: and the life which I now live in the flesh I live by the faith of the Son of God, who loved me, and gave himself for me" (Gal 2:20).

The understanding just presented of these and similar passages from Scripture is not something that has only recently come to light. That is, such interpretation is not a solitary brainstorm on my part. These understandings are the mainstream of Christianity throughout the ages, though they must be constantly renewed. You may wish to compare what we have just said to the section on "Several Manners of the Divine Presence" in Jeremy Taylor's *Holy Living*.[11] This section provides a sense of the solidarity of what I have said here with what has been taught in past times.

In concluding this chapter it will be useful, as a further clarification of the view presented, to single out three interpretations of God's guidance that are commonly accepted but are surely mistaken and certainly very harmful to the search for divine guidance.

Message-a-Minute

There is, first, *the message-a-minute view*. In this view, God is either telling you what to do at every turn of the road, or he is at least willing and available to tell you if you only would ask him.

I do not believe that either the Bible or our shared experience in the Way of Christ will substantiate this picture. There is no evidence in the life of Peter or Paul, for example, that they were constantly receiving communications from God.

The union Christ had with the Father was the greatest we can conceive of in this life, if indeed we can conceive of it. Yet there is no indication that he was constantly awash with revelations as to what he should do. His union with the Father was so great that he was at all times obedient. Yet this obedience was something that rested in his mature will and understanding of his life before God, not on always being told "Now do this" and "Now do that" with regard to every detail of his life or work.

Putting it this way returns us to our theme that *divine guidance is ultimately for the mature personality.* This is not to say that people on conversion, or as they first enter the church or begin to come alive in their experience of God, do not have guidance. God meets us where we are. Yet the aim of God in working through the Holy Spirit and the indwelling Christ to guide us is not to keep us constantly under his dictation. Too much intrusion on a seed that has been planted, or on the life of a plant or a child, makes normal, healthy growth impossible.

Thus, E. Stanley Jones helpfully observes:

> I believe in miracle, but not too much miracle, for too much miracle would weaken us, make us dependent on miracle instead of our obedience to natural law. Just enough miracle to let us know He is there, but not too much, lest we depend on it when we should depend on our own initiative and on His orderly processes for our development.[12]

A redemptive community does not consist of robots, but of mature people who know how to live together and who know how to live with God. And for that reason, I think this model of a message-a-minute is mistaken and very harmful in our search for guidance. Extensive observations of individuals who try to live with this model, or at least so profess, show that they simply cannot actually do it and that any sustained effort to do so leads quickly to disaster.

Of course, the question is not whether God *could* give a message each minute. Surely he could do that. He could give ten or a thousand messages a nanosecond. Even more, if that would suit his purpose of bringing forth the cosmic family of God. But it does not. Sometimes we get caught up in trying to glorify God by praising what he can do, and we lose sight of the practical point of what he actually does do.

All of this must be kept in mind as we develop our educational programs, hold our evangelistic meetings, run teaching missions, and carry on with all of the activities of the church. In our services and in our models of the ministry and of ministers, we must remember that we are not making robots who sing, clap, pray, give, and show up for meetings when they are supposed to. We are bringing forth the sons and daughters of God to live their unique lives in this world to his glory. We must do all we can to suit the means we employ to that end.

It's-All-in-the-Bible

The second view of guidance that I believe is seriously misguided and very harmful is the *it's-all-in-the-Bible* view. This is a view that intends to honor the Bible, but with a zeal that is not according to knowledge.

About many questions in our lives, the Bible gives direct instructions. We do not need to make long inquiries into God's will in order to know whether we should worship an idol, take something that is not ours, engage in illicit sex, or mistreat our parents. But many other questions force us to realize that *we* and the specific circumstances of our lives are simply not dealt with in the Bible.

The Bible will not tell which song you are supposed to sing next Sunday or which verse you should take as a text for a talk or a sermon. Yet God's special leading is claimed more frequently for the selection of texts and sermon topics than for anything else.

The Bible will not tell you what to do about most of the details of your life. Say you want to know how to raise your children. The Bible will tell you some very important things, but not everything you need and want to know on that subject. Your family, your work, your community will face you with many, many choices and issues that the Bible says nothing specific about.

But, on the other hand, the *principles* are all there. I happily insist that, so far as principles are concerned, the Bible says all that needs to be said or can be said. But the principles have to be applied before they can be lived out. And it is largely at the point of application that almost everything that we can imagine has been "proven" from the Bible. This is in part because the principles of "proof" have to be scandalously loosened before one can get the applications so desperately desired.

Our reverence for and faith in the Bible must not be allowed to blind us to the need for personal divine guidance within the principles of but beyond the details explicitly stated in the Bible. A distinguished minister recently said on a nationally televised program that if we would only accept the Bible as the Word of God, all differences among Christians would be resolved. But in fact, it is Bible-believing Christians who disagree with one another most often and most heatedly.

Nearly every faction in Christendom claims the Bible as its basis but then disagrees as to what the Bible says. An exalted view of the Bible does not free us from the responsibility of learning to talk with God and learning to hear him in the many ways he speaks to humankind.

It is a misguided expectation of the Bible with reference to individual guidance that leads some people to play the "Bible roulette" earlier mentioned. They allow the Bible to fall open where it will and then stab their finger at random on the page to see which verse they land on. Then they read the verse thus selected to see what they should do.

Despite of the greatness of some Christians who have used this technique, it certainly is not a procedure recommended by the Bible, and there is no *biblical* reason why one might not just as well use the dictionary or the *Encyclopedia Brittanica* or the morning newspaper or why one might not as well open the Bible and wait for a fly to land on a verse.

A novel approach was recently suggested by a minister who stated in all seriousness that we should look up the year of our birth to cast light on what we should do. Unless you were born in the first half of this century, and the earlier the better, this method will do you no good because there are few verses numbered beyond twenty or thirty. I was born in 1935, so I thought I would see what direction I could get from Genesis 19:35. I will leave it to your curiosity to see what that verse says, but one shudders to think what "guidance" might be derived from this method.

Of course, God is so great that he sometimes does use almost any-thing one can imagine for his purposes in the life of one sincerely seeking him. Even truly superstitious methods are not beyond his for-bearance and use. But that does not certify these as methods he chooses for the spiritual life.

In the upper room (Acts 1:26), lots were cast—something like flip-ping a coin or drawing straws—to determine who would replace Judas among the twelve apostles. This method was often used in biblical times, and Proverbs 16:33 (KJV) assures us that although the lot is cast into the lap, "its every decision is from the Lord."

However, even the most biblically oriented churches of today would not think of rolling dice or flipping a coin to determine policy for the church or to settle an issue in some individual member's life. This is true even though all might agree that God *could* influence the coin or the dice to come out as he wished.

So we have made some progress. Nevertheless, you still hear peo-ple tell of opening the Bible at random and reading a random verse to decide whether to undertake some enterprise, or move, or marry a certain person. Many devout people will do such things to get "guid-ance," so great is their need and anxiety, though they may later try to hide it or laugh at it when revealed. Worse still, many actually act on this "guidance" to the great harm of themselves and others about them. They are the losers at "Bible roulette."

What a stark contrast to this unhappy condition is the simple word of Jesus: "My sheep hear my voice, and I know them, and they follow me" (Jn 10:27).

Whatever-Comes

A third mistaken view of guidance is *the whatever-comes view.* This view is very commonly adopted and has much to recommend it in terms of the peace of mind and freedom from struggle it provides. But, in fact, it amounts to giving up any possibility of guidance as a conscious interchange between God and his children.

The view even shows up in some of our most loved hymns. There is a well-known hymn titled "If Thou But Suffer God to Guide Thee."

This may seem to be exactly what we are talking about: allowing God to guide us. But when we study the hymn closely, we find that there is in it a council to accept *everything* that happens to us as the guidance of God.

But if you wish to know what God would have you do, it is no help at all to be told that whatever comes is his will. For you are precisely in the position of having to decide in some measure what is to come. Does this mean that whatever you do will be God's will? I certainly hope not.

We can at least say that if Moses had accepted this view, there would have been no nation of Israel. Perhaps there would have been a nation of "Mosesites" instead. When the people made and worshiped the golden calf while Moses was on Sinai receiving God's commandments, God said, "I will destroy them, and make of thee [Moses] a great nation" (Ex 32:10). Moses not only did not accept "whatever comes," he actually and successfully withstood God's own declared intent in the matter, appealing to God's reputation before the surrounding nations and to his friendship with Abraham. "And the Lord repented of the evil which he thought to do unto his people" (Ex 32:14).

Many things that happen are not the will of God, although obviously he does not act to stop them. "It is not the will of God that any should perish, but that all should come to repentance" (2 Pt 3:9). But countless people nevertheless *do* perish and fail to come to repentance.

God's world is an arena in which we have an indispensable role to play. The issue is not simply What does God want? but also What do we want and will? To accept whatever comes is not guidance. Merely that something happens does not indicate that it is God's will.

With respect to many events in our future, God's will is that *we* should determine what will happen. What the child does when not told what to do is the final indicator of what and who that child is. And so it is for us and our heavenly Father. We shall return to this point in the last chapter.

Against these three mistaken views of divine guidance we set a conversational view in which, in a manner to be further explored later, there is appropriate, clear, specific communication through conscious experience from God to the individual believer within the context of a life immersed in God's Kingdom.

> Then you shall call, and the Lord shall answer; you shall cry, and he shall say, Here I am. . . . And the Lord shall guide you continu- ˙ ally, and satisfy your soul in drought, and make your bones fat: and you shall be like a watered garden, and like a spring of water, whose waters fail not. (Is 58:9, 11)

There will be many who still wonder if we really do live in a universe in which this could happen. Does the human and physical reality of our universe call for it? Does it even allow it? This is an issue to which we must now turn.

SOME TOPICS FOR REFLECTION

1. Have you known people who were so close to God that they were never lonely? What do you think of the prospects of such a relationship for you? For others in the contemporary world?

2. Do the four basic forms of being "with" God and God "with" us adequately cover that relationship? What would you add? Or take away?

3. How important do you think "blind" faith is to the stability of the Christian's walk?

4. Discuss some cases in which you are sure God *acted* with you. How can one learn more about this from experience?

5. Can you explain to someone else the two main types of guidance (mechanical and personal) and the two aspects of personal guidance?

6. Do you think that the critiques are sound of the three interpretations of guidance said to be erroneous? What would you disagree with in them?

Notes

1. Anglican hymn #315 in *The Hymnal* (Oxford, England: Oxford University Press, 1889).
2. Thomas à Kempis, *The Imitation of Christ* (Chicago: Moody Press, 1958), 106–7. A. W. Tozer sharply states the contemporary need in this connection: "What we need very badly these days is a company of Christians who are prepared to trust God as completely now as they know they must do at the last day. For each of us the time is coming when we shall have nothing but God. Health and wealth and friends and hiding places will be swept away and we shall have only God. To the man of pseudo faith that is a terrifying thought, but to real faith it is one of the most comforting thoughts the heart can entertain." (Quoted from *The Root of Righteousness* [Harrisburg, PA: Christian Publications, 1955], 50.)
3. St. Augustine, *The City of God*, trans. by Marcus Dods (New York: The Modern Library, 1950), 867.
4. "Shorter Catechism," *Westminster Confession of Faith*, first paragraph.
5. St. John of the Cross, *Dark Night of the Soul* (Garden City, NY: Image Books, 1959), 36–39. The phrase "dark night of the soul" covers a larger sphere of our experience of God than is dealt with in our discussions here.
6. Richard J. Foster, "Praying in the Desert," *Christianity Today*, July 20, 1992, p. 25. This is an exerpt from Foster's *Prayer: Finding the Heart's True Home* (San Francisco: HarperSanFrancisco, 1992).
7. A. P. Fitt, *The Shorter Life of D. L. Moody* (Chicago: Moody Press, 1900), 67.
8. Fitt, *Shorter Life*, 76.
9. Brother Lawrence, *Practice of the Presence of God*, 37–38.
10. Leslie Weatherhead, *The Transforming Friendship* (London: Epworth Press, 1962), 54.
11. An excellent supplementary discussion to the above is found under the heading "Several Manners of the Divine Presence" in Jeremy Taylor's *The Rule and Exercise of Holy Living* (London: Henry G. Bohn, 1858), 19–27. (First published 1650)
12. E. Stanley Jones, *A Song of Ascents* (Nashville, TN: Abingdon Press, 1979), 191.

4   *Our Communicating Cosmos*

Earth's crammed with Heaven, and every common bush afire with God; but only he who sees
take off his shoes.

ELIZABETH BARRETT BROWNING

In him we live, and move, and have our being.

ACTS 17:28

The preceding chapters have offered a large number of stories about
God's guidance of well-known and unknown Christians, especially
about their being *spoken* to in various ways. There is a practically endless supply of such stories, and each is of considerable interest in its own
right. I love to dwell on them myself, and I have noticed that people
rarely tire of hearing them, even when they don't entirely believe them.
Although none is to be treated as "canonical," taken together they
serve as an essential point of reference for research into divine guidance.

Another favorite of mine concerns Peter Marshall, the Scotsman
who in the middle years of this century became one of our most widely
acclaimed ministers and, by his outstanding qualities as a person and
as a minister, gained a new level of prominence for the office of the
chaplain of the United States Senate.

One foggy, pitch-black Northumberland night, he cut across the
moors of his native land in an area where lay a deep, deserted limestone

quarry. As he plodded blindly forward, an urgent voice called out, "Peter!" He stopped and answered: "Yes, who is it? What do you want?" But there was no response.

Thinking he was mistaken, he took a few more steps. Then again, even more urgently, "Peter!" At this he stopped again and, trying to peer into the darkness, stumbled forward and fell to his knees. Putting down his hand to brace himself, he found nothing there. As he felt around in a semicircle he discovered that he was right on the brink of the abandoned quarry, and one step more certainly would have killed him.[1]

Many widely read religious papers and magazines from almost every denomination and theological persuasion provide us with a constant stream of such stories. In his book *Does God Speak Today?* David Pytches compiled "real life accounts" of "words" given to disciples of Jesus in recent years. He adds fourteen cases of what are pretty clearly *mistaken* claims of guidance from God.[2] Study of these latter cases is also very useful in understanding God's guidance, because we need to know both what it is and what it is *not*.

Mary Geegh, a long-time missionary to India, recorded many remarkable experiences of herself and others hearing from God during her years there. In her little booklet *God Guides,*[3] she explains a special method of listening and obeying that she has followed and taught with outstanding success.

What Lazarus Could Not Do

But we have now come to a point in our study where we must recognize that there is a limit to what can be accomplished for the growth of our faith by contemplating such stories, no matter how well attested they may be or how reliable are the minds and characters of the people involved. This limit is not neglected in the teachings of the Bible itself.

According to the account given by Jesus in Luke 16, "a certain rich man" died and found himself tormented in Hades. There he saw poor Lazarus, who used to beg at his gate, across from him at a great distance and at peace in close company with Abraham. The rich man then saw how wrong he had been during his lifetime and wished to keep his five brothers still on earth from joining him in the place of torment.

He asked father Abraham to send Lazarus back to tell them of his fate so that they might avoid it. This instructive conversation then follows: "Abraham said unto him, 'They have Moses and the prophets; let them hear them.' And he said, 'Nay, father Abraham: but if one went unto them from the dead, they will repent.' And Abraham said unto him, 'If they hear not Moses and the prophets, neither will they be persuaded, though one rose from the dead'" (Lk 16:29–31).

The Limits of Signs

We also recall from the New Testament record that Jesus refused to do religious stunts or "signs" for those who demanded them (Mt 12:39–40; Mk 8:11–12; Lk 23:8–9; Jn 2:18, 6:30). I believe that this was because he knew that such deeds, no matter how wondrous, would be fruitless against the false ideas and mind-sets of the observers. We cannot imagine that he would have withheld signs if they truly would have helped people have genuine faith in him.

But they could not. It is precisely our preexisting ideas and assumptions that largely determine what we *can* see, hear, or otherwise observe. These general ideas, which are so often held because they express how we *want* things to be, determine what stories can mean to us. They cannot, therefore, be changed by stories and miraculous events only, since they prevent correct perception of those very stories and events.

Agnes Sanford relates how, as the young wife of an Episcopal minister, she reacted when her child came down with a serious ear infection. It lasted for six weeks, during which she prayed fearfully and fruitlessly. Then a neighboring minister called to see her husband and learned that the child was sick. He quite casually, though intently and in a businesslike manner, prayed for the little one, who immediately shut his eyes, lost his fever flush, and went to sleep. When the child awoke, the fever was gone and his ears were well.

Mrs. Sanford remarks:

> The strange thing is that this did not immediately show me a
> new world. Instead, it perplexed me greatly. Why did God answer
> the minister's prayers when He had not answered mine? I did not
> know that I myself blocked my own prayers, because of my lack of
> faith. Nor did I know that this [successful] prayer could not come
> from resentment and darkness and unhappiness, as a pipeline can
> be clogged with roots and dirt. This doubt and confusion remained
> in my mind, even though the child himself, whenever he subse-
> quently had a bit of an earache, demanded that I pray for him.[4]

Necessity of General Understanding of God

We find such a failure to "see a new world" strange only because we
do not pay attention to how our minds work. This inability only illustrates the fact that beholding or being told of God's specific interventions in our lives—whether to guide us, speak to us, or perform
saving deeds in our behalf—does not automatically clear up our confusions or straighten out the entanglements of our hearts. Such events
may, in fact, only entertain us. Or they may stimulate us to *seek* faith
and understanding. But they do not of themselves *give* us faith and understanding.

Our understanding must grow *before* we can have any significant
appreciation of what we are experiencing on occasions in which God
intervenes in our lives. We must have a correct general understanding
of God and his ways, which is why the rich man was told, "Let them
hear Moses and the prophets."

The role of the Scriptures and scriptural interpretation is to provide
us with a general understanding of God and to inspire and cultivate
a corresponding faith. The power of stories alone to generate life-
changing faith is much overestimated today.

Lack of general understanding may also limit the effects of a word
truly given by God to the individual. Very often, in my experience, the
word given *to* me is actually spoken by me. In a way I've come to recognize through repeated occurrence, it simply "comes out," with no
preliminaries. But I do not always understand its true significance at

the time. Many others have had the same experience. This is exactly what happened to Peter on the occasion of his great confession: "Thou art the Christ, the Son of the living God" (Mt 16:16–17).

Notice what followed in Peter's case. First, Jesus authenticated that the word to Peter was indeed from his Father in the heavens. Then Jesus began to explain further what was going to happen to himself: persecution, death, resurrection.

Immediately, Peter showed that he did not understand what he himself had just uttered. He had been given to recognize Jesus as the Christ, but he did not know what the Christ would be. Consequently, he tried to cast him in a strictly human role. Jesus had to tell him to get out of his way, because Peter had his mind in the wrong place and was actually playing the role of adversary (Satan).

God is always trying, in many ways, to teach us of himself. And certainly he will meet us with inward illumination as we study and as we strive to understand:

> If you cry out for insight
> and raise your voice for understanding,
> if you seek it like silver
> and search for it as for hidden treasures;
> then you will understand the fear of the Lord
> and find the knowledge of God.
>
> *(Prv 2:3–5, RSV)*

All of this must be kept clearly in mind as we go on in this chapter in which we will be dealing with the basic questions: *What kind of world do we live in?* and *How does God relate to us enclosed within it?* Admittedly, we are entering an intellectual and spiritual "hard-hat area." We must deal with a number of difficult problems that trouble many thoughtful Christians and non-Christian alike, problems about the *very idea* of our being in a conversational relationship with God. The Bible has been given to us to help us with these problems, but we still have to work hard to resolve them.

If you are one of those who have no difficulty along these lines, perhaps you should just count your blessings and immediately skip to chapter 5, which deals with the various ways God uses to communicate personally with us. But if you find that you do not have any real confidence that God *would* or *could* guide you and speak to you, this chapter is intended to be of use. Put on your hard hat, your hard nose, your best brains, and prayerfully dig in.

Four Negative Responses

In fact, and I have verified this on many occasions, the honest response of many people (including some of those who heartily confess and practice faith in Christ) to what has been said in the foregoing chapters will be that (1) God *would not* communicate with run-of-the-mill human beings by surrounding them with his presence and speaking to them, or (2) he *does not* communicate with *them* in that way, or even (3) he *cannot* do so.

Perhaps others, motivated by the need to control the Divine Presence and Word for what they sincerely regard as proper ends, will even think that (4) God *should not* communicate with individuals as has been indicated in this book. But consider the following replies.

1. God Would

When we are considering whether God would be with ordinary human beings in a conversational relationship, we must remember not to conceive of him in the likeness of human dignitaries. The famous, the rich, and the great among humanity are still severely limited in their powers of communication by the fact that they are merely human. Their abilities to interact personally with others are very narrowly limited, and it is possible for them to be in intimate contact only with a small number of other people, despite all the "wonders" of modern communications technology. Their span of consciousness, their capacity to pay attention, and the scope of their willpower permits nothing more.

But beyond such factual limitations, human "greatness" is often taken to mean, and essentially to *require,* having nothing to do with those who are "just ordinary people." Greatness is seen as involving a certain exclusiveness, insularity, or snobbishness. If we are unable to clear our minds of such associations with greatness, we will be unable to think that the great God would talk to *us*. We will think of him as a dignitary who is too busy for that, or who is too conscious of his "status," too "high up."

How hard it is for us to adequately conceive of the *lowliness* of God! It is precisely his greatness that makes him able, available, and ready to hear and speak personally with the most insignificant of his creatures.

This lowliness is, of course, at the very center of Jesus' teaching about God. In his actions and words, Jesus made clear how totally accessible God is to the weak, to the downtrodden and castaway, to the little children. "Suffer little children, and forbid them not, to come unto me: for of such is the kingdom of the heavens" (Mt 19:14). In saying "of such," many interesting characteristics certainly were intended by our Lord, but here we stress the element of unimportance. The unimportant ones are important to God. God being who he is, and now revealed in the person of Jesus Christ, *we should be surprised if he did NOT speak to us.*

As E. Stanley Jones has written:

> Does God guide? Strange if he didn't. The Psalmist asks: "He that planted the ear, shall he not hear? He that formed the eyes, shall he not see?" (Ps 94:9). And I ask: "He that made the tongue and gave us power to communicate with one another, shall he not speak and communicate with us?" I do not believe that God our Father is a dumb, non-communicative impersonality.[5]

2. And God Does—Though We Can Miss or Prevent It

But what of those who believe that God just simply and as a matter of fact does not speak to *them?* Here we must consider, I believe, two separate lines along which the cause of the difficulty may be found.

First of all, *that we do not hear does not mean that he is not speaking to us.*

It is a very common thing, even at the strictly human level, for us not to hear those who speak to us. It has probably happened to most of us this very day. Someone spoke to us but we did not know it, did not hear it. Moreover, we know that messages of radio and television programs are passing through our very bodies and brains at all hours of the day, messages that an appropriate receiver appropriately tuned could pluck from the air we breathe.

In certain circumstances, the human body can act as an antenna to a radio set. As a child I had a radio set that required me to hold the aerial wire in order to bring in faraway stations. As you now read this, radio waves bearing a vast number of messages flood around you and even right through you: messages from television or radio news, from ships at sea, from citizens' band or police radio, possibly even from outer space.

Astronomers who seek for signs of life on other planets and in other galaxies of our universe say it may well be that earth is constantly bombarded by messages from outer space and that we simply don't know how to pick them up, organize them, or recognize their patterns.

What an apt picture this is, it seems to me, of the human being in relation to God: showered with messages that simply go right through us or by us. We are not *attuned* to God's voice. We have not been taught how to hear it sounding out in nature—as we read in Psalm 19, "The heavens announce the glory of God"—or in a special communication directed by God to the individual mind or soul.

Thus some of Jesus' deepest teachings are about hearing. He taught in parables so that those who did not really want to hear truth could avoid it. He realized that not everyone has ears for the purpose of hearing, but that some use their ears to sort out what they want to hear and leave the rest aside. Thus one of his most repeated sayings was "If anyone has ears to hear, let them hear." But he also urged his hearers to make a great effort to hear, assuring them that what they got would be proportional to their desire and effort (Mk 4:23–24).

A Ready Vessel?

This brings us to our second way of understanding those who say, "God just does not speak to me." In this case, a bit of honest soul-searching may be required. Possibly these individuals are being spoken to and do not hear. But it may also be that *they could make no good use of a word from God because of how they are living.*

Do they stand ready to obey and change, should that be what God directs? Do they *want* to know if they are on a wrong path? It is, in general, a good thing for God to speak to us. But there may be reasons in an individual case why it would be best for God to speak very little or even not at all. If it is true that God does not speak to me, then I must inquire whether or not I am such a case.

The question must be asked, To what use would I try to put a word from God? True, God is not a snob, and he is not far away: "Behold, the Lord's hand is not too short to reach us and save, nor is his ear heavy and unable to hear" (Is 59:1). But when he speaks, it is to accomplish his good purposes in our lives and through his creation.

Divine guidance is not a gimmick we can keep on tap for our gain. Its purpose is not to enable us to win in our competitions with others. We cannot invoke it to help us win bets on football games or horse races or to prove that we are theologically correct. Although it is available to all those who walk with God, it is not *at their disposal as they see fit*, without regard to the purposes of God's government. Nor should it be, for that would be very dangerous.

We have already briefly touched on this point, but it must be hammered home relentlessly. Divine guidance is not for any form of self-aggrandizement. It is not for the enhancement of the ego, for the building up of pride. It is not to prove that "I'm okay." How many times have we heard others invoke God's support for their cause, saying "God says" or "God told me," sometimes subtly, sometimes blatantly using the voice of God to prove that they are right! But as with all of God's activities in human life, guidance is for the promotion of his kingdom and our good in that kingdom.

We pray: "Our Father which art in heaven, hallowed be thy name, thy kingdom come, thy will be done on earth as it is in heaven." This preamble to the Lord's Prayer beautifully expresses the purpose of all of God's activities in us: "Hallowed be *thy* name. *Thy* kingdom come. *Thy* will be done." Divine guidance, as a reliable, day-to-day reality for people with good sense, is for those who are devoted to the glory of God and the advancement of his kingdom. Guidance is for disciples of Jesus Christ who have no higher preference than to be like him.

Admittedly, this does not mean that it never comes to anyone else. And in the next chapter we will see how God speaks to some very unlikely people. But we cannot too often recall that his speaking to someone does not mean that they are right or that they are particularly good. It means only that he wills to communicate to them in order to accomplish his purposes concerning them.

In Business with God

So if you find yourself in the position of the one who can honestly say, "God has never spoken to me," then you well might ask, "Why *should* God speak to *me?* What am I doing in life that would make his speaking to me a reasonable thing for him to do? Are we in business together in life? Or am I in business just for myself, trying to 'use a little God' to advance my projects?"

When our lives are devoted to the will of God, there is reason for him to speak to us. If our lives are not devoted to his purposes, he still may speak to us, even use us for his ends if we are strategically placed. After all, we are his creatures, no matter how misguided or rebellious. But for a willing walk in conscious, loving cooperation with God, we must come to grips with this issue: *What are we living for?* We must face it *clearly.*

It may well be that I have never come to the place where I can truly say, "I am living for one thing and one thing *only,* and that is to be like Christ and do his work and live among his people and serve them and him in this world. My life is to bless others in the name of God." If we have not come to that place, then the question that normally arises as How do we hear the word of God? is replaced by the more basic question What would we do if we heard it?

We borrow a few incisive words on this point from G. Campbell Morgan. Having mentioned that when God speaks to us, his word comes as a disturbing element into our lives, Morgan continues:

You have never heard the voice of God, and you say: "The day of miracles is past. I am never disturbed. I make my own plans and live where I please and do as I like. What do you mean by a disturbing element?". . . Beloved, you are living still among the fleshpots and garlic of Egypt. You are still in slavery. . . . You know no disturbing voice? God never points out for you a pathway altogether different from the one you had planned? Then, my brother, you are living still in the land of slavery, in the land of darkness.[6]

Perhaps we do not hear the voice because we don't expect to hear it. But then again, perhaps we don't expect it because we know that we fully intend to run our lives on our own and have never seriously considered anything else. The voice of God would therefore be an unwelcome intrusion into our plans. By contrast, we expect the great ones in the Way of Christ to hear that voice just because we see their lives wholly given up to doing what God wants.

Frank Laubach tells of the immense change that came over his life at the point when he resolved to do the will of God:

As for me, I never lived, I was half dead, I was a rotting tree, until I reached the place where I wholly, with utter honesty, resolved and then re-resolved that I *would* find God's will, and I *would* do that will though every fiber in me said no, and I *would* win the battle in my thoughts. It was as though some deep artesian well had been struck in my soul. . . . You and I shall soon blow away from our bodies. Money, praise, poverty, opposition, these make no difference, for they will all alike be forgotten in a thousand years, but this spirit which comes to a mind set upon continuous surrender, this spirit is timeless.[7]

3. Certainly God Can: The Open Creation

Many fear that the physical universe, being what it is, makes communication with God impossible. It puts him "too far away." Even some who understand the lowliness of God's greatness and the greatness of God's lowliness and really live to do the will of God are yet troubled by the thought that brutal nature interposes itself as a barrier between us and him. After the death of his dear friend A. H. Hallam, the poet Tennyson speaks as if he were addressed by the personage of Sorrow:

"The stars," she whispers, "blindly run";
A web is woven across the sky;
From out waste places comes a cry
And murmurs from a dying sun.

Especially in times when the word of God does not come and we are not at peace with him, the very face of nature becomes cold and hard and forbidding: "And I will break the pride of your power; and I will make your heaven as iron, and your earth as brass: and your strength shall be spent in vain: for your land shall not yield her increase, neither shall the trees of the land yield their fruits" (Lv 26:19–20). "And your heaven that is over your head shall be brass, and the earth beneath you shall be iron. The Lord shall make the 'rain' of your land to be powder and dust: from heaven shall it come down upon you, until you are destroyed" (Dt 28:23–24).

Then we cry out, "Oh that you would rip the heavens open, that you would come down" (Is 64:1), but the heavens remain intact, God keeps his distance, and nature rolls on. Amidst the ravages of war, accident, and physical and mental illness, we suffer, shed our tears, and bury our loved ones and our hopes. All the while it seems that God is known only by his absence and is anything, we think, but "our refuge and strength, a very present help in trouble" (Ps 46:1).

The "Warfare" Between Science and Theology

But even beyond such *experiences* of the seemingly "godless" course of nature common to all generations of humanity, there is a special burden of unbelief born by Western civilization for several hundred years past. This is the idea that it is *unscientific* to believe that God could speak to us or guide us. Today it is readily assumed that "scientific knowledge" excludes the presence of God from the material universe of which we human beings are supposed to be a pitifully small and insignificant part.

The discovery of the immensity of space and of the forces of nature, which appear to determine everything that happens and *seem* to run their course with no assistance from the hand of a personal God, can be quite overwhelming. When the great French mathematician and astronomer Laplace presented the Emperor Napoleon with a copy of his book on celestial mechanics, the emperor asked him where God fitted into his system. Laplace indignantly drew himself up and replied: "Sir, I have no need of any such an hypothesis!"

And so the current model of the natural sciences proceeds, without invoking God. You will not find any laboratory manual, any statistical analysis of social processes—even in a Christian school or seminary!—that introduces God as a factor in its calculations.

The social institution of higher education, the university system, stands in our culture as the source of unquestioned authority as far as *knowledge* is concerned. Without making a special point of it, the university now throws its weight behind a picture of reality without God, where human beings are entirely "on their own." This is the view known as "naturalism" or "secularism." Regardless of what might be said for public relations purposes, the system presumes in its processes that you can have the best education possible and be ignorant of God.

Thus we seem to have had imposed on us a picture of reality according to which humanity is encapsulated *within* a material world. God, if he really exists, is pictured as wholly *beyond* that material world, which seems to run without God.

Given such a view of things, one of the most difficult issues we face in trying to think about guidance concerns the "how" of it all.

How Could God "Get Through" to Us?

For example, if you want to talk to someone in Germany, you will have to produce a chain of events in the physical substance, the inorganic matter, between here and there. You will perhaps begin by dialing a number on your telephone. This will cause electrical impulses to propagate themselves by various means across the intervening space. A physical apparatus located in Germany will be sensitive to those impulses and will convert them into a form your friend can hear or see and understand. That is how it will be done.

The point is that to communicate, as is ordinarily done, *we must go through the intervening physical reality.*

Even if I am standing next to you and want to speak directly to you, I must do the same thing. I make some sort of noise that strikes your eardrum. Somehow, in a way no one fully understands, registering this noise causes you to think of specific things or events. I *bring about* your thinking, and that is what my communication with you consists of.

What I have been doing on these very pages is a case in point. I have been guiding you, guiding your thoughts. You have, of course, accepted my guidance and cooperated with me.

Another illustration of how a physical medium intervenes in human communication can be found in art. In our experience of art, the physical medium of communication, whether it is written or spoken words or color or form, becomes the field of creativity. When you go to a movie, the room is made dark, and you fix your eyes on the screen with its moving images. What are you doing? You are accepting guidance through a physical medium. The variegated light reflecting from the screen into your eyes controls the processes of your experience.

Given the picture of communication presented by these models, the questions we now must face are as clear as they are compelling:

1. Is *this* the only way God can communicate with us?
2. Does God always have to go *through* physical substance?
3. Does the entire realm of organic and inorganic matter stand *between* us and God?
4. *Where* is God in relation to that realm?
5. How does God come into relation to us if he is "far off" from us?

But Space Is Not the Whole of Reality

For many, these will be the most difficult questions we take up in this chapter, or even in this book. I hasten to say, however, that God does *not* have to go through physical intermediaries of any sort to reach us, though on some occasions he obviously chooses to do so.

The material world in which we are placed by him permits him to be "nearer" to us than even our own eyes, ears, and brain. It is "in him" that we "live, and move, and have our being" (Acts 17:28).

Our faith may all too easily fall victim to the tendency of the human mind to *spatialize* everything. If we think of God as being literally "outside" of the physical realm, then it will seem as if he were utterly out of reach for us and we out of reach for him. The edge of the known universe is now thought to be something like thirteen or fourteen million light-years away. Beyond that, even light waves, traveling at the speed of 186,284 miles per second, can never reach us! How then can we reach God or he us, if he is "out there"?

Blaise Pascal, the great scientist and Christian, remarks:

> When I see the blind and wretched state of man, when I survey the whole universe in its dumbness and man left to himself with no light, as though lost in this corner of the universe, without knowing who put him there, what he has come to do, what will become of him when he dies, incapable of knowing anything, I am moved to terror, like a man transported in his sleep to some terrifying desert island, who wakes up quite lost and with no means of escape. Then I marvel that so wretched a state does not drive people to despair.
>
> I see other people around me, made like myself. I ask them if they are any better informed than I, and they say they are not. Then these lost and wretched creatures look around and find some attractive objects to which they become addicted and attached. For my part I have never been able to form such attachments, and considering how very likely it is that there exists something besides what I can see, I have tried to find out whether God has left any traces of himself.[8]

The "traces" of God that have always stood forth to the earnest seeker consist in *the purposeful order* that appears within nature and history, as well as purposeful interventions that seem to show up in history and in our individual lives. To fully develop this point is impossible here. But the *order* of events large and small throughout our world strongly suggests to those who are not already set against it—and thus, as opinion surveys clearly demonstrate, to the overwhelming mass of humanity—that there is a providential and personal oversight of our world and our lives.

This is what the Apostle Paul has in mind when he says in his sermon on Mar's Hill in Athens that God has so arranged our world that we should seek the Lord and, as the Jerusalem Bible translates it, "by feeling [our] way towards him, succeed in finding him. Yet in fact he is not far from any of us, since it is in him that we live, and move, and exist" (Acts 17:27–28).

The New Testament presents Christ the Son as continuously "sustaining all things by his powerful word" (Heb 1:3) and as the very "glue" of the universe. "In Him all things hold together" (*sunistemi*, Col 1:17). As A. H. Strong spells this out:

> Christ is the originator and the upholder of the universe. . . . In him, the power of God, the universe became an actual, real thing, perceptible to others; and in him it consists, or holds together, from hour to hour. The steady will of Christ constitutes the law of the universe and makes it a cosmos instead of a chaos, just as his will brought it into being in the beginning.[9]

Hints from Current Physics

And now we come to a most important point, for our present concerns. The current state of the physical sciences, in opposition to the crudely mechanical view that was dominant for several centuries past, is very congenial to the view of God's presence in his world that we find in the New Testament. Sir James Jean interpreted the result of developments in physics during this present century as follows:

> Today there is a wide measure of agreement, which on the side of Physics approaches almost to unanimity, that the stream of knowledge is heading towards a nonmechanical reality; the universe begins to look more like a great thought than like a great machine. Mind no longer appears as an accidental intruder into the realm of matter; we are beginning to suspect that we ought rather to hail it as the creator and governor of the realm of matter.[10]

More recently, in his essay "Remarks on the Mind-Body Question," Nobel Prize laureate Eugene Wigner points to a general recognition among physicists that thought or the mind is primary to physical reality: "It is not possible to formulate the laws of quantum mechanics in a fully consistent way without reference to consciousness."

Princeton physicist John A. Wheeler even goes so far as to hold that subjective and objective reality, consciousness and matter, mutually create each other. Another leading physicist, Jack Sarfatti, remarks that "an idea of the utmost significance for the development of psychoenergetic systems . . . is that the structure of matter may not be independent of consciousness."[11]

I do not wish to make more of these recent interpretations of physics than is strictly warranted. In particular, there is offered here no suggestion that physics "proves" any theological position, or even that it "proves" matter to be dependent on mind, as the New Testament itself teaches.

Our sole point is that *on some influential contemporary views* of physical reality there is, so to speak, an "inside"—or, better, a *nonside* or *un-side*—to matter that allows for a *nonspatial and yet causal dimension* to be in action within the physical world. This dimension could very well accommodate the biblical view of God's relation to his world in creation and sustenance. The "mental" side of reality does not have to traverse space to have its effects.

In all of this we at least find some further support for our contention that there is no reason, drawn from established truths of science, to suppose that God *cannot* reach us to guide us and communicate with us. There is plenty of room left for God in the picture of the world presented to us by contemporary science.

We remain comfortable, then, with our view that we live in the kind of material universe in which divine guidance is possible. We are confident this is so *precisely because our universe seems to be pervaded by mind and the power or energy of mind.* Biblically, John 1, Hebrews 1, and other texts confirm this. Is it not then reasonable to *expect* guidance, since it is the nature of mind to always and everywhere guide?

Such Explorations Clarify Faith

We must not suppose that such discussions as the foregoing are irrelevant to our confidence in divine guidance. A popular song says, "If you believe in things you don't understand you will suffer!" Over and over, humanity has proven this true. Perhaps it is a slight oversimplification, but the heart *is* largely dependent on the head. A lack of understanding does weaken faith and misdirect life.

Even though not everything can be understood, our faith will be strengthened by such understanding as it is possible to acquire. Science, vaguely understood as it may be, is a power of our age, a weighty authority whether we like it or not. And if you really believe that guidance is *unscientific*, you will have great difficulty in dealing with it practically or being open and intelligent concerning it.

As you come to understand that the whole of reality is something penetrated through and through by God, then you can begin to open yourself up to the possibility of divine guidance.

A comparison may help. God's relation to the world is similar, though not identical, to your relation to your body. You inhabit your body, but *you* cannot, nor can any act of your consciousness or any element of your character, be located or physically identified *at* any point in your body. Similarly, God inhabits space, though he infinitely exceeds it as well (1 Kgs 8:27). "The whole earth is full of his glory" (Is 6:3). The Heavens are the throne of God, and the earth is his footstool (Is 66:1; Mt 5:34, 23:22).

Your whole body is accessible to you, and you are accessible through it. As your consciousness plays over and through your whole body, so do "the eyes of the Lord run to and fro throughout the whole earth, to show himself strong on behalf of those whose heart is perfect toward him" (2 Chr 16:9).

Chariots of Fire

In this world we are too much obsessed by practical concerns, governed by a fallen ideology—in part the ideology of the "scientific"— that shapes our minds away from God. We need to have done for our understanding what Elisha did for his young assistant on one occasion when they were in great danger.

The king of Syria was at war with Israel, but every time he laid his battle plans, Elisha would tell them to the king of Israel. The king of Syria naturally supposed that there was an Israelite spy in his confidence, but his aides all denied it, explaining that "Elisha, the prophet who is in Israel, tells the king of Israel the words that you speak in your bedroom" (2 Kgs 6:12, NASB). Talk about guidance!

Such extrasensory events are a part of the very life of the Bible. If we cannot approach them with openness to what the experience would be like for us, then—to reemphasize an earlier theme—we will not be able to believe them, *really* believe them. Our very reading of the Bible may then force us into skepticism about what is most important: a genuine, living relationship with God.

The king of Syria, for his part, went right to the heart of the problem: "Get Elisha!" So, when Elisha's young helper stepped out the door one morning, he found they were completely surrounded by Syrian troops. The scriptural account of what then happened is too good to do anything but quote: "When the attendant of the man of God had risen early and gone out, behold, an army with horses and chariots was circling the city. And his servant said to him, 'Alas, my master! What shall we do?' So he answered, 'Do not fear, for those who are with us are more than those who are with them.' Then Elisha prayed and said, 'O Lord, I pray, open his eyes that he may see.' And the Lord opened the servant's eyes, and he saw; and behold, the mountain was full of horses and chariots of fire all around Elisha" (2 Kgs 6:15–17, NASB).

What did the young man see? The spiritual is a type of reality that can reveal itself if it wants to. This is also true in some measure of the spiritual side of you and me. We may hide from others in our body, or reveal ourselves there. God enabled the young man to see the powers of his realm, which totally interpenetrated and upheld all of the visible reality around him (even the Syrian army itself). Every working of visible reality is a movement within the encompassing Logos, the sustaining Word of God, which rests on nothing else but God through his Son (Heb 1:1–3).

How we need our Elishas today, who, by life and teaching as well as prayer, might open our eyes to see the reality of God's presence all around us in every bit of matter as well as beyond!

We in our "existence as usual" are like Jacob, wearily asleep on our rock in our own desert ravines. Jacob went to sleep in his sorrow, alienation, and loneliness, seeing only the physical landscape. In his dream—or was he only then truly awake?—he beheld the commerce of God with that ditch, and awakening cried out: "Surely the Lord is in this place, and I did not know it. . . . How awesome is this place! This is none other than the house of God, and this is the gate of heaven" (Gn 28:16–17, NASB).

> The angels keep their ancient places,
> Turn a stone and start a wing,
> 'Tis ye, 'tis your estranged faces,
> That miss the many splendored thing.[12]

4. And God Should! But—Chaos in the Church?

> Would God that all the Lord's people were prophets, and that the Lord would put his spirit upon them. (Nm 11:29)

One further serious objection to the individual believer's living in a conversational relationship with God comes from a feeling that *this would lead to chaos in the church,* the community of believers.

In 1 Peter the faithful are described as "living stones" (2:5). Think of trying to build a wall with stones or bricks that have a mind of their own. You fit them in here, and soon you find that they have waddled over there. Stones joined together in the wall discover that they do not get along, and those set apart want to be together. The wall will fall.

Many beleaguered pastors can understand what this means. Perhaps the last thing they want is to be contradicted and criticized on the basis of the private "conversations with God" of these "living stones."

These church leaders may find attractive a logic that goes counter to the very essence of the Protestant (as in "protest") movement, a movement that continues apace today in an ever-increasing number of sects emerging within and on the fringes of Christendom. This logic, driving toward a rigorous hierarchy of authority and subordination, naturally eventuates in *one person alone speaking for God and thus enforcing conformity.*

What is in question here is nothing less than the model of leadership and authority that is adequate to the redeemed community living out the good news of God's reign in the context of human life. "Living stones" in conversation with God himself begin to look much better, despite all their problems, when we compare them to the alternative—dead stones.

Dead stones are fine for the building of walls, but not for accomplishing the aim of building a community of persons, a living temple for a living God. Dead stones would be robots that simply do what they are told. This just will not do as a picture of the fellowship of Jesus Christ, a fellowship of friends united by knowledge and love in freehearted devotion to Christ. It will not do as a picture of *you*.

Sheepdogs or Shepherds?

Yet far too much in our examples and in our training for Christian leadership is oriented toward getting others merely to do as they are told. In this regard, the church far too greatly conforms to the leadership structures of the world. Indeed, *leadership* is normally an empty euphemism as applied to our standard communal efforts, whether in a church or out.

To manipulate and manage people—to drive them—is not the same thing as to *lead* them. The sheepdog nips and harasses the sheep, while the shepherd simply calls as he calmly walks ahead of the sheep. This distinction between the sheepdog and the shepherd is profoundly significant for how we think of our work as leaders of Christ's people. We must frequently ask ourselves which role we are fulfilling and constantly return ourselves, if necessary, to the true posture of the shepherd.

When we lead in the style of the shepherd, our confidence is in one and only one thing: the word of the Great Shepherd coming through us or otherwise to his sheep. We know that they know his voice and will not follow another (Jn 10:1–14). We do not *want* them to follow another, even if *we* are that other. This supreme confidence, and this alone, frees us to be the ministers of Christ.

We are then sure that "every plant, which my heavenly Father has not planted, shall be rooted up" (Mt 15:13). And we have heard the Master say: "All that the Father gives to me shall come to me; and those that come to me I will under no conditions reject" (Jn 6:37).

Thus we would never stoop to drive, manipulate, or manage, relying only on the powers inherent in unassisted human nature (see 1 Pt 4:11). Those who follow Christ in their ministries will substitute no "Ishmaels" of effort for the promised "Isaac" of gift. Their authority over their flocks is beyond successful challenge for God's purposes as long as they patiently count on him to do the work.

Not only do these undershepherds lead their flocks, but also they rely on their flocks to minister the word of God—as well as "all good things" (Gal 6:6)—*to them*. Ministry of the Word is never a one-way street when it is functioning rightly in a group. "A redemptive teaching relationship," as Henri Nouwen says, "is bilateral. . . . The teacher has to learn from his student. . . . Teachers and students are fellow men who together are searching for what is true, meaningful, and valid, and who give each other the chance to play each other's roles."[13]

At this point we must abandon the metaphor of sheep, for if we take it further, they may become sheep for slaughter. Whatever the metaphor, the point is that we are to lead "willingly," not for "filthy lucre," "neither as being lords over God's heritage, but being ensamples to the flock" (1 Pt 5:2–3). In this way we are indeed to be "servant of all" (Mk 9:35). Redemptive "mutual submission" (Eph 5:21) is achieved.

How desperately out of line with these scriptural injunctions is so much current religious work! This misalignment inevitably occurs if those who lead do not intelligently rely on Christ's power and readiness to govern and guide his people effectively. They will invariably turn to controlling the "flock," depending on their own abilities to organize and drive, which will be, of course, suitably clothed in a "spiritual" terminology and manner.

And as is their faith, so shall it be. It will be in fact "my church" and "my ministry"—as is often explicitly said—and we will never know by experience how completely and in what manner *Christ* is Lord of *his* church.

Leadership: Cultic or Christlike?

Spokesmen for the Christian community, as well as the general public, frequently lament the way in which "cults" turn their adherents into mindless robots. In our highly fragmented society, dominated by gadgetry and technology, lonely and alienated people are ready prey for any person who comes along and speaks with confidence about life and death, especially when they have some degree of glamour about them and profess to speak for God.

There are now more than twenty-five hundred distinct cults active in the United States, all based on the premise that God speaks to one or several central persons in a way not possible for the ordinary cult member. The members, on the other hand, are taught not to trust their own minds or their own communications with God unless they operate within the context of the group, with all its pressures toward conformity to the word from "on high." Frequently, adherents are taught to accept what is explicitly self-contradictory and flies in the face of all common sense, if the leader says it is so.

Here we have a common factor between many of the cults and the even more extreme groups that form around such personalities as Jim Jones and Charles Manson. But the more "mainline" religious groups, if they would be honest, should ask themselves to what extent their own models of leadership actually prepare the way for the cult phenomenon. I must ask myself, as a Christian minister, to what extent *I* might be prepared to have people put away their minds and their own individual experiences of guidance and communication with their Lord in order to secure the conformity and support adequate to maintain and enlarge *my* programs.

A Great Pastor Speaks

In contrast to the cultish mentality, consider the immense spiritual healthiness of that good man Charles Haddon Spurgeon:

> For my part I should loathe to be the pastor of a people who have nothing to say, or who, if they do say anything, might as well be quiet, for the pastor is Lord Paramount, and they are mere laymen and nobodies. I would sooner be the leader of six free men, whose enthusiastic love is my only power over them, than play the director to a score of enslaved nations.
>
> What position is nobler than that of a spiritual father who claims no authority and yet is universally esteemed, whose word is given only as tender advice, but is allowed to operate with the force of law? Consulting the wishes of others he finds that they are glad to defer to him. Lovingly firm and graciously gentle, he is the chief of all because he is the servant of all. Does not this need wisdom from above? What can require it more? David when established on the throne said, '[It is He] who subdueth my people under me,' and so may every happy pastor say when he sees so many brethren of differing temperaments all happily willing to be under discipline, and to accept his leadership in the work of the Lord.
>
> . . . Brethren, our system will not work without the Spirit of God, and I am glad it will not, for its stoppages and breakages call our attention to the fact of His absence. Our system was never intended to promote the glory of priests and pastors, but it is calculated to educate manly Christians, who will not take their faith at second-hand.[14]

What then are we to say? No doubt having everyone personally conferring with God does risk disagreement and noncooperation. If the spirit of the prophets is subject to the prophets, individual prophets may from time to time find themselves earnestly questioned and examined—and perhaps overturned—by those they are appointed to lead. It will then require a real security before other human beings, as well as a genuine authority from the Lord, for these prophets to succeed in leading, in addition to a true humility—everyone thinking the other better than him- or herself (*see* Phil 2:3)—if they are to carry on with their work.

Leading Like Jesus

But how could we have ever thought that anything other than just this is required in a minister of the Kingdom of God?

For my part, I cannot help but say: This is exactly what we want in our leaders of the Church of the Lord Jesus Christ. It is exactly the spirit in which he led. The spirit and the manner of the Chief Shepherd should be the one adopted by the undershepherds. We can minister Christ only as we teach what he taught in the manner in which he taught it.

With this kind of spirit of Christ in the leaders, the individuals of the fellowship will have a correct and formative model of how they should respond to and bear their communications with God. Of course there is a subordination within the fellowship of believers, but it is not one that comes from a clever or crude struggle for ascendancy. Rather, the subordination stems solely from authority given by experience in the Way and by the speaking of what is truly God's Word.

If we but count on the Christ whose church it is to bring to pass that subordination which is right, we shall then see significantly actualized the true unity and power of the glorious Body of Christ, the living temple inhabited by God, which in its full realization is the light of the world, the end and aim of all human history.

But it must never be forgotten that the social and outward dimension of the church is not the whole—nor, finally, the basic dimension—of redemption. Ultimately, the social dimension, in all of its glory, is derived only from the individual's communion with God. The advice of Saint Francis de Sales to his student in the Way gives a proper practical balance. Describing as "inspirations" all of "those interior attractions, motions, reproaches and remorses, lights and conceptions which God excites in us," he directs her as follows:

Resolve, then, Philothea, to accept with a ready heart all the inspirations it shall please God to send to you. When they come, receive them as ambassadors sent by the King of Heaven, who desires to enter into a marriage contract with you. Attend calmly to His proposals, think of the love with which you are inspired, and cherish the holy inspiration. Consent to the holy inspiration with an entire, a loving and a permanent consent.[15]

But Always Check

Then Saint Francis wisely proceeds to say, directing his friend back into the fellowship of the church: "But before you consent to inspiration in things which are of great importance, or that are out of the ordinary way, always consult your adviser."[16]

Similarly, Joyce Huggett passes on advice she received from her friend Jean Darnall: "If you believe God has told you to do something, ask him to confirm it to you three times: through his word, through circumstances, and through other people who may know nothing of the situation."[17] This is not a law, but it is a good rule of thumb in an area where rules of thumb are required.

No man or woman is an island, though we always remain much more than the sum of our relationships to others—even in the redemptive community. Our relationships to others, as essential and helpful as they may be, finally must rest on our personal relationship to God himself. When both relationships are right, we find perfect safety and

> . . . this full and perfect peace!
> Oh, this transport all divine!
> In a love that cannot cease,
> I am His and He is mine.[18]

SOME TOPICS FOR REFLECTION

1. Do you agree with the author about the limits of what stories and signs can do to increase our faith—in guidance or elsewhere?

2. "We *mistakenly* try to think of God's dignity in terms of what we experience of the 'great ones' among human beings. But God's dignity and greatness is seen precisely in His lowliness and accessibility to all." Do you have any problems with this?

3. What is "naturalism" and how does it affect the possibilities of divine guidance for the individual?

4. Do you personally believe that "science" makes divine guidance questionable? Can you trace out your thinking on this matter in detail? Or you might want to articulate the thinking of someone else you know well on this matter.

5. What are the main characteristics of a "cultic" style of leadership? Have you noticed any cultic behaviors in religious groups you are associated with or informed about? What would it cost organized religious groups to give up such behaviors?

6. How should I relate my private experiences of "God speaking to me" to my own spiritual traditions (for example, denominational) and my present fellowship?

Notes

1. Catherine Marshall, *A Man Called Peter* (New York: Fawcett Book Group, 1962), 24.

2. David Pytches, *Does God Speak Today?* (Minneapolis: Bethany House Publishers, 1989).

3. Mary Geegh, *God Guides*, published by the author, c/o Samuel Geegh, 6325 Lakeshore Drive, West Olive, MI 49460.

4. Agnes Sanford, *Sealed Orders* (Plainfield, NJ: Logos International, 1972), 98.

5. E. Stanley Jones, *A Song of Ascents* (Nashville, TN: Abingdon Press, 1968), 188.

6. G. Campbell Morgan, *How to Live* (Chicago: Moody Press, n.d.), 78.

7. Frank Laubach, *Letters by a Modern Mystic* (Syracuse, NY: New Reader's Press, 1955), 14.

8. Blaise Pascal, *Pensees* (Baltimore, MD: Penguin Books, 1966), 88.

9. A. H. Strong, *Christ in Creation* (Philadelphia: Griffith & Rowland Press, 1899), 3.

10. James Jean, *The Mysterious Universe* (New York: Dutton, 1932), 27.

11. Michael Talbot, *Mysticism and the New Physics* (New York: Bantam Books, 1981), introd. and chap. 1.

12. Francis Thompson, "The Kingdom of Heaven," in *British Poetry and Prose*, Vol. 2, 3d Ed., (Boston: Houghton Mifflin Co., 1950), 804.

13. Henri J. M. Nouwen, *Creative Ministry* (New York: Doubleday, 1978), 12–13

14. David Otis Fuller, ed., *Spurgeon's Lectures to His Students* (Grand Rapids, MI: Zondervan, 1945), 187.

15. St. Francis de Sales, *Introduction to the Devout Life*, Ryan translation (New York: Doubleday, 1957), 106.

16. St. Francis de Sales, *Introduction*, 106.

17. Joyce Huggett, *Listening to God* (London: Hodder & Stoughton, 1986), 141.

18. G. Wade Robinson, "Loved with Everlasting Love," in *Hymns of Glorious Praise* (Springfield, MO: Gospel Publishing House, 1969), Hymn #289.

5   *The Still Small Voice and Its Rivals*

Therefore Eli said unto Samuel, "Go, lie down:
and it shall be, if he calls you, that you shall say,
'Speak, Lord, for your servant hears.'"

I SM 3:9

And, behold, the Lord passed by, and a great and
strong wind rent the mountains, and brake in
pieces the rocks before the Lord; but the Lord was
not in the wind: and after the wind an earthquake; but the Lord was not in the earthquake:
and after the earthquake a fire; but the Lord was
not in the fire: and after the fire a still small voice.
And it was so, when Elijah heard it, that he
wrapped his face in his mantle, and went out, and
stood in the entering in of the cave. And, behold,
there came a voice unto him, and said, "What are
you doing here, Elijah?"

I KGS 19:11–13

Guidance Takes Many Forms

So now we know what guidance is. We have seen that it is a process
in which some person or thing or sequence of events is brought to
follow a definite course.

In this inclusive sense, the train is guided by the rails on which it
runs, the driver guides the automobile, the writer guides the pen or

typewriter, the radar guides the airplane, the stars guide the ship, the teacher guides the class, and the parent guides the child.

God can, certainly, *determine* the course of our lives by manipulation of our thoughts and feelings or by arranging external circumstances—what is often called the "closing" and "opening" of doors in the "sovereign will" of God. But he can and he does also guide us by *addressing* us. Humanity's actual experience of God, profusely documented in history, shows that God does address us.

God addresses us in various ways: through dreams, visions, voices, the Bible, extraordinary events, and so forth. This is a plain fact about humanity's experience of God in general and is clearly marked out within the biblical accounts. But confusion about the *significance* of the various ways God encounters us and communicates with us is a cause of serious problems for those who seek to live a life within his guidance.

All the ways God communicates with us have their own special uses, but they are not all of equal significance for our life with him. The written Word and Jesus, the living Word, are not to be compared in overall importance to a voice or vision used by God to speak to an individual. And, from among our individual experiences, the "still small voice" has a vastly greater role in divine guidance than does anything else.

What is this "still small voice"? The phrase is taken from the Elijah story just quoted. The translation could also have been "a gentle whisper of a voice," or "a gentle whispering." Each of these ways of describing the event places the emphasis on the unobtrusiveness of the medium through which the message came.

In the still small voice of God, we are given a message that bears the stamp of his personality quite clearly in a way we will learn to recognize. But the medium through which the message comes is diminished, often to the vanishing point, taking the form of thoughts that are our thoughts, though tangibly not *from* us. In this way, as we shall see, the "spirit of man" becomes the "candle of the Lord."

Unfortunately, this gentle word may be easily overlooked or disregarded and has even been discounted or despised by some who think that only the more explosive communications can be the "real thing."

A *life* of guidance would then have to be a life of constant fireworks from heaven.

But this dramatic view is hard to square with the actual course of daily life. Thus many have been led to attack visions and the like as illusions or even as satanic. A cloud of confusion and mistrust therefore spreads over the whole issue of God's guidance. Clearly, we must dispel it by examining the many forms of guidance in their relation to one another.

A Personal Appearance of Jesus?

A letter sent out by the staff of *Guideposts* magazine tells of an ordinary suburban housewife who one day, for reasons unknown to her, began to weep and continued weeping for four days. As the letter tells her story:

> On the morning of the fourth day, alone in her living room, there was a sudden hum and crackle in the air. She saw a ball of white light through a window, spraying showers of multicolored light in its wake and approaching her with amazing speed. Then it was right there, beside her, and as she looked at it she saw a face.
>
> "He is perfect," was her first thought. His forehead was high. His eyes were large, but she could not fix their color any more than she could the color of the sea. His features were lost in the overwhelming impression of life brimming over with power and freedom.
>
> Instantly she knew this was Jesus. She saw His utter lack of condemnation; saw that nothing she had ever done or ever would do could alter the absolute caring or the unconditional love in His eyes.

According to her account, Jesus was present with her in the manner described for three months, and then his presence began to fade. When this woman, named Virginia Lively, last saw him, he said to her, "I will always be with you." She, Thaddeus-like (Jn 14:22), asked how she would know this if she could no longer see him. He replied, "You will see me," and then he was gone.

Some years later, while speaking to a church group, she found his eyes looking into hers again, but the eyes belonged to a woman in the second row. "And suddenly she saw His eyes looking at her from the eyes of every person in the room."[1]

Reactions

It is useful to take note of certain common reactions to such stories as this. Some people immediately conclude that the whole thing is of the devil, because "Satan himself is transformed into an angel of light" (2 Cor 11:14). We cannot simply dismiss this concern. In fact, such experiences are always dangerous, in various ways.

But we also must not overlook the fact that light only serves as Satan's disguise because God really *is* light (1 Jn 1:5), because we are children of light (Eph 5:8) and saints in light (Col 1:12), and because "His messengers are a flame of fire" (Ps 104:4). It would be strange if we came to shun the genuine simply because it resembled the counterfeit.

Others will suppose that Mrs. Lively just hallucinated or suffered a "nervous breakdown" due to stress she could not cope with or even face. And yet others may simply be at a loss as to *what* was going on with her but remain unconvinced that Jesus Christ himself came to her, as she thought, on the occasions described.

At the other end of the spectrum, there are those who will consider her as especially favored by God *above all* who have not had such an experience. They may go so far as to confuse the medium with the message and worship the experience rather than the One who, supposedly, was present through it.

These folks often feel spiritually inferior until something similar happens to them. This sense of spiritual inadequacy is one of the burdens of religious groups that insist that their members reproduce the experiences of their leaders.

These members will be tempted to try to *make* the great event happen, in whatever specific form it must take, and may deceive themselves or pressure others into *faking* it. They may even judge those lacking the required experience to be incapable of any significant spiritual ministry or service to God or even of being received into heaven when they die. Experiences of such unusual types as Mrs. Lively's obviously pose problems for the understanding of guidance, as for the understanding of the spiritual life generally.

The Primacy of the "Inner Voice"

This is not to question whether such "spectacular" experiences occur or whether they are, sometimes at least, given by God. But it is a major point of this book that the "still small voice"—or the "interior" voice, as it also is sometimes called—is the preferred or highest form of individualized communication for God's purposes.

The still small voice is the usual way in which God individually addresses those who walk with him in a mature, personal relationship, proclaiming and showing forth the reality of the Kingdom of God as they go. We must therefore compare and contrast it to the other ways— the "rival" ways—in which God encounters human beings.

I hasten to add that to perform its function, the "voice" need not be very self-conscious. And one need have no theory or doctrine about it in order for it to occur. When the voice came to little Samuel, he did not know what it was, or even that there was such a thing.

And I believe it possible for one who regularly interacts with the voice of God not even to recognize it as something "special." In contrast to those who have some of the more spectacular experiences, those most adept at the divine-human conversation are often reluctant to speak much about the inner voice—which is completely as it should be. God's guidance is not for show-and-tell any more than are intimate personal interchanges in general.

But when an understanding of guidance is sought, as we seek it here, discussion of "the voice" is indispensable. Our procedure will be to consider the various ways in which God addresses men and women in the course of guiding them, in the hope of gaining a better general understanding of the nature and function of *the one way* that is most common and most suited to communion between God and humankind. We will begin by providing a brief, and undoubtedly an imprecise and incomplete, catalog of epiphanies taken chiefly from the Bible. Most of these are also reported in extrabiblical sources, but we regard the biblical accounts as normative.

Reaffirming Our Commonality with Biblical Experience

However, before beginning this discussion we must remind ourselves to read the biblical accounts we are about to consider as if what
is described were happening to *us*. We must make the conscious effort
to think that such things might happen to us and to imagine what it
would be like if they did. This will be difficult at first, for we are accustomed to thinking that God does those marvelous things only with
other people.

So we must give ourselves a little talking to, recalling our earlier
discussion of how Elijah, Moses, and Paul were people "subject to like
passions as we are." When misunderstood or mistreated, they felt as
we do. They too experienced hunger, weariness, nervousness, confusion, and fear. They too doubted their abilities and their self-worth.
They too—witness Moses and Gideon—often said, "Oh, no! Not *me*.
I can't do it."

Generally speaking, God will not compete for our attention. Occasionally a Saul gets knocked off his horse. But we must expect that
God will *not* run over us. And if we are not open to the possibility of
God's addressing us in whatever way *he* chooses, then we may walk right
by the burning bush instead of, like Moses, saying, "I will now turn
aside, and see this great sight, why the bush is not burnt" (Ex 3:3).

I say in all seriousness that we may take the voice of God to be
someone's radio turned up too loud, or to be some accidental noise,
or, more likely still, to be "just another one of my thoughts."

Guidance does not make seeking unnecessary. And when I seek
for something, I look for it everywhere. It is when we *seek* God earnestly,
and thus are prepared to go out of our way in examining those things
that might be his overtures toward us—including, of course, the most
obvious of things, like the Bible or our own thoughts—that he promises
to be found (Jer 29:13). But we will be able to seek him only if we honestly believe that he might explicitly address *us*, meet us, in ways suitable to his purposes in our lives.

With this reminder, and a plea for the use of our imagination to
identify with the experiences of individuals we shall be considering, we

turn now to six ways in which people are addressed by God within the biblical record. These are:

1. Phenomenon plus voice
2. Supernatural messenger or angel
3. Dreams and visions
4. Audible voice
5. The human voice
6. The "human spirit," or the "still small voice."

Phenomenon Plus Voice

This first category of divine-human encounter is richly represented in the events of Scripture. The Abrahamic covenant, a major foundation of the Judeo-Christian reality, was solemnized on such an occasion. A fire from God passing through the air consumed the sacrifice Abraham had prepared, while God intoned the promise to Abraham and his seed (Gn 15:12–21).

Moses received his call to deliver Israel from Egypt by the hand of God while standing before the bush burning but unburnt, from which God spoke (Ex 3:3–6). The nation of Israel as a whole was called to covenant by God's voice from within a mountain on fire, pulsating with the energy of God's presence (Dt 5:23). Ezekiel was spoken to in the context of a meteorological display that defies all but poetic description (Ez 1–2).

At the baptism of Jesus, "the Heavens" appeared to open up, and the Spirit visibly descended on him in conjunction with a voice from heaven that said, "This is my beloved Son, in whom I am well pleased" (Mt 3:17). Saul's encounter with Christ on the road to Damascus involved a blinding light from the heavens and an audible voice heard not only by Saul but by those with him as well (Acts 9:3–8).

Supernatural Messenger or Angel

In his recent book on angels, Mortimer J. Adler, the distinguished philosopher and historian of ideas, described the opposition from his scholarly colleagues when, for a major publication, he wished to include angels among the great ideas of Western humanity.[2] There is no doubt whatsoever that, purely in terms of the amount of attention they have received—not only in religion, but also in art, literature, and philosophy—angels deserve the place in Western civilization assigned to them by Adler. And it certainly is not going too far to describe the Bible itself as a book full of angels, from Genesis 16:7 onward.

Strictly speaking, the word *angel* means nothing more than "emissary" or "messenger." But it is normally understood that such "messengers," although persons, are not mere human beings. They are supernatural beings on a divine mission. God addresses humans through them, though they don't always "show their driver's licenses."

Sometimes in the biblical record it is difficult to decide whether an angel or the Lord himself is on the scene. Thus, for example, we have in Genesis 18 an account of three "men" appearing at the door of Abraham's tent. In the middle of this chapter the text casually shifts from "they" and "the men" to "the Lord." There then follows the well-known dialogue between Abraham and the Lord concerning the fate of Sodom.

Strangely, at the opening of chapter 19, it is only two "angels"—two who apparently were with "the Lord"—that appear to Lot in Sodom to finish off the episode. Some take it as referring back to this story in Genesis when Hebrews 13:2 exhorts us to "be not forgetful to entertain strangers: for thereby some have entertained angels unawares."

Joshua, in front of the city of Jericho (Jos 5:13–15), encounters "a man . . . with his sword drawn in his hand," who has come to help as "captain of the host of the Lord." He directs Joshua to take off his shoes because of the holiness of the ground where he is standing. The "host of the Lord" here is mainly made up of angels—no doubt the same as those legions that became visible in 2 Kings 6:17, as we have seen, and who later stood at the beck and call of our incarnate Lord (Mt 26:53). "Lord of Hosts" becomes a primary name for God as redemptive history progresses in the Old Testament (Ps 24:10, 46:7, 59:5, and so on).

A few verses later, at Joshua 6:2, the "captain" now seems to be "the Lord" himself, giving that famous and unorthodox military strategy whereby the walls of Jericho were to be brought down. (By the way, did they just fall or were they pushed?)

Human beings are so commonly addressed by angels in Scripture that here we shall list only a few more of the outstanding cases: Balaam (Nm 22:22–35), Gideon (Jgs 6:11–24), the parents of Samson (Jgs 13), Isaiah (Is 6:6–13), Daniel (Dn 9:20–27), Joseph (Mt 1:20–25), Zacharias (Lk 1:11–20), Mary (Lk 1:26–38), the women at the empty tomb (Mt 28: 2–5), Peter (Acts 5:19–20) and Paul (Acts 23:11, 27:23–24).

We should take note that encounters with angels seem to occur in an otherwise "normal" state of mind, as distinct from dreams and visions, although the content of the conversations recorded sometimes suggests (as with Gideon, with Samson's parents, and with Zacharias, for example) that the people involved felt things were more than a little out of control.

Dreams and Visions

These two categories of divine communications can be treated together here because our purposes do not require scholarly depth and precision. Sometimes dreams and visions seem to coincide, perhaps because they often come at night and the recipients may have been unable to tell with certainty whether they were awake or asleep.

Thus as with Paul: "And a vision appeared to Paul in the night; there stood a man of Macedonia, and begged him, saying, 'Come over into Macedonia, and help us'" (Acts 16:9; see also Acts 18:9, 2 Cor 12:1). Both visions and dreams involve some degree of a trancelike condition, a certain detachment from actual surroundings, that marks them off from ordinary waking consciousness.

On the other hand, some visions clearly are not dreams, as with Ananias, to whom the Lord spoke in a vision (Acts 9:10–13), and with Peter in his rooftop "trance," which is also specifically called a vision (Acts 10:9–19). And many dreams are not visions, as was the case with Jacob's dream (Gn 28), Joseph's dream (Gn 37), those of his jailmates (Gn 40), Pharaoh's (Gn 41), and Nebuchadnezzar's (Dn 4).

Gustave Oehler points out that the difference between a dream and a vision is not sharply marked out in the Bible.[3] However, as he concedes, the dream is regarded as being a lower form of communication from God than a vision is. Both are unusual states of consciousness, but the dream characteristically requires greater interpretation, often of great difficulty, in a manner the vision does not.

By the time of Jeremiah, the understanding of the ways in which God speaks to us had progressed to the point where the "dreaming" prophet was treated with some contempt. The dream is like straw or chaff when compared to the "wheat" of God's *Word* (Jer 23:25–32). The Word, on the other hand, is like fire, like a hammer that crushes rock. The dream has no comparable power.

Oehler sees emerging here "the principle that a clear consciousness when receiving revelation is placed higher than ecstasy or other abnormal states of mind."[4] This is a point that is very important to keep in mind as we attempt to understand our own experiences of God's communications and the significance of the different ways in which he meets us today.

Audible Voice

However we are to understand the mechanisms involved, it is clear that on occasion God has addressed human beings through what was experienced as an audible voice with no visible speaker present.[5] Something like this, though involving an angel "in heaven," seems to have occurred with Abraham on Mount Moriah as he was about to sacrifice his son Isaac (Gn 22:11, 15).

A most touching, informative, and profound story is that of the child Samuel learning to recognize God's voice, which he clearly experienced as an audible voice (1 Sm 3). As this young boy lay on his pallet "ere the lamp of God went out in the temple of the Lord, where the ark of God was" (v. 3), he heard his name called out. He rose and ran to his old master, Eli, thinking that it was he who had called.

This was during a period in the history of Israel when God rarely spoke and no visions were occurring. Such things as voices and visions were not commonly discussed. Hence, "Samuel did not yet know the Lord, neither was the word of the Lord yet revealed unto him" (v. 7).

On the third time that Samuel came to Eli, maintaining that Eli certainly had called him, Eli recognized what was happening. "Therefore Eli said unto Samuel, 'Go, lie down; and it shall be, if he calls you, that you shall say, "Speak, Lord; for your servant hears"'" (1 Sm 3:9–10). And so it happened. With this there began one of the most remarkable careers of any person who has ever lived before the Lord, justifying fully the use of the phrase "conversational relationship" between God and man.

This brings us to the two most important ways God speaks to us: in conjunction with the language of human beings, and through the "inner" voice of our own thoughts. These two ways are the ways most suited to his presence in our lives as a close personal friend shared by the redemptive community and to the development of our personalities into his likeness.

The Human Voice

We have seen that an audible voice with no visible speaker was present both at the baptism of Jesus and on the Damascus Road. But no means of communication between God and humankind is more commonly used in the Bible or the history of the church than the voice of a specific individual human being.

In such cases God and the person "used" speak *conjointly.* And it may be that the one spoken *to* is also the one spoken *through.* This is frequently my experience. The word is at once the Word of God, God speaking, and the word of a human being who also is speaking.

The two do not exclude each other any more than humanity and divinity exclude each other in the person of Jesus Christ. We can say that God speaks *through* us, as long as this is not understood to automatically rule out our speaking *with* God and even, in an important sense, through God. The relationship must not be understood as essentially mechanical, with God simply using us as we might use a telephone. No doubt God could choose this option is he wished, but usually he does not.

Samuel Shoemaker has written the following excellent description of our experience of God in this connection:

> Something comes into our own energies and capacities and expands them. We are laid hold of by Something greater than ourselves. We can face things, create things, accomplish things, that in our own strength would have been impossible. . . . The Holy Spirit seems to mix and mingle His power with our own, so that what happens is both a heightening of our own powers, and a gift to us from outside. This is as real and definite as attaching an appliance to an electrical outlet, though of course such a mechanical analogy is not altogether satisfactory.[6]

Now we may say with assurance that this action in union with the human voice and human language is the primary *objective* way in which God addresses us. That is, of all the modes in which the message concerned comes from *outside* the mind or personality of the person addressed, in the most common of cases it comes through another human being.

This manner of its coming is best suited to the purposes of God precisely because it most fully engages the faculties of free, intelligent beings socially interacting with *agape* love in the work of God as his co-laborers and friends. That it is so suited is obvious from the contents of the Bible. And of course the Bible is itself a case of God speaking *with* human beings, both in the past as it was delivered to humankind and now as it continues to speak to us.

When God speaks conjointly with human beings, it often seems that "weaker vessels" are purposely chosen. In the encounter of Moses with God through the burning bush, his last line of protest against the assignment God was giving him was that he did not speak well: "Please, Lord, I have never been eloquent, neither recently nor in time past, nor since Thou has spoken to Thy servant; for I am slow of speech and slow of tongue" (Ex 4:10, NASB). The Lord's reply was that he, after all, had made human mouths, and presumably could assist them to accomplish his assignments: "Now then go, and I, even I, will be with your mouth, and teach you what you are to say" (v. 12).

When Moses still begged God to send someone else, God angrily gave him Aaron as *his* spokesman: "You are to speak to him [Aaron] and put the words in his mouth; and I, even I, will be with your mouth and his mouth, and I will teach you what you are to do. Moreover, he shall speak for you to the people; and it shall come about that he shall be as a mouth for you, and you shall be as God to him. And you shall take in your hand this staff, with which you shall perform the signs" (vv. 15–17).

Some New Testament passages suggest that the Apostle Paul also was not an eloquent person. We know from his own statements that, whether by choice or necessity, he came among the Corinthians "not . . . with superiority of speech or of wisdom," but was with them "in weakness and in fear and in much trembling. And my message and my preaching were not in persuasive words of wisdom, but in demonstration of the Spirit and of power, that your faith should not rest on the wisdom of men, but on the power of God" (1 Cor. 2:1–5, NASB). His only confidence was in God speaking *with* him, "electrifying" his words, as it were, when he spoke.

It is significant, I believe, that those chosen by our Lord to bear his message and carry on his work were, for the most part, "unlearned and ignorant men" (Acts 4:13). The pattern seems amply to prove that in selecting them God would have no mistake made about where they got their words and authority. He would use ordinary human beings and would dignify them by the association. But just as this is wholly suitable to his redemptive purposes, so it is wholly appropriate that everyone—and especially the individuals involved—should be clear about the source of power manifested.

There must be no misallocation of glory, not because God is a cosmic egotist, but because to do so would destroy the *order* that is in the beatitude of the blessed life and would misdirect us away from God. Thus, "He that glorieth, let him glory in the Lord" (1 Cor 1:31).

The success of the redemptive plan therefore requires that possibly some but "not *many* wise men after the flesh, not *many* mighty, not *many* noble are called" (1 Cor 1:26) into the work.

Two of the people most responsible for the human authorship of the Bible, Moses and Paul, were accordingly weak with words so that they might have the best chance of clinging constantly to their support in God, who spoke in union with them, and might unerringly bring their hearers into contact with that God.

Does the Word of God then literally overpower us? In some parts of the Bible record, those who speak with God seem compelled by force, as we see in the case of Balaam. Balak, king of Moab, offered Balaam great riches and honor to curse Israel, for he knew that Balaam spoke in unison with God so that "he whom thou blessest is blessed, and he whom thou cursest is cursed" (Num 22:6). Balaam was obviously greatly tempted by the offer. Even after God told him not to go to Balak and not to curse Israel, because Israel was indeed blessed (vv. 12–14), he kept on toying with the idea.

Eventually he at least thought that he had God's permission to go to Balak (v. 20). But even while in Balak's camp, he was *unable* to curse Israel. He explained to Balak that he did not have "any power at all to say anything. The word that God puts in my mouth, that shall I speak." And when, after great preparations, the moment came for him to curse Israel, only a stream of blessings came forth (Num 23:7–10), to the exasperation of Balak (vv. 11, 25).

It would be a great mistake, however, to take these and similar cases to mean that the one who speaks with God, and thus speaks the Word *of* God, literally cannot help speaking. Perhaps this is true in some cases. On the other hand, it is certainly true that he or she cannot force God to speak. But the compulsion of these individuals to speak, though often great, is normally resistible. They are not mere *tools*.

The experience of Jeremiah in this connection has been replicated innumerable times in the experience of those who understand what it is to speak for and with God. Speaking God's Word had made him a laughingstock and a subject of derision on the part of those who knew him. Hence, he resolved to speak no more for the Lord. "But if I say, 'I will not remember Him or speak any more in His name,' then in my heart it becomes like a burning fire shut up in my bones; and I am weary of holding it in, and I cannot endure it" (Jer 20:9, NASB).

Thus the Word of the Lord is often treated by the prophets as a *burden*. Later, in his sermon against the false prophets, Jeremiah cries: "My heart is broken within me, I tremble in all my bones, I am like a drunken man, a man overcome with wine—because of Yahweh and his holy words" (Jer 23:9, JB).

But the prophet may also exalt in the power he feels surging within him, as did Micah: "I am filled with power—with the Spirit of the Lord—and with justice and courage to make known to Jacob his rebellious acts, even to Israel his sin" (Mi 3:8, NASB). Jeremiah also, we recall, had experienced the Word to be of great power, like a fire that scorches or a hammer that breaks rocks.

J. B. Phillips somewhere said that, when doing his well-known translation of the New Testament, he often felt like an electrician working on the wiring of a house with the power *on*.

In a later chapter we will explore in detail the idea of the Word of God as an agency, a substantial power, in the cosmos and in human affairs—an agency that could "come unto John . . . in the wilderness" (Lk 3:2); have dominion over unclean spirits (Lk 4:33–36) like the finger of God (Lk 11:20); be spirit and life (Jn 6:63, 68); increase (Acts 6:7), grow, and multiply (Acts 12:24); not be bound in prison (2 Tm 2:9); function as the sword of the Spirit (Eph 6:17), being more dexterous and powerful than any mere two-edged human sword, since it has a life of its own and is so acute that it can dissect thoughts and intentions (Heb 4:12); and simultaneously hold all of creation together (Col 1:17).

This picture of the *Word of God* must be closely examined before we conclude our study. But for now we rest with the fact that this Word can and does come to us through the living personality, mind, and body of other human beings as they, in unison with God, speak to us.

The Human Spirit, or the "Still Small Voice"

The final instrumentality considered here through which God addresses us is our own spirits—our own thoughts and feelings, toward ourselves as well as toward events and people around us. And this, I believe, is the primary *subjective* mode through which God addresses us. That is, of all the ways in which the message concerned comes from *within* the experience of the person addressed—such as dreams and visions or other mental states—it most commonly comes, for those who are living in harmony with God, in the form of their own thoughts and the attendant feelings.

Of the subjective routes, this manner of coming is best suited to the redemptive purposes of God because, once again, *it most engages the faculties of free, intelligent beings in the work of God as his co-laborers and friends.*

The King James version of Proverbs 20:27 says: "The spirit of man is the candle of the Lord, searching all the inward parts of the belly." This is better put in the Jerusalem Bible: "Man's spirit is the lamp of Yahweh, searching his deepest self."

In a passage of great significance for our subject, the Apostle Paul makes a comparison between man and God with respect to self-knowledge. "For who among men knows the thoughts of a man except the spirit of the man, which is in him? Even so the thoughts of God no one knows except the Spirit of God" (1 Cor 2:11, NASB). But, in contrast to the proverb, in which *the Lord's* use of *our* spirit is emphasized, Paul then points out that we have received the Spirit of God and concludes that we can therefore search out and know the very mind of God by means of his Spirit. Quoting the question from Isaiah 40:13, "For who has known the mind of the Lord, that he should instruct Him?" the apostle replies, "But we have the mind of Christ" (1 Cor 2:16, NASB).

So the Lord uses our self-knowledge or self-awareness, heightened and given a special quality by his presence and direction, to search us out and reveal to us the truth about ourselves and our world. And, on the other hand, *we* are able to use his knowledge of himself, made available to us in Christ and the Scriptures, to understand *his* thoughts and intentions toward us and to help us see his workings in our world.

In the union and communion of the believer with God, their two beings are unified and reciprocally inhabit each other as Jesus prayed:

"That they all may be one; as thou, Father, art in me, and I in thee, that they also may be one is us: that the world may believe that thou hast sent me" (Jn 17:21).

Accordingly, his laws are increasingly, as we grow in grace, the constitution of our hearts; his love is our love; his faith, our faith. Our very awareness of our actions and intentions and surroundings then bears within it the view that God takes and brings things into the clarity of *his* vision as a candle illumines for us what is present on our dinner table.

The spirit of the individual truly is, therefore, the candle of the Lord, in the light of which we see ourselves and our world as God sees. So we are addressed by him, spoken to by him, through *our own* thoughts.

This is something you can and should test by experiment. Those who will begin to pray that God will illumine them as to the nature and meaning of the processes that go on in their own soul will begin to understand and see their spirit functioning as the candle of the Lord.

The soul's self-awareness passes through every part of the self, touching on family, possessions, profession, reputation, sexual life, concern with physical appearance, health, fear of death, attitudes toward God— all of these and more.

Our spirit, as a candle in the Lord's hands, may turn to many other things than our own internal condition, although the primary point of the passage from Proverbs deals with the illumination of the inner life. Russ Johnston points out the importance of *recurrent thoughts* in God's guidance of his children:

> We would see wonderful results if we would just deal with the thoughts that continue in our minds in a godly manner. But most people don't. . . . As thoughts come into your mind and continue, ask God, "Do you really want me (or us) to do this?" Most of us just let those thoughts collapse—and God looks for someone else to stand in the gap."[7]

But are not our thoughts automatically bad? A well-intended but mistaken teaching about our thoughts has done much harm to the understanding of divine guidance.

The great Puritan minister Thomas Goodwin wrote a powerful discourse on *The Vanity of Thoughts*, taking as his text Jeremiah 4:14: "How long shall your vain thoughts lodge within you?"[8] Goodwin is fairly careful and helpful in the manner in which he describes these "vain" thoughts. But he leaves an impression, which is widely shared and insisted on, that if a thought is *our* thought, it could not possibly be trusted.

Does not Isaiah 55:8 tell us that "my [God's] thoughts are not your [human] thoughts"? And does not Jeremiah (17:9) also tell us that our hearts are desperately wicked beyond our powers of comprehension?

Of course there is an important point in all of this that emphasizes the difference between God's view of things and that of the normal person *apart from* God. But this point must not be allowed to obscure the simple fact that God comes to us precisely in and through *our* thoughts, perceptions, and experiences and can approach our conscious life *only* through them, for they are the substance of our lives.

We are, therefore, to be transformed by the renewing of *our* minds (Rom 12:2). His gracious incursions into our souls can make our thoughts his thoughts, and he will help us learn to distinguish when the thought is *only* ours and when it is also his.

We shall later discuss at length, in chapter 8, how we can know which thoughts are from God, but for now, keep this practical advice in mind: when thoughts recur, we should always stop prayerfully to consider whether or not this may be an appearance of "the Lord's candle" or whether it may have some other significance. Although repetitious thoughts are not *always* an indication that God is speaking, they are not to be lightly disregarded.

So the thoughts and attendant feelings in the mind and spirit surrendered to God make it as if God were walking through the personality with a candle, directing our attention to one thing and then another. And as we become used to the idea that God is friendly and helpful, that he is there to straighten, to inform, and to correct for our good, as well as to comfort and encourage, and that he really does love us, then we can begin to pray heartily with the psalmist, "Search me, O God, and know my heart!" (139:23).

We are then praying, "Bring the light to bear on my life, please," somewhat as we might go to the dentist or physician and say: "Examine me, please, and see if there are needed corrections of my physical condition. Find out what is needed and repair it." Here our own spirit works together with the Almighty God, utilizing our own thoughts and feelings to bring the truth of his word and his understanding of us to bear on our heart and life and world.

Having now brought before us some major ways in which, in the biblical record, God addresses our conscious mind and will in order to inform and guide us, let us now give some thought to their meaning for our quest for guidance.

God Speaks Today

The first thing that must be said is that *there is no foundation* in Scripture, in reason, or in the nature of things *why any or all of these types of experiences might not be used by God today* to communicate with his creatures and his children.

No one should be alarmed or automatically thrown into doubt by such experiences coming to them or by reports that others have experienced them. Here as always, with hearts at peace, we simply follow the Pauline admonition to "prove all things; hold fast that which is good" (1 Thes 5:21).

It is true that the existence and history of the church and the presence of the full written Scripture changes the circumstances of, and gives new dimensions to, the way in which God deals with human beings. But there is nothing *in* Scripture to indicate that the biblical modes of God's guidance to humans are superseded and abolished by the presence of the church or by the close of the scriptural canon.

This is simply a fact, as it is simply a fact that God's children have continued, to the present age, to find themselves addressed by God in most of the ways common to biblical characters.

The testimony of these individuals, when they are generally admitted to be honest, clearminded, and devout—many of whom are the very greatest Christians throughout the ages—should not be discarded in a blanket dogmatic denial.

Of course there will always be some fakery and confusion. But such a blanket denial has, to repeat, no scriptural foundation. Moreover, such denial often is no more than an attempt to substitute for living communications from God, accessible to people of the plainest sort, the safe, dead words of the ponderous scholar and the "letter-learned scribe."

The close of the scriptural canon marks the point in the divine-human conversation (which is, nevertheless, still ongoing) where the *general* principles and doctrines that constitute the substance of Christian faith and practice are so adequately stated in human language that nothing more need be said *in general*. It is the faith of the biblical Christian that nothing further will be said by God to extend or contradict those principles.

But the biblical Christian is not just one who holds certain beliefs *about* the Bible. Rather he or she is one who leads the kind of life shown forth in the Bible: a life of personal, intelligent interaction with God. Anything less than such a walk with God makes a mockery of the priesthood of the believer.

A book by Garry Friesen titled *Decision Making and the Will of God* describes a certain "traditional view," according to which:

> The Bible only reveals God's moral will, but His ideal will is more specific. And direct revelation (i.e., verbal communication by God to the individual) is not to be sought or expected. So when someone holding the traditional view says, "I have discovered God's will concerning which school I should attend," he is not claiming to have received supernatural revelation, nor did he find such leading from a direct statement of Scripture.[9]

This "traditional view" is further presented by the author as if it held "inner impressions" to be *the* mode of direct revelation from God to the individual, even though the term *verbal communication* is used in the above quotation. Friesen proceeds to say that "the problem with the traditional view is not that it recognizes the reality of inner impressions, but that it requires too much of them"—namely, that they should provide "objective guidance pointing to one 'right' decision."[10]

The emphasis of this book is on making specific decisions. Speaking generally, however, it seems to me that one of the most damaging things we can do to the spiritual prospects of anyone is to suggest or teach that God will not deal with them specifically, personally, intelligibly, and consciously or that they cannot *count on* him to do so as he sees fit. Once we have conveyed this idea to them, it makes no sense to attempt to lead them into an honestly personal relationship with God.

Conversing with God

Rosalind Rinker relates how after years of service on the mission field and many fruitless efforts at a satisfactory prayer life, she found herself rebellious and spiritually empty. Then, through a serious illness and other grave difficulties, "God began to take care of my rebellions through His great love. He began to teach me to listen to His voice."[11]

Almost by "chance," as she was praying with a friend for some of their students, she interrupted the friend's prayer with thanksgiving on a point that was being prayed for. After a moment of awkward silence, they sat back and laughed with great relief and then settled down again to prayer, but now "with a sense of joy, of lightness, of the Lord's presence very near."

They then asked in prayer if the Lord was trying to teach them something about prayer. "Should we give Thee more opportunity as we are praying to get Thy ideas through to us? Would that give the Holy Spirit more opportunity to guide us as we pray?" Then Ms. Rinker stopped praying, and said to her friend:

> Do you know what? I believe the Lord taught us something just now! Instead of each of us making a prayer-speech to Him, let's talk things over with Him, including Him in it, as we do when we have a conversation.[12]

I personally recall that when her book *Prayer: Conversing with God* came on the scene in the United States, group after group was brought to life as they learned to listen to God as well as "make prayer-speeches" to him. Their talk of a life with God now had real, objectively shareable content.

Silence Is NOT an "Answer"

Nowhere is it more important to be in a conversational relationship with God than in our prayer life. Often God does not give us what we ask for, but I believe that he will always answer, always *respond* to us. It is interesting that we commonly speak of answered prayer only when we are given our requests. Is there to be no response, then, when the request is denied?

Some people are heard to say that God's silence is an answer in these cases. But I think that, if we know how to listen, God will normally tell us something when he does not give us our requests. And we will hear it, and grow through it, if we have learned to recognize and acknowledge his voice.

This was certainly true in the case of Paul's famous "thorn in the flesh," which he three times begged the Lord to remove from him (2 Cor 12:7–8). The Lord was not silent to Paul, even though he turned down his request: "*And he said unto me, 'My strength is sufficient for you; for my strength is made perfect in weakness'*" (v. 9, italics added).

God is not impassive toward us, like the pagan idol, but calls us to grow into a life of personal interchange with him that does justice to the idea of our being his children.

Do We Need Anything More Than the Bible?

To many this will be an inflammatory question, but it is one that must be faced. One of the strange premises put forward to disallow any significant continuing usage of voices, visions, dreams, prophetic personages, and individual thoughts as communications from God is that these, allegedly, are no longer needed. "We have the Bible and we have the church. Let *them* speak for God." But a number of things should be said in response to this contention.

First of all, if by "needed" we refer to what is minimally required to enable human beings to know God, this, according to the Bible itself, is available independently of the Bible and of the church. Hence they too would not be "needed." And yet here they are.

As the New English Bible renders Romans 1:19–21: "For all that may be known of God by men lies plain before their eyes: indeed God himself has disclosed it to them. His invisible attributes, that is to say his everlasting power and deity, have been visible, ever since the world began, to the eye of reason, in the things he has made. There is therefore no possible defense for their conduct; knowing God, they have refused to honor him as God, or to render him thanks."

But if by "needed" we refer to what is required to constitute a truly redemptive and personal *relationship* between God and the individual soul, then certainly the existence of the Bible and the church is not enough. These must, at least in addition to merely being there, have an individualized function in the life of each person. And in order for this to happen, they—both church and Bible—must become the instrumentality through which God personally and uniquely addresses each individual.

Referring to the question, "Were not the miracles and gifts of the Spirit only for the apostolic Church?" Andrew Murray replied:

> Basing my views on scripture, I do *not* believe that miracles and the other gifts of the Spirit were limited to the time of the primitive Church, nor that their object was to establish the foundation of Christianity and then disappear by God's withdrawal of them. . . . The entire scriptures declare that these graces will be granted according to the measure of the Spirit and of faith.[13]

He further dismisses the idea that such a particularized presence of the hand of God was necessary only in the early days of Christianity:

> Ah, no! What about the power of heathenism even today wherever the gospel seeks to combat it, even in our *modern society,* and in the midst of the ignorance and unbelief which reigns even in the Christian nations.[14]

One of the most amazing conceits of the "flesh" that from time to time creeps into the Western branches of the church is the following attitude: "We are so much better now than in more primitive times that it is enough to have a written Word of God without the kind of divine presence and interaction with humanity described in that written Word."

How much more obviously mistaken is this approach now, at the end of the twentieth century, when biblical truth and ideas less and less serve to guide the course of human events and when service to the old gods and goddesses of the pre-Christian world is explicitly reasserting itself in the highest levels of culture!

By assuming that a particularized relationship with God is not now needed, we shut ourselves off from God's resources for life and ministry in the present age. C. H. Spurgeon, by contrast, is right on the mark with his comments on Psalm 103:2:

> Ought we not to look upon our own history as being at least as full of God, as full of His goodness and of His truth, as much a proof of His faithfulness and veracity, as the lives of any of the saints who have gone before? We do our Lord an injustice when we suppose that He wrought all His mighty acts, and showed Himself strong for those in the early time, but doth not perform wonders or lay bare His arm for the saints who are now upon the earth. Let us review our own lives. Surely in these we may discover some happy incidents, refreshing to ourselves and glorifying to our God. Have you had no *deliverances?* Have you passed through no rivers, supported by the divine presence? Have you walked through no fires unharmed? Have you had no *manifestations?* Have you had no choice favors? . . . Surely the goodness of God has been the same to us as to the saints of old.[15]

Bible Deism

Frankly, there is abroad in the world today, and very strongly present in conservative religious circles, a position we may aptly characterize as "Bible deism." Classical deism, associated with the extreme rationalism of the sixteenth through the eighteenth centuries, held that God created his world complete and perfect and then went away, leaving humanity to its own devices. There was no individualized intervention in the lives of human beings, no miracle.

Bible deism holds, similarly, that God gave us the Bible and then went away, leaving us to make what we could of it, with no individualized communication through the Bible or otherwise.

Bible deism is very like the Sadducean doctrine current in the time of Jesus and Paul—namely, that God quit speaking when he finished talking with Moses, so that no alleged communications via angels or spirits could possibly be valid. The Sadducees did not accept individual communications with God, and they rejected angels, disembodied spirits, a resurrection, and an afterlife. (That's why they were sad, you see!)

It will be recalled that Paul—himself a Pharisee, and having actually dealt with angels and spirits—was able to divide his accusers on one occasion and defuse a dangerous situation by invoking the resurrection, which the Pharisees, but not the Sadducees, accepted.

The Pharisees then, to make a point important to them, sided with Paul: "We find no evil in this man: but if a spirit or an angel has spoken to him, let us not fight against God" (Acts 23:9). Far too many who intend to honor the Bible adopt, similar to the Sadducees, an unbiblical teaching about God's relationship to his children.

Turning People On, Not Off

From the pastoral point of view, one of the greatest harms we can do to those under our care is to convince them that God is not going to meet them personally in their experience or that he is really doing so only if we approve of what is happening. If our gospel does not free up the individual for a unique life of spiritual adventure in living with God daily, we simply have not fully entered into the good news Jesus brought.

The Lord does take care of his church, and all our efforts must be directed toward fostering each individual's adventure with him. We can trust him, and we cannot trust anything else, not even the sterling soundness and sobriety of our own "faith and practice."

If we trust anything else, we will cause our charges to trust something else, which may result, at best, in our having proper "spiritual corpses" to fill our pews. We should tremble and take heed on hearing the words of Jesus to ministers of his day: "You travel about on sea and land to make one proselyte; and when he becomes one, you make him twice as much a son of hell as yourselves" (Mt 23:15, NASB).

And yet there are dangers, of course. The adventure can get disastrously out of hand. We know that people do "go off the deep end." And this problem must be addressed. After gravely warning that death and disaster also may come from going off the "shallow end," what we must do as pastors is to lead people into an understanding of the voice of God and how it works in their lives.

Most important, and right at the outset, they must be made to see that recognizing God speaking is something that they *must learn to do through their own course of personal experience and experimentation.* They must especially be encouraged to do so if they do not expect God to speak to them. We may even at the outset have to help identify the voice of God for them and instruct them on how to respond. Those who are older in the Way should be prepared to do this by their own experience.

How wonderful that Eli recognized what was happening to young Samuel and could tell him what to do to begin his lifelong conversational walk with God! It might well have been years, in the prevailing circumstances, before Samuel would have found his way. We must not foolishly assume that, if God speaks, one automatically knows what is happening and who is talking. If Samuel did not know, surely many others also will not.

How wonderful that Abraham could assure his puzzled servant (Gn 24:1–7) of God's guidance back to the city of Nahor to find a wife for Isaac! How wonderful that the servant could come to an utterly new understanding of God because he *was* experientially guided—and indeed, guided into knowledge of guidance itself! You may enjoy reading and meditating on this great story of one who learned by experience to work with our God *who is available.*

The Priority of the Voice

Knowledge and experience of guidance teaches us many things that can keep us from harm and from harming others in our spiritual adventure of life in God's Kingdom. One of the most important things we can learn is *the superiority of the voice* over the other epiphanies, however the voice may come, even as the "still small voice," within the silence of our own minds. This superiority lies in two things: (1) the clarity of its cognitive content, and (2) the advanced spiritual condition of those who can hear and receive it.

In Numbers 12 we find Aaron and Miriam, brother and sister of Moses, criticizing him because he had taken a black woman from Ethiopia for a wife. Really, they were jealous of the way God spoke to Moses: "Has the Lord indeed spoken only through Moses? Has He not spoken through us as well?" (v. 2, NASB).

Now this certainly was no problem for Moses. He wanted everyone to prophesy (Nm 11:29), and he was a very unassuming man. But the Lord did not disregard what Miriam and Aaron were doing. He called the three of them into the meeting tent. He then came down in a cloud and called Aaron and Miriam forward: "Hear now My words: If there is a prophet among you, I the Lord shall make Myself known to him in a vision. I shall speak with him in a dream. Not so, with My servant Moses. He is faithful in all My household; with him I speak mouth to mouth, even openly, and not in dark sayings, and he beholds the form of the Lord. Why then were you not afraid to speak against My servant, against Moses?" (Nm 12:6–8, NASB).

"Not in dark sayings"—this phrasing is important for our contemporary understanding of God's guidance. "Dark" sayings are, of course, *obscure,* barely intelligible sayings. They lie on a continuum with the "squeaking and gibbering" of the "ghosts and familiar spirits" from which people sought guidance in Isaiah's day as well as currently (Is 8:19, NEB). We cannot know for sure what they mean, and they provide a too-fertile field for wild conjectures and manipulative interpretations.

Many who claim to speak for God refer to their visions, dreams, and other unusual phenomena or to their vague impressions or feelings but with no clear, sane meaning. This does not mean that they are not truly spoken to. But Moses was spoken to directly, "mouth to mouth," or *conversationally.* His meaning when he spoke for God was, therefore, always specific, precise, and clear.

We notice as we proceed on through Bible history that the greater the maturity, the greater the cognitive clarity of the message and the lesser is the role played by dreams, visions, and other "strange" phenomena and "altered states" in the process of communication.

Of course, we cannot argue conclusively from silence. But we do notice in the lives of New Testament personalities, and especially with reference to Jesus himself, a great preponderance of strictly spiritual communications between God and humans. Visions, dreams, and angels continue to play some part, as I think they may do today. But it is not too much to say that when these were the main, as opposed to occasional, means of interaction between God and man, *there was a less developed spiritual life in the individual and in the church group.*

We turn again to the words of E. Stanley Jones, who so greatly believed in and practiced interaction with divine guidance throughout his life:

> God cannot guide you in any way that is not Christlike. Jesus
> was supreme sanity. There was nothing psychopathic about
> Him. He went off into no visions, no dreams. He got His guidance
> through prayer as you and I do. That is, He got His guidance
> when in control of His faculties, and not when out of control as in
> dreams. I do not say that God may not guide through a vision or
> dream; but if He does, it will be very seldom, and it will be because
> He cannot get hold of our normal processes to guide them. For
> God is found most clearly and beneficially in the normal rather
> than in the abnormal. And Jesus is the Normal, for He is the
> Norm.[16]

The More Spectacular Is the Less Mature

I believe that the predominance of the spectacular encounter does, in general, go along with the *less* mature levels of the spiritual life, though the mere absence of such spectacular events must not be taken as indicating great spiritual development. After all, such an absence is also consistent with utter spiritual deadness.

And it is, of course, well that this should be so. The spectacular encounters are obscure in their meaning, in their cognitive content. This protects us, for, in general, knowledge tends to be destructive when not held in a mature personality thoroughly permeated by love and humility. This is true even in the "secular" areas of life.

Few things are more terrifying in the spiritual realm than those who *absolutely know*, but are also unloving, hostile, proud, superstitious, and fearful. *That Aaron and Miriam COULD be jealous of Moses is a sure indication that God could not trust them with the kind of knowledge he freely shared with Moses.* That Moses was untroubled by their attack, and glad to share the prophetic ministry, just as surely indicated that he *could* be trusted with such knowledge.

When the spectacular is *sought*, this is because of childishness in the personality. Children love the spectacular and show themselves as children by seeking it, running heedlessly after it. It may be given by God, even may be necessary, because of our denseness or our hard-heartedness. However, it is *never* to be taken as a mark of spiritual superiority. Those who are advanced in the Way of Christ never lightly discuss the spectacular things that come to them or, especially, invoke them to prove that they are right or "with it" in some special way.

How Obscurity Can Serve Us

God in his mercy often speaks to us in obscure ways to allow us the room and time we need to respond, and by so doing lets us know that we indeed are being addressed but stretches us out in growth in order to receive the message. Perhaps we often think: "Well, God, why don't you just come out and say it? Tell me in detail how to live." But this is usually said in a context of our own misguided ideas about what that would amount to.

Our minds and values have to be restructured before God's glory and our interests are truly appreciated and understood. We may be tempted to cry out, like Isaiah, for God to rend the heavens, come out of hiding, and stand here before us telling us what to do (Is 64:1). But we do not really understand what it is we are asking for when we do that. And it probably would literally kill us, or at least destroy our personality and our ability to lead a normal life, if this actually happened. So God in his mercy continues to approach us obliquely, in one way and another, but increasingly less so as we mature, until that time when we can safely know him as he now knows us (1 Cor 13:12).

So it is natural and right that the Word comes to us in forms we must struggle to understand. This is even true of the Bible, which is very explicit but still requires persistent and energetic work to understand. In the process of struggling, we grow to the point where we can appropriate and assimilate the content of truth as it becomes clear. It is one of the oldest and most common stories of human life that in its most important moments we have little more than the foggiest idea of what it is we are doing and saying. And our ignorance is for our good.

Did you know what was happening when you got married or brought a child into this world? In some vague sense you did, but you also had very little idea of what it meant. Had you at the time appreciated all that it meant, you probably would not have had the courage to proceed. Then you would have missed much good that has come to you through those events.

In religion, also, we come very slowly to appreciate what is happening to us. James and John came to Jesus and said, in effect, "Lord, when you become King we want to be your Secretary of State and Secretary of Treasury." He replied: "You do not know what you are asking. Can you drink the cup that I will drink of, be baptized with my baptism?" With great assurance they replied: "Oh yes, Lord, we are able to do that; bring it on" (Mk 10:37–39).

But they had no idea. And it turned out that, by the Lord's mercy, they *were* able to drink his cup and take his baptism. They were prepared when the time came. James was the first one of the apostles to be martyred. According to tradition, John lived longer than any of the apostles. But he was tortured with hot oil. And we know that he was exiled on the barren island of Patmos, where he experienced the revelation of Jesus Christ in a form utterly new to all previous experience.

These experiences were not what John and James had in mind, by any means. But they met their trials very well when they came, because

God was with them. They grew to the vision and the task as they stepped forward in faith. They lived and they finally died as the friends and co-laborers of Jesus and of his Father and theirs.

The "Signs" Are Not the Reality

Bob Mumford, discussing the spectacular forms of guidance, remarks:

> Signs are given to us, because God meets us on the level where we operate. . . . In guidance, when God shows us a sign, it doesn't mean we've received the final answer. A sign means we're on the way. On the highway we may pass a sign saying, "New York: 100 miles." The sign doesn't mean we've reached New York, but it tells us we're on the right road.[17]

But, on the other hand, he continues:

> God wants to bring us beyond the point where we need signs to discern His guiding hand. Satan cannot counterfeit the peace of God or the love of God dwelling in us. When Christ's abiding presence becomes our guide, then guidance becomes an almost unconscious response to the gentle moving of His Holy Spirit within us.[18]

How glad I am that history was finally ready to be addressed in the "still small" voice of Jesus! How good it is that God left the spectacular forms that were necessary—and perhaps still are necessary for some purposes—and came to deal with us by the very whispers of God's Spirit. Once again, who of us would really know what to do if the great God came down in full splendor and stood before us? In the language of Job, "Lo, these are but the outskirts of his ways; and how small a whisper do we hear of him! But the thunder of his power who can understand?" (Jb 26:14, RSV).

The Incarnate Son comes without strife, so gentle that his voice is not to be heard above the chatter of the street (Mt 12:19). It is because of this approach that the Gentiles, or people generally, can come to trust in his name.

I am so thankful for the quiet written Word, for the history and presence of the Church of the Lamb, for the lives of the saints, and for the tireless, still conquests of the Spirit of God. These approach me. These I can approach, and through them approach God while he safely draws ever closer to me.

The "rivals" of the voice—still and small, still and within—are necessary and have their place, then. But once we are earnestly seeking God and get beyond the need to have "big things" happen to reassure ourselves that somehow we are right and alright—and possibly that others are not—then we begin to understand and rejoice that, as Jesus so clearly lived and taught, the life of the Kingdom "is righteousness, peace and joy in the Holy Spirit" (Rom 14:17).

Then we begin to understand that God's whole purpose is to bring us to the point where he can walk with us quietly, calmly, constantly, leaving us space to grow to be his (often fumbling) co-laborers, to have some distance from him and *yet* be united with him because we have been conformed to the image of his Son. We bear the family resemblance.

Beyond Words

Even at the merely human level, one of the highest forms of communication is that kind of communion in which no overt word is needed or wanted. What are we to make of a poet who says, "Drink to me only with thine eyes, and I'll but pledge with mine"? We must say that he has touched on an element of that to which God would finally bring us in the communion with him that is a union sometimes beyond communication and in a constant life before him in this world and the next.

There is, finally, a silence that speaks, that, paradoxically, "says" all:

> Love culminates in bliss when it doth reach
> A white, unflickering, fear-consuming glow;
> And, knowing it is known as it doth know,
> Needs no assuring word or soothing speech.
> It craves but silent nearness, so to rest,
> No sound, no movement, love not heard but felt,
> Longer and longer still, till time should melt,

A snow-flake on the eternal ocean's breast.
Have moments of this silence starred thy past,
Made memory a glory-haunted place,
Taught all the joy that mortal ken can trace?
By greater light 'tis but a shadow cast:—
So shall the Lord thy God rejoice o'er thee,
And in His love will rest, and silent be.[19]

SOME TOPICS FOR REFLECTION

1. Do you see any reasons for concern about the Virginia Lively story? Should such testimonies be suppressed in a local congregation? Encouraged?

2. What do you think of Gustave Oehler's "principle that a clear consciousness when receiving revelation is placed higher than ecstasy or other abnormal states of mind"? How would this relate to cases like Moses and the burning bush or Joshua and "the captain of the Lord's host"?

3. The cases of "audible voice alone" are today most likely to be associated with mental unbalance. Is this justified? Is there any well-based objection to God simply producing the sound waves appropriate to audible language? Or does skepticism about such cases really rest on outright disbelief in God?

4. Have you experienced any cases that could be described as God speaking with the words of some human being? With Biblical words? With those of a contemporary? What is it about these cases that leads you to so describe them?

5. It is very common to hear religious leaders speak of "having a *personal relationship* with God (through Jesus Christ)." In your opinion, can such a "personal relationship" make sense without God speaking directly to the individual? How could it?

6. Some reasons are given above for regarding the "voice" as the superior form of guidance, given God's announced purposes in interacting with humanity. Do you find those reasons convincing?

7. What is "Bible deism"? Have you ever seen it in action? What might make it attractive?

Notes

1. Letter no. 117-2, *Guideposts*, December 1982.

2. Mortimer J. Adler, *The Angels and Us* (New York: Macmillan, 1982), pref. See also Billy Graham, *Angels: God's Secret Agents*, rev. ed. (Waco, TX: Word Books, 1986); and A. C. Gaebelein, *What the Bible Says About Angels* (Grand Rapids, MI: Baker Book House, 1987).

3. Gustave Oehler, *Theology of the Old Testament* (Grand Rapids, MI: Zondervan, n.d.), 143.

4. Oehler, *Theology*, 143.

5. Today we unfortunately do not have on hand an adequate, common vocabulary to discuss the movements of God within and on the soul. We are now without a psychology of the spiritual life. Distinctions in the individual's experience of God that once were widely understood and utilized are now either unknown or wholly the object of scholarly curiosity. On vital distinctions to be drawn in experiences of voices and visions, Teresa of Avila, for example, has this to say: "Some of them [voices] seem to come from without; others from the innermost depths of the soul; others from its higher part; while others, again, are so completely outside the soul that they can be heard with the ears, and seem to be uttered by a human voice." (from Chapter III of the Sixth Mansion in *Interior Castle*, trans. E. Allison Peers [Garden City, NY: Image Books, 1961], 139.) See also the remarkably analytical and sane discussion of the experience of "Voices and Visions," in part 2, chapter 5 of Evelyn Underhill's *Mysticism*, 12th ed. (New York: New American Library, 1974).

6. Samuel Shoemaker, *With the Holy Spirit and with Fire* (New York: Harper & Row, 1960), 27.

7. Johnston, *How to Know the Will of God*, 13.

8. Thomas Goodwin, *The Vanity of Thoughts and Let Patience Have Its Perfect Way* (Wilmington, MA: Classic-A-Month Books, 1964), 4.

9. Garry Friesen, *Decision Making and the Will of God* (Portland, OR: Multnomah Press, 1980), 129.

10. Friesen, *Decision Making,* 144.

11. Rosalind Rinker, *Prayer: Conversing with God* (Grand Rapids, MI: Zondervan, 1959), 17.

12. Rinker, *Prayer,* 19.

13. Leona Choy, *Andrew Murray: Apostle of Abiding Love* (Ft. Washington, PA: Christian Literature Crusade, 1978), 152.

14. Choy, *Andrew Murray,* 152.

15. Charles H. Spurgeon, *Morning by Morning* (London: Passmore & Alabaster, 1865), 191.

16. E. Stanley Jones, *The Way* (Nashville, TN: Abingdon-Cokesbury Press, 1946), 283.

17. Bob Mumford, *Take Another Look at Guidance: Discovering the Will of God* (Plainfield, NJ: Logos International, 1971), 140–41.

18. Mumford, *Take Another Look,* 140–41.

19. Frances Ridley Havergal, sonnet.

6

The Word of God and the Rule of God

By the word of the Lord the heavens were made,
and all their host by the breath of his mouth.

PS 33:6, RSV

He gives an order; his word flashes to earth: to
spread snow like a blanket, to strew hoarfrost like
ashes.

PS 147:15–16, JB

Then they called to Yahweh in their trouble and
he rescued them from their sufferings; sending his
word and curing them, he snatched them from
the Pit.

PS 107:19–20, JB

Where the word of a king is, there is power.

ECCL 8:4

The very phrase "still small voice" could suggest that what lies at the heart of divine guidance is something weak and marginal. But the guided life is operating from the very foundation and framework of all reality, not from the fringe. We must explore this point in depth.

Astonishing Faith in the Power of Words

He is known to us only as "a certain centurion" (Lk 7:2). He was a Gentile, a Roman soldier of considerable rank, the top man, possibly, in the area of Capernaum. He also was a good governor who sacrificed his private wealth to help his subjects (Lk 7:5) and a good man who loved his servant, sick to the point of death. And he was humble. But all this was not what impressed Jesus when the man came requesting healing for his servant.

Jesus was particularly impressed by the quality and magnitude of the man's faith. The centurion seemed to understand, from his own experience of authority, how Jesus accomplished what he did. Therefore he had complete trust in his power.

So, in a manner almost casual and offhand, he said to Jesus: "Don't trouble yourself, Sir! I'm not important enough for you to come into my house—I didn't think I was fit to come to you in person. Just give the order, please, and my servant will recover. I am used to working under orders and I have soldiers under me. I can say to one, 'Go,' and he goes, or I can say to another, 'Come here,' and he comes; or I can say to my slave, 'Do this job,' and he does it" (Lk 7:6–8, Phillips).

Jesus looked at this man with astonishment. Then, turning to the group following along after him, he said, "I have never found faith like this anywhere, even in Israel" (v. 9, Phillips).

What! Did not John the Baptist have greater faith? Did not those who heralded and welcomed the child Jesus as the Messiah? Did not his own family and disciples have greater faith than this Gentile soldier? Apparently not.

Great faith, like great strength in general, is evidenced by the *ease* of its workings. As "the quality of mercy is not strained," so also with faith. Most of what we think we see as the struggle *of* faith is really the struggle to act *as if* we had faith when in fact we do not. We will return to this centurion later. He has much to teach us about faith and about its dependence on a proper understanding of the Word of God.

Words and THE Word

God *created,* God *rules,* God *redeems* through the instrumentality of his Word. God creating, God ruling, God redeeming *is* his Word. This is the single basic truth about the overall relationship he has to his creatures. We see in it the all-encompassing mediatorship of the Son Word. If we would understand God's personal relationship to us, including guidance provided to our individual lives, we must understand what in general the Word of God is and how both the Son of God and the Bible are the Word of God.

So we must think in depth about what words are. If you find a word written on a wall or simply overhear one spoken, you cannot tell whose word it is. Its ownership does not reside within itself, considered merely as a mark or sound. *My* word is not just *a* word. It is me speaking or me writing. Even my name written on a check ever so clearly is not my word, not my "signature," if I did not write it and thereby express my *self*—my thoughts and my intentions.

What is essential to the word of a person is the meaning given to it by them—that is, what thought, feeling, or action *they* associate with it and hope to convey to others. Through our words we literally give to others a "piece of our mind." Through their words we may know their thoughts and feelings and share in their very lives.

Through words, soul impacts soul, sometimes with a spiritual force equivalent to that of planets in collision. As marks or sounds alone, of course, words are nothing. It is their mental side, their spiritual force, that hooks into the hidden levers of mind and reality and gives them their immense power. If we do not understand Spanish or Greek, we may hear the sounds, but they have little or no effect because they are without meaning for us.

The power of the word lies finally in the personality it conveys. Children learn to say: "Sticks and stones may break my bones, but words can never hurt me." Adults teach them to say this in order to assuage the terrible pain that really is inflicted on them by the words of their playmates.

How deeply children can be hurt from words! The schoolyard and playroom become a chamber of horrors where the souls of little ones are drawn and quartered or left permanently crippled and scarred by malicious or mindless chatter and prattle.

Jesus saw this, no doubt, for *he* had eyes that saw. And he also saw adults ravaging the lives of little children with their words. Surely it was largely his sense of the damage thus done that made him say: "But whoso shall offend one of these little ones which believe in me, it were better for him that a millstone were hanged about his neck, and that he were drowned in the depth of the sea" (Mt 18:6).

The true view of the power of words is forcefully given in the book of Proverbs: "Death and life are in the power of the tongue" (18:21); "A soft tongue may break down solid bone" (25:15, NEB); "The tongue that soothes is a tree of life; the barbed tongue, a breaker of hearts" (15:4, JB).

This theme is carried into the New Testament. James remarks that the tongue is "only a tiny part of the body, but it can proudly claim that it does great things. Think how small a flame can set fire to a huge forest" (Jas 3:5, JB). Jesus himself regarded words as a direct revelation of the state of the soul: "By your words you shall be justified, and by your words you shall be condemned" (Mt 12:37, NASB).

Words as Spiritual Forces

We cannot afford to overlook *the spiritual nature of words*. Spirit is nonbodily, personal force. It is personal reality that can, and often does, work independently of physical or bodily forces. Spirit also can work in conjunction with the physical. We are most clearly presented with spirit in ourselves as the force that belongs to thought, emotion, and intention, although in the biblical view spirit reaches far beyond mental qualities as we know them and ultimately serves as the foundation of all reality.

The view of words as spiritual forces is one common both to Scripture and to pagan philosophers. Jesus said to his followers on an occasion where they were putting too much weight on the material realm: "It is the spirit that gives life, the flesh has nothing to offer. The words I have spoken to you are spirit and they are life" (Jn 6:23, JB).

This meant, in accordance with what we have just said about the nature of words, that through his words Jesus imparted himself and in some measure imbued those who received his words with the powers of God's sovereign rule. Through him they "tasted the good word of God, and the powers of the world to come" (Heb 6:5). This power imparted is seen in his later explanation: "If you abide in Me, and My words abide in you, ask whatever you wish, and it shall be done for you" (Jn 15:7, NASB).

Plato, the great philosopher of ancient Greece, also spiritualizes words by treating our very thinking itself as an inner "conversation" the soul holds with itself.[1] In thus treating thought as a language—hence as words, but words hidden away in the nonphysical realm—Plato sets a pattern that many thinkers have followed up to the present day.

Our brother Saint Augustine carried on this tradition, joining it to Christian thought, in saying that "he who thinks speaks in his heart." He explicitly founded his view in part on Gospel passages such as Matthew 9:2–4 in which "certain of the scribes *said within themselves,* 'This man blasphemeth.'"[2] (See also Lk 12:17.)

The word, as *person speaking,* is therefore to be understood as a spiritual power, whether of man or of God or of other personal agency and whether for evil or for good. It is the power of the person who speaks. It is precisely in this realm that God seeks for those who would worship him "in spirit and in truth" (Jn 4:23). He desires truth in the "inward parts," and "in the hidden part thou shalt make me to know wisdom" (Ps 51:6).

William Penn says, with the characteristically Quaker emphasis:

> For the more mental our worship the more adequate to the nature of God; the more silent, the more suitable to the language of the spirit.
>
> Words are for others, not for ourselves: nor for God who hears not as bodies do; but as spirits should. If we would know this dialect we must learn of the divine principle in us. As we hear the dictates of that, so does God hear us.[3]

The Word of God, when no further qualification is added, is God speaking, God communicating. When God speaks, he expresses his mind, his character, and his purposes. Thus he is always present with his Word.

All expressions of his mind are "words" of God. This is true whether the specific instrumentality is *external* to the human mind—as in natural phenomena (Ps 19:1–4), other human beings, the incarnate Christ (*Logos*), or the Bible—or *internal* to the human mind—as in thoughts, intents, and feelings.

His Kingdom rules over all things, including the affairs of mankind, and is carried out through his word thus understood.

A Kingdom of Words

Humanity in its present condition is under constant temptation to think of the universe as a place in which there are only certain physical or mechanical relationships between things. We are drawn to think of the blind forces pushing and pulling among physical objects as *the* way in which all things relate to one another.

This is the naturalistic outlook discussed in an earlier chapter. But such a view can never understand the common deeds and affairs of human beings, and much less still can it understand higher culture or the religious life. After centuries of attempts at such understanding, this outlook still today falls pathetically short of its goal as we enter the twenty-first century.

The religious life and the religious outlook on the universe—and, of course, we are especially concerned with the one identifiable with the mind of Christ and with life in his steps—is one that sees the universe as *a kingdom*. And a kingdom does not work merely by pushes and pulls. It essentially works by communication of thoughts and intentions through words or other symbols.

This point is about the nature of social reality and is one we cannot afford to miss. Some of our greatest problems in understanding and entering into life in the Kingdom of God come from inadequate appreciation of how that Kingdom, like *all* kingdoms, works by communication: by the speaking of words or the use of words for the expression of minds. We turn now to the Scriptures to illustrate ways in which the speaking of a word works in the Kingdom of God.

Creation by "Words"—God's and Ours

We begin, naturally enough, with the first chapter of the first book of the Bible, at the creation of the heavens and the earth. We are told that in the beginning God created the heavens and the earth. And how did he do it? By speaking. By a sequence of directly *creative words*.

It should come as no surprise, given what the advance of knowledge has demonstrated about the physical universe, that the first creative act of God was to create light, a form of physical energy (Gn 1:3). And how did he create light? According to the record, he *said,* "Let there be light." We recall that God speaking—the Word of God—is simply the expression of his mind. By the expression of his mind, then, he created light.

Conversely, the coming into being of light and the result (light itself) is to be viewed as a Word of God. The writer of the book of Hebrews observes (1:1–3) that the things that are seen (light, and so on) were not made of things that are visible. The Word of God is the invisible, the spiritual, reality that produces all that is visible (see 2 Pt 3:5–7 and 2 Cor 4:18).

Is it possible to illuminate these passages from Genesis in some small measure by reflecting on how *we* create? I think so. You yourself may express your mind through creation and in what you create. Generally, if you do so you will have to do *more* than just "speak." For example, if you are to create a bouquet of flowers or a cake, you cannot just think or say: "Let there be a bouquet!" or "Let there be angelfood cake!"

Here we have before us the very essence and meaning of finitude. Finitude means limitation or *restriction*. You and I are under some restrictions regarding how we can make a cake. We must work with and through the eggs and the flour and the sugar and the heat of the oven and the time. We must adapt ourselves and our actions to their natures. One cannot make a silk purse from a sow's ear, as the saying goes— nor a sow's ear from a silk purse, for that matter. The structures within the substances with which we must deal dictate the order in, and limitations of, our actions.

But finally the cake comes forth, if we know what we are doing, and it is an expression of our self, our thoughts and feelings and intentions. Without these the cake would not exist. The husband or wife or child who only eats the cake, making no comment, has not got this point. They must find it good and say so. Better yet, they must say, in so many words, "How good of you to make this cake for me!" *You* are invested in the cake.

At a still more creative level of human life we have what are called "inventions." Normally the cake will be thought of as just something nice you were able to produce by following the directions or knowing how to make it. But if a person conceives of a new type of engine or clothing or communicative device, *that* is an invention. It also is an expression, at a deeper level of individuality, of the mind of its creator.

Hence we glorify inventors and authors as special kinds of individuals. Here, also, thought—the internal word—governs events in the material world. But here, too, it works under restrictions. We cannot create a jet engine just by saying or thinking, "Let there be a jet engine!"

But this is not yet the end of human powers of creation. There is one domain where the human mind but "speaks" and it is done. That realm is in the voluntary motions of the body—of the hands, the feet, the face—and over wide ranges of our inward thoughts themselves. God, of course, is *always* able to speak and to create thereby, without "going through channels," without working under restrictions— though he does not always choose to do so. This lack of limitations constitutes God's infinity.

Within a range—very narrow, in contrast to God's—we too have been given in our own "natural" powers a similarly unrestricted ability. In the realm of our familiar finitude we learn how to do things. We learn how to break the eggs and how to stir the batter, how to steer the automobile and put on the brakes.

But we do not *know* how to move our finger or our tongue or our foot. Here there are no "channels" to go through in the normal case. The action is immediate, and in our conscious processes there is no "how" about it. The thought, the intent, is there; the body, with all of the physical intricacies involved, just moves.

Similarly, we know how to interpret a passage of Scripture or how to read music or how to solve a crossword puzzle or how to dissect an argument from the editorial page of the newspaper. There is, accordingly, a "how to" across broad ranges of the mental life as well. But at a certain point, one can only *directly* think of certain things or decide on a course of action. If I ask you to think of a kitten, you do so with no "how to." To ask, under normal circumstances, How shall I think of a kitten? makes no more sense than to ask, How shall I move my little finger?

This all goes to make the following point: here, in this restricted range of direct action, God has given us an immediate power that, as far as our conscious governance is concerned, is as immediately creative as his own. This is what it means for us to have *life*. And, in this life given to us, he even permits us to use our little power to oppose him, even to hate him, in order that our compliance, if and when it comes, might be the free and intelligent response of a person to a person.

It seems there is no very clear boundary, or at least not a clear understanding of the boundary, between what we can influence directly by our thoughts and intents and what we cannot. We are astonished at great feats of "willpower." Also, if you can bend nails or spoons by "mental force"—or if you can even make it seem that you are doing so—you will certainly be invited to appear on television talk shows and in other circuses.

Biofeedback techniques have proven that by the immediate direction of our thoughts and our imagery, we can control the rate of our heartbeat and the level of our blood pressure. But, again, the creative Word of God is without any limitations at all, unless such limitation is purposely adopted by God himself. He says, "Let there be light," and there *is* light. Similarly, as you intend your arm to rise now, it rises.

Our own *experience* of thought, or of the "inner word," translating itself into "creation" is absolutely vital to our gaining any appreciation of God's rule through his Word. And only if we have some sense of what it is for his word to *act* will our understanding of guidance provide support for a robust faith.

Returning to Genesis 1 we see God continuing to create by the direct action of his Word on the results of his *first* creative word, which produced light and energy from itself alone, energy we now know to be the substance of matter. Thus, in verse 6, "Let there be a firmament in the midst of the waters, and let it divide the waters from the waters"; and verse 9, "Let the waters under the heaven be gathered together." He spoke and thereby formed these specific things into existence, as in verse 14, "Let there be lights in the firmament of the heaven"; verse 20, "And God said, Let the waters bring forth abundantly the moving creature that hath life"; verse 24, "God said, Let the earth bring forth"; and verse 26, "And God said, Let us make man in our image."

In all these cases, as God spoke, the object concerned came into existence—whether in an instant or over a more or less extended period of time does not matter—just as your hand goes up in response to your thought and intent. That is the creative power of the Word of God.

The thought, the mind, the Word of God continues its presence in the created universe as the *upholding* word. "Lasting to eternity, your word, Yahweh, unchanging in the heavens: your faithfulness lasts age after age; you founded the earth to endure. Creation is maintained by your rulings, since all things are your servants" (Ps 119:89–91, JB).

"Natural laws," then, must be regarded as God's thoughts and intents as to how the world should run. Because of this, as the Christian philosopher and Anglican bishop, George Berkeley, has said, echoing Psalm 19: "God Himself speaks every day and in every place to the eyes of all men."[4] The events in the visible, material world—the unfolding of a rosebud, the germination of a seed, the conception and growth of a child, the evolution of galaxies—constitute a "visible language" manifesting not only a creative mind but also, Berkeley continues,

> a provident Governor, actually and intimately present, and attentive to all our interests and motions, who watches over our conduct and takes care of our minutest actions and designs throughout the whole course of our lives, informing, admonishing, and directing incessantly, in a most evident and sensible manner.[5]

With all of this in mind you may wish to engage Psalm 104 in a meditative and worshipful reading.

The Word of God as the Son of God

This "visible language," this "Word," present as the upholding order of the universe, "was in the world, and the world was made through Him, and the world did not know Him. He came to His own, and those who were His own did not receive Him" (Jn 1:10–11, NASB).

The *redemptive* entry of God on the human scene was therefore no intrusion into foreign territory, but a move into "His own"—a focusing into the finite form of one human personality of that Divine "Thought" that is the order of all creation. He, as the ancient prayer says, "did not abhor the Virgin's womb." Therein, as always, the control panel of the whole universe lay ready to hand, though by voluntarily "emptying" himself (Phil 2:7), he refrained from all but a very selective use of it.

The seeming paradox of the incarnation is that Christ's infleshment *really* was no imposed restriction, but instead was the supreme exercise of the supreme power, as the end of human history will make abundantly clear: "Here is my servant, whom I have chosen, my beloved, on whom my favor rests; I will put my Spirit upon him, and he will proclaim judgment among the nations. He will not strive, he will not shout, nor will his voice be heard in the streets. He will not snap off the broken reed, nor snuff out the smoldering wick, until he leads justice on to victory. In him, the nations shall place their hope" (Mt 12:18–21, NEB).

The story of the New Testament is the story of increasing understanding of who Jesus was. Those among whom he was reared said, "This is Mary and Joseph's boy. We know him." His own disciples thought he might be Elijah or one of the old prophets risen from the dead. In a flash of divine revelation, Peter announced, as Jesus quizzed them on his identity: "Thou art the Christ!" (Mt 16:16).

Only in the later parts of the New Testament does there emerge the concept of Jesus as in fact a *cosmic* Christ spanning all geographical and ethnic differences but also providing, as we have seen, the "glue" of the universe (Col 1:17), upholding all things by the *Word* of his power (Heb 1:3)—or, as the Jerusalem Bible translates it, "Sustaining the universe by his powerful command." Thus he is the "alpha and omega" of the book of Revelation, the "Faithful and True," "the Word of God" leading the armies of heaven, "the King of Kings and Lord of Lords" (Rv 19:11–16).

In all of its manifestations in nature and in the incarnate Christ, the Word of God is characterized by overwhelming power. It is the awareness of this power that brings the prophet Isaiah to contrast the thoughts of man with the thoughts of God, which in their expression are the words of God. Mere human thoughts, though efficacious within their appointed range, are as far below the power of God's thoughts (and words) as the earth is below the heavens (Is 55:7–9).

With a force comparable to the forces of nature—the rain and seed bringing forth plants, seed and bread to nourish the hungry (v. 10)— "So shall My word be which goes forth from My mouth; it shall not return to Me empty, without accomplishing what I desire, and without succeeding in the matter for which I sent it" (v. 11, NASB).

The *unity* of the natural order and God's redemptive community under the Word of God is seen in Psalm 29. Here the behavior of the waters and of the forests are attributed to the voice of the Lord. "The voice of the Lord makes the deer to calve, and strips the forests bare" (v. 9, NASB). But while "the Lord sat as King at the flood," he also will "give strength to His people; the Lord will bless His people with peace" (vv. 10–11, NASB).

This same unity is of course exhibited in the life of Jesus. He could turn water into wine, calm the billowing waves with his word, and walk on them like a sidewalk. But he could also place the Word of God's Kingdom rule into the hearts of men, where it would bring forth fruit, "some an hundredfold, some sixty, some thirty" (Mt 13:23).

This, then, is the Word of God and the Son of God and their unity in the governance of the cosmos. But to understand how the Word of God is related to the *family* of God, we must consider more closely the role of ordinary human words in ordinary human life. This should enable us to see how the power of the Word of God, operating among human beings, *differs from superstition, magic, and voodoo.*

The Power of a Word

In the book of Ecclesiastes a wise man reflects in depth on how human life and society work. Among other things he considers how kings or governments function. We have seen in Psalm 29 how the Lord sat as King at the flood, and we know that he is indeed King over all the earth and master of the most terrible of situations. But a king, contrary to what is often thought, does *not* rule simply by brute force.

The emperor Napoleon was on one occasion about to use great force to subdue a certain population. But a wise lieutenant, one of his aides, said to him: "Monseigneur, one cannot *sit* upon bayonets." This man understood that the use of mere force could not lead to a settled political rule. Truly, all government is in some significant degree by consent of the governed. No one can totally rule a people by force. Instead, the ruler rules by words, understandings, allegiances, and alliances.

The writer of Ecclesiastes, himself a king, was amazed at what the word of a king could do. He remarks: "Where the word of a king is, there is power: and who may say unto him, What doest thou?" (8:4).

Take his authority, his role, away from him, and a king is like any other person. But when he is indeed kingly, his smallest word has awesome effects. Heads roll, nations prosper, cities burn, armies march. Those who oppose are crushed. Seeing clearly what occurs at the merely human level may help our faith to rise to an understanding of the power of the creative Word of God in his Kingdom.

Poets are in the business of seeing, and no poet has seen and inscribed the power of an "official" human word better than Dylan Thomas:

> The hand that signed the paper felled a city;
> Five sovereign fingers taxed the breath,
> Doubled the globe of dead and halved a country;
> These five kings did a king to death.
> The mighty hand leads to a sloping shoulder,
> The finger joints are cramped with chalk;
> A goose's quill has put an end to murder
> That put an end to talk.
> That hand that signed the treaty bred a fever,
> And famine grew, and locusts came;
> Great is the land that holds dominion over
> Man by a scribbled name.
> The five kings count the dead but do not soften

The crusted wound nor pat the brow;
A hand rules pity as a hand rules heaven;
Hands have no tears to flow.[6]

Words in the Kingdom of God

Now as we turn to the Kingdom of God with an understanding that it *is* precisely a kingdom and that it too works in large measure by words, numerous events from the life of Jesus on earth are easier to appreciate and enter into.

At the opening of this chapter we met "a certain centurion" who knew how words of authority work. He had implicit faith in Jesus, not, it seems, on a religious basis but from his quite secular knowledge of the power of authoritative words. So far as one can tell from the story, he did not have any special degree of faith in God, though he was a good man and respected the Jewish religion. He simply knew how authority worked, and he recognized that Jesus was working with authority to heal.

When (as recorded in Mt 8) Jesus entered into the city of Capernaum on one occasion, this centurion came "beseeching him, and saying, 'Lord my servant lieth at home sick of the palsy, grievously tormented'" (vv. 5–6). Palsy is paralysis, often accompanied with involuntary tremors. Without being asked, Jesus said, "I will come and heal him." Just like that! It was nothing extraordinary. We must remember that for Jesus this would be like me saying, "Now I'll raise my hand."

The centurion was in a position to understand Jesus' response. He replied: "Lord, don't bother. I'm not worthy that you should come under my roof." This was both an act of humility and a courtesy on the part of the centurion. He knew that he was speaking to a Jew, and that proper Jews thought that entry into the house of a Gentile would defile them. So, in an act of courtesy, the centurion said, "You don't need to come. Just *speak the word only* and my servant shall be healed."

"Speak the word only"? Yes, for where the word of a king is, there is power! The word is enough. This centurion understood that fact because he was, within his own arena, a "king," authorized to speak for a higher king, Caesar.

In both scriptural accounts of his meeting with Jesus, the centurion is allowed to explain fully how it is that he knows Jesus can just "speak the word only" and heal his servant: "For I am a man under authority, having soldiers under me: and I say to this man, 'Go,' and he goes; and to another 'Come,' and he comes; and to my servant, 'Do this,' and he does it" (Mt 8:9; compare Lk 7:8).

What we see here is *trust* based on *experiential knowledge of the power that words of authorized individuals have.* In a personal universe, the word directs actions and events. The centurion understood this, and Jesus marveled at his understanding: "I'm telling you the truth, I have not found so great faith, no, not in Israel" (Mt 8:10).

This is one of those points at which our practical atheism may abruptly emerge. We are apt to find ourselves saying (or silently thinking), "Things just aren't like that!" But what is it, exactly, that we find wrong? What is amiss with a universe in which reality responds to a word? What is wrong with a universe in which reality responds to thoughts and intentions? Surely we live in precisely such a universe, but our faith does not normally rise to it—or at least not to the extent to which it is true.

In part, no doubt, our skepticism about this framework is produced by the fact that we often speak words that are unaccompanied by faith and authority. Such words, of course, do not have the effect on reality of words freighted with faith in the fulfillment of an authoritative role. Thus *our* experience, unlike the centurion's, hinders rather than helps our faith.

We must not miss the point here. For the centurion, it was all perfectly easy, because he recognized that he was dealing with someone in high authority. He knew what authority was. He knew what it was to command an event. He knew that Jesus was doing the same kind of thing. So it was a simple matter for him to step into the situation by faith.

Where *he* had no authority—and thus could not himself say, "Be healed!"—he yet could recognize the One who did have such authority. He could in faith ask that person to use his authority to direct processes within the material universe, namely, the healing of the centurion's servant.

This Power Given to Human Beings

> "But to prove to you that the Son of Man has authority on earth to forgive sins,"—he said to the paralytic—"get up, and pick up your bed and go off home." And the man got up and went home. A feeling of awe came over the crowd when they saw this, and they praised God for giving such power to men. (Mt 9:6–8, JB)
>
> Miracles of grace must be the seals of our ministry; who can bestow them but the Spirit of God? (C. H. Spurgeon)[7]

According to the biblical record, powerful words such as Jesus spoke *have* been given to human beings to speak. In Numbers 20:8–12 we find a fascinating case study of this point. The situation is one in which the Israelites, in their wilderness wanderings, are dying for lack of water. Moses' leadership is under violent criticism from his people. This drives him to prayer, as it ought. Then God appears to him to tell him to *speak* to a rock that was close by, "and it shall give forth its water, and you shall bring forth to them water out of the rock" (v. 8).

But instead of doing this, Moses took the rod God had earlier given him as a sign and, with Aaron, called the people together. "'Hear now, ye rebels,' he said, 'must we fetch you water out of this rock?' And Moses lifted up his hand, and with his rod he smote the rock twice: and the water came out abundantly, and the congregation drank, and their animals also" (20:10–11).

Pretty impressive. But, having struck the rock instead of speaking to it, Moses had disobeyed God, who dealt sternly with Moses for his disobedience. He did not allow him to cross into the land of promise, "Because ye believed me not" (v. 12). But was it truly such a serious offense? Did it deserve such a strong reaction from God? And if so, why? Without understanding the matters discussed above, one might see little wrong in what Moses did. How could it possibly hurt a rock to strike it with a stick?

Possibly Moses was attempting to answer those who criticized *his* power. Or possibly he did not believe that merely speaking to a rock could bring water out of it. Possibly he thought he had to bring forth the water by his own physical strength—"must *we* fetch you water out of this rock?"

But the rock he struck, we learn in 1 Corinthians 10, *was Christ*. Rocks—if what we have come to understand about the *Logos*, or Word, in creation and nature is true—are things that well might respond to words spoken with the appropriate authority and vision of faith.

The transfer of the power of God's Word to "ordinary" humans was something that Jesus, in his days of humility, approached experimentally. *He* could exercise this power of God's government. But could it be transferred to his followers? That was the question they faced together.

So he commissioned his disciples to do what they had so often seen him do, and he sent them on their way: "Go, preach, saying, 'The kingdom of the heavens is at hand.' Heal the sick, cleanse the lepers, raise the dead, cast out devils: freely ye have received, freely give" (Mt 10:7–8; compare Lk 9:1–10). This first trial run was conducted with his twelve apostles only. When they returned and reported good success in acting in the power of God's Word, the question then became Can this transfer of God's power be extended even beyond the close followers and to even more "ordinary" believers? And so, according to Luke 10:1, Jesus sent out "other seventy also."

It seems to me to be a matter of great significance that these "other seventy" were not his closest associates—not, we might say, the best trained troops in the army of the Lord. Yet they too returned rejoicing in the knowledge that even demons were subject to them through the name of their Master (Lk 10:17).

This seems to have had the effect of settling the mind of our Lord on the extended incarnational plan of saving humankind. It apparently was only at *this* point that Jesus saw Satan in defeat, through the transfer of the Word of God and its power to ordinary people who could then speak with God in his government (Lk 10:17).

In this touching passage (Lk 10:21–23), Jesus seems positively gleeful, as in no other scriptural passage. He "exulted in the Holy Spirit," as the New English Bible translates it. The Greek word *agalliao* (v. 21) used here suggests the state of mind in which people may jump up and down with joy.

Then he turned aside, perhaps, for a moment of thanks to his Father: "I praise Thee, O Father, Lord of heaven and earth, that Thou didst hide these things from the wise and intelligent and didst reveal them to babes. Yes, Father, for thus it was well-pleasing in Thy sight" (v. 21, NASB).

Under the vivid realization of the meaning of these events, he then informed his followers with assurance that his Father had turned everything over to him—"All things have been handed over to Me by My Father"—and that he, Jesus Christ, was to be totally in charge of the revelation of the Father to humanity (v. 22, NASB). He then congratulated those around him on their good fortune in being able to witness what had happened, as "just plain folks" who had succeeded in operating with the power of God's authoritative Word. Prophets and kings had longed to see this, but had not been able to (v. 23–24).

Thus did the governmental rule of God, *through* the actions and words of human beings, reaffirm itself within the people of Israel just before its removal from their exclusive control. Because of their failure to fulfill their divine appointment of being the light of the world, of showing the world how to live under God, Jesus finally said to the Israelites of his day: "Therefore I say to you, the kingdom of God will be taken away from you, and be given to a [people] producing the fruit of it" (Mt 21:43, NASB).

It wasn't as if the Jews were to be excluded as individuals from exercise of the word of power in God's kingdom. Far from it. But it was no longer to be exclusively their role *as* Jews. The Jewish people would not longer exclusively be the people of God. The story of the transfer indicated by Jesus is precisely the story of the New Testament book of Acts, which begins in Jerusalem and ends in Rome.

Prayers, Actions, and "Words"

A proper understanding of the ways of the Word of God among humanity, within the Kingdom rule of God, illuminates something that has troubled many thoughtful students of the New Testament. It casts light on the fact that rarely does Jesus ever pray for a need brought before him. Rather, he normally *addresses* it or performs some *action* in relation to it.

Such a case comes before us in Mark 9, which relates that while Jesus was on the Mount of Transfiguration, a man brought his child to be healed. The child was possessed of a spirit that rendered him mute. The disciples tried to cast the spirit out, but they failed. When the Master then arrived back on the scene, he scolded his disciples for their inability (v. 19). After some conversation with the father about the child's condition and about the father's own faith, Jesus cast the demon out by a command. When the disciples then asked why they could not cast it out, for apparently they had previously had some success in such matters, Jesus replied, "This kind cannot come out by anything but prayer" (v. 29, NASB). And yet Jesus did not pray on this occasion. What is the explanation?

I believe we see illustrated here a principle to the effect that, as experience readily shows, there are degrees of power in speaking the Word of God and that prayer is necessary to heighten that power. Prayer is more fundamental in the spiritual life than "speaking a word" and is the indispensable foundation thereof. If we want to understand why the speaking role has such little play today, as it obviously does, we will find the explanation in the general lack of understanding of such speaking, together with the generally low quality of the life of prayer.

Surely in some situations we will encounter, and perhaps in most, a *direct* word or action from God himself is what is required. And for that we can only pray. But sometimes, we should be in a position to speak, to say on behalf of God and in the name of Christ how things are to be.

To do this will be more or less difficult, as Jesus indicates, depending on the specifics of the case. "This kind" of situation will frequently differ from other kinds in other cases and will call for other abilities, which we may or may not have available at the time. But I believe we are called to grow into this capacity to "speak with God" in the measure appointed by him for us individually.

Certainly in the works done by the apostles of Jesus, we see them *speaking with* God, namely, in the book of Acts and, less so, in the Gospels. The apostles did not always pray to God for help in the matter at hand. When Peter and John are confronted with the lame beggar as they enter the Temple in Acts 3, Peter commands the man in the name of Jesus Christ—commands on his behalf, that is—to rise up and walk. Then he takes the beggar by the hand and pulls him to his feet (vv. 3–7). Peter does not kneel down and pray, nor does he pass on with a "We'll be praying for you!" He puts his whole bodily being on public display as an agent of Christ. Scary, isn't it?

When dealing with Dorcas, the deceased sister "full of good works and almsdeeds" (Acts 9:36), Peter put everyone out of the room. (Did he not learn this from Jesus?—Mt 9:25.) Kneeling down, he prayed. Then he faced the body and commanded Dorcas to arise, and she returned to life (Acts 9:40). Perhaps Peter also learned from Elisha's practice in a similar situation (2 Kgs 4:32–35). Elisha, as we know, was one of the all-time greatest practitioners of Kingdom rule.

Paul at Lystra spoke the redemptive Word of God to a lame man whose faith had been raised by hearing Paul preach. Paul loudly commanded the man, "Stand upright on your feet." And the man leaped and walked (Acts 14:10).

In our day, with the return of the *charismata,* or "gifts" of the Spirit, to prominence across all denominational boundaries, multitudes of disciples once again dare to *speak* in the name of Jesus to the needs and dangers that confront them. More recently still, the practice of "spiritual warfare" has prepared countless others to "speak to the mountain," as Jesus said (Mk 11:23). Testimonies of remarkable results find their way into many fellowships and into an abundance of Christian literature. Such testimony is only what will be expected as we grow in our confidence that reality is, ultimately, a kingdom in which authority and personal relationship and communication are basic.

But This Calls Us into Question

Of course there are multitudinous ways in which such speaking and its results might be misunderstood. They will be especially unsettling if we are already used to living our lives untouched by them and are convinced that they must have nothing to do with our faith or our service to God. Thus if it should be suggested that we possibly should be healing the sick, casting out demons, or raising the dead by our participation in the Word and power of God, we may feel baffled, rebellious, guilt-ridden, and angry.

Once, after I spoke in a certain church on accomplishing things through prayer, a woman confronted me in great agony and tears and with not a little anger. As we talked, it became clear that she had earlier believed that our prayers could actually make a difference in the course of events around us, and she had tried very hard to make prayer work in her life. But she had, for whatever reason, failed in the attempt, and, obviously, that failure had left her feeling guilty and deeply hurt.

To protect herself she had readjusted her faith, at least on the surface, to consist of believing the creeds, helping out at church, and being a good person generally, as that is commonly understood in our society. My words had reopened the old wounds and disturbed her hard-won peace. I have since come to understand that she is representative of many fine people who think well of Christ and would like to be his followers but are convinced that the biblical mode of life in God's Kingdom just cannot be a reality for them.

On another occasion, a very devout woman, who had been raised in a fellowship in which receiving a "second work of grace" was stressed, had been driven to distraction in her frantic efforts to obtain this "deeper life" and cease being a "second-class citizen" among her religious friends. She too felt she had "failed" and had recoiled into a life of mental assent to the truth about Jesus and some degree of service to the local church with which she was associated.

In this case I was only teaching about the joyous possibilities of life opened up by Jesus' invitation to enter his Kingdom and about how gladly that invitation was received by his hearers. But this woman was thrown into agony by hearing of a life of real interaction with God in the manner of those described in the Old and New Testaments.

I cannot in these pages effectively deal with all of the issues involved in such cases, but there is one thing we can and must rest in: when we consider the life of participation in God's kingdom rule, we are not looking at anything we must make happen. The extent of our obligation is *to be honestly willing and desirous to be made able.*

If we are to exercise the Word and rule of God in ways regarded as spectacular by human beings, Jesus here, as always, is our model. And that means, above all, that there will be nothing forced or hysterical about our efforts and that we can count on God himself to lead us into whatever we are to do. He will do this in such a way that it is suitable to our lives and his calling for us.

Beyond this we should always keep in mind the words of Jesus to his seventy friends on their return from their mission: "Nevertheless do not rejoice in this, that the spirits are subject to you, but rejoice that your names are recorded in heaven" (Lk 10:20, NASB).

With this firmly in mind, we turn to consider two final questions of this chapter: How does a life in which one speaks the creative word of God differ from superstition, magic, and voodoo? and What does the Bible have to do with the Word of God as thus far discussed?

Voodoo, Magic, and Superstition

By "magic" we have in mind here not sleight of hand or mere trickery, but the attempt to influence the *actual* course of events, as distinct from their *appearance,* by manipulation of symbolisms or special substances such as effigies and incantations. Voodoo and witchcraft—sometimes lumped together as "black" magic—are forms of magical practice most familiar to the Western mind.

Satanism and demonism operate on yet a different principle, as service to or from a personal evil power, though they sometimes merge with magic. Magic and witchcraft, by contrast, are forms of *superstition.* That is, they work from belief that some action or substance or circumstance not logically or naturally or even supernaturally related to a certain course of events does, nonetheless, if "correctly" approached, influence the outcome of those events.

The word *superstition* itself is derived from words meaning "to stand over," as one might stand in wonder or amazement over something incomprehensible. The famous Connecticut Yankee in King Arthur's court, in Mark Twain's fictional portrayal, was able to lead the ignorant and generally superstitious people of ancient England to attribute unusual powers to his own actions, while he himself understood the natural causes of the events he manipulated.

Thus, Martin Buber rightly says that "magic desires to obtain its effects without entering into relation, and practices its tricks in the void."[8]

Superstition, then, is belief in magic, and magic relies on *alleged* causal influences that are not mediated through the natures of the things involved. Suppose, for example, someone says that they can throw you into great pain or even kill you by mutilating a doll-like effigy of you. This is a practice common in voodoo and other forms of witchcraft and rests on superstition or magical thinking, for there is no real connection between sticking a pin in a doll and you feeling pain.

I am sure that in some cases there is much more reality to the *effects claimed* than we might wish to credit, from a commonsense or scientific point of view. There seems to be good evidence that in some settings people do suffer or die when certain rituals concerning them are performed.

However, it is not the mutilation of the doll or the incantations over it that produce the effects. Rather, the effects—where there are effects—come from the realm of the mind or spirit in a social context in which a certain set of beliefs about voodoo or magical rituals are shared.

This does not mean that the *effects* are illusory or unreal, but rather that whatever actual causation is involved has nothing magical about it. *No* causation has magical properties. The "voodoo process" is an entirely natural process in the context of the prevailing psychosocial order.[9] The power involved is not the power of the ritual, but rather the power of personal force, and often involves something like hypnotism, the social context, and perhaps the satanic dimension of the spiritual realm.

Why Christ's Faith Is Not Superstition

When we return to the ways in which Moses, Jesus, Peter, and Paul did the work of God, by exercising his rule through speaking and acting his Word, there is neither magic nor superstition to be found.

Similarly, neither is there superstition nor magic involved in the astonishing results of "speaking," which increasingly are a part of the life of the ordinary Christian today.

Many of my readers who have difficulty conceptualizing the more spectacular episodes of the Word working, such as we have seen in the Scriptures, still believe in the healing power of prayer and in the capacity of some individuals or some rituals practiced by the church to minister at the physical level in the healing of the body and so forth. Why is this belief not just more superstition?

The answer is that in our faith *we do not believe the power concerned to reside in the words used or in the rituals taken by themselves.* If we did, we would be engaged in superstitious practices. Instead, we regard the words and actions employed as simply the ways ordained in the nature of things, as established by God, for accomplishing the goal in question. Such rituals work as part of living in the Kingdom of God and enlist the personal agency of that Kingdom to achieve their ends. Hence they are not tools by which we engineer our desired result. We are "under authority" and not "in control."

The specific condition of understanding, faith, love, and hope present in those who work with the Word of God is, *in its very nature,* connected to the effect to be brought about, relating, as it does, the nature of the human body or mind (in the case of healing) to the creative and redemptive Spirit who is God. That condition forms, as part of the Kingdom, the appropriate channel from the supply to the need. It forms a "natural" order of influence and causation.

We may understand this better by returning briefly to the matters discussed at the beginning of this chapter. We saw there that it is the very nature of the material universe to be subject generally to the Word of an all-present, all-powerful, all-knowing Divine Mind. This Mind is what mediates between the Word spoken by his servant on his behalf, on the one hand, and the physical structure of the waves or the rocks, or the body or mind to be healed, on the other. This is why Moses, Jesus, Peter, and Paul were not magicians and did not practice anything like voodoo.

Sometimes, however, I fear that we Christians do engage in truly superstitious usages of words and rituals, especially so when our activities are not an expression of any understanding of the connection between the consequence desired and our faith and union with God.

A few years ago many Christians in the United States were caught up in a fad involving the phrase "What you say is what you get." Some still are. It was suggested that if you would just affirm what you wanted, you would get it. Further, if you *say*, or give verbal expression to, what you do not want—for example, voice something you are worried may happen—it will happen to you.

This *is* superstition, and places us in the category of those, described by Jesus, who in prayer use "vain repetitions," thinking "that they shall be heard for their much speaking" (Mt 6:7). Possibly there is nothing but superstition in the religious activities of many people. They may have no understanding of the nature of God's Kingdom and of how, through his Word, he rules in the affairs of humanity and especially within the family of the faithful. We each must search our own heart on this matter. It does not have to be so, if we will "seek above all the kingdom of God."

Legalism Is Superstition

The *legalistic* tendencies of the religious and cultural life also thrust us toward superstition. "Legalism" holds that overt *action* conforming to rules for explicit behavior is what makes us right and pleasing to God and worthy of blessing. Jesus called it "the righteousness of the Scribes and Pharisees" (Mt 5:20). Legalism, superstition, and magic are closely joined because they share an interest in *controlling* people and events. The legalist is forced toward superstitious behavior because, in the interest of controlling life through his laws, he departs from the natural connections of life. He bypasses the realities of the heart and the soul from which life really flows.

Life does not come by law (Gal 3:21), nor can law adequately depict or guide it. The law is letter, and "the letter killeth, but the spirit giveth life" (2 Cor 3:6). The legalist is evermore forced into merely symbolic behaviors, which he superstitiously supposes have the good effects sought by him. Magic or superstition, as is well known, places absolute emphasis on doing everything "just right," which is the essence of legalism.

"Speaking the Word" and Magic Confused

But living and acting from the power of God through reliance on Christ has nothing to do with superstition, as it has nothing to do with legalism or salvation through the law. In two different cases in the book of Acts, the work of God was mistaken for magic by those without understanding.

The first case is that of Simon the Sorcerer in Acts 8. Beholding Peter and John conferring the Holy Spirit on others, with the attendant manifestations, Simon offered money to them if they would but give him power to do the same (v. 18). Peter saw from this that Simon, though a "believer," did not have his heart right with God. He rebuked Simon severely for thinking "that the gift of God may be purchased with money" (v. 20).

In the nineteenth chapter of Acts, we find a rather more humorous story. A traveling troop of Jewish exorcists, the seven sons of Sceva, saw the miracles worked by God with Paul and Paul with God. They listened to the *words* Paul used, mistaking them for incantations rather than intelligent, rational discourse within a society or kingdom.

They then tried pronouncing the name "Jesus" over a person possessed of demons, saying, "I command you by Jesus preached by Paul" (v. 13). The scriptural account of what then happened is so good that it must be simply quoted: "The evil spirit replied, 'Jesus I recognize, and I know who Paul is, but who are you?' and the man with the evil spirit hurled himself at them and overpowered first one and then another, and handled them so violently that they fled from that house naked and badly mauled" (vv. 15–16, JB).

This greatly impressed everyone in Ephesus, and the name "Lord Jesus" was held in great respect. Believers who had been using spells and practicing magic forsook such practices, realizing the great disparity between the realm of the magical and the Kingdom of God. They burned magic books worth fifty thousand pieces of silver, while, for its part, "the word of the Lord was growing mightily and prevailing" (v. 20, NASB).

We as followers of Christ are not to believe or act on things that make no sense and that we only hope to make work for our own ends, no matter how fine.

The Bible and the Word of God

Finally, we come to the question of how we are to understand the relationship of the Bible to the Word of God we have just seen "growing mightily and prevailing" around Ephesus and to that Word that is God and that upholds the world.

The Bible is *one* of the results of God speaking. It is the *unique* written Word of God and, in conjunction with it, God himself presently speaks to the devout heart ever anew. It is inerrant in its original form and infallible in all of its forms for the purpose of guiding us into a saving relationship with God in his Kingdom. It is infallible in this way precisely because God never leaves it alone.

The inerrancy of the original texts is rendered efficacious for the purposes of redemption only as that text through its present-day derivatives are constantly held within the eternal living Word. Inerrancy by itself is not a sufficient theory of biblical inspiration, because, as everyone knows, the Bible in our hand is not the original text.

Inerrancy of the originals also does not guarantee sane and sound, much less error-free, interpretations. Our dependence as we read the Bible is on God, who now speaks in conjunction with it, and our best efforts to understand.

In the light of our discussions thus far it is clear that *the Bible is the written Word of God, but the Word of God is not simply the Bible. The way we know that this is so is, above all, by paying attention to what the Bible says.*

If you take just the passages studied thus far and carefully examine what they say about the Word of God, you will see that that Word is much greater than the Bible, though inclusive of it. The Bible is the

Word of God in its unique written form. But the Bible is not Jesus Christ, who is the living Word. It was not born of a virgin, crucified, resurrected, and elevated to the right hand of the Father.

And the Bible is not the Word of God that is settled eternally in the heavens, as the psalmist says (Ps 119:89), expressing itself in the order of nature (Ps 19:1–4). The Bible is not that Word of God that in the book of Acts expanded and grew and multiplied (Acts 12:24). It is not the Word that Jesus spoke of as being sown by the active speaking of the ministry (Mt 13). But all of these are God *speaking*.

To reemphasize: the Bible is the unique, infallible written Word of God. But the Word of God is not just the Bible, and if we try to dignify the Bible by saying false things about it—that is, by simply *equating* the Word of God with it—we do not dignify it. Rather, we betray its content by denying what *it* says about the nature of the Word of God.

God reigns in his Kingdom through speaking. That "speaking" is reserved to himself but may in some small measure be communicated through those who work in union with him. The Bible is a finite, written record of what saving truth the infinite, living God has spoken, and it reliably fixes the boundaries of what he will ever say to humankind. It fixes those boundaries in principle, though it does not provide the detailed communications God may have with individual believers, as we have earlier discussed.

The Bible has its own special and irreplaceable role in the history of redemption. We can refer any person to it with the assurance that if they will approach it openly, honestly, intelligently, and persistently, God will meet them through its pages and speak peace to their souls. This is assured to any person whose deepest self cries out:

> Beyond the sacred page I seek Thee, Lord;
> My spirit pants for Thee, O Living Word.[10]

Paul therefore instructed his protege, Timothy, that "the sacred writings . . . are able to give you the wisdom that leads to salvation through faith which is in Christ Jesus. All Scripture is inspired by God and profitable for teaching, for reproof, for correction, for training in righteousness; that the man of God may be adequate, equipped for every good work" (2 Tm 3:15–17, NASB).

The word of God in the larger sense portrayed *in* the Bible is therefore available to every person *through* the Bible, the *written* Word of God. All may hear the living Word by coming to the Bible humbly, persistently, with burning desire to find God and live in peace with him.

As for others, the Bible may prove a deadly snare, as it did for those in Christ's earthly days who actually used the Bible to dismiss his person and his claims on them (Jn 5:36–47). Because of this we are warned in the Bible that we can destroy ourselves by Bible study, specifically by the study of Paul's epistles "in which are some things hard to understand, which the untaught and unstable distort, as they do also the rest of Scriptures, to their own destruction" (2 Pt 3:16, NASB).

Our only protection from our own pride and fear and ignorance and impatience as we study the Bible is fellowship with the living Word, the Lord himself, invoked in constant supplication from the midst of his people.

> O send Thy Spirit, Lord, now unto me,
> That He may touch my eyes, and make me see;
> Show me the truth concealed within Thy word,
> And in Thy book revealed, I see the Lord.
>
> *Mary Ann Lathbury* [11]

> Light up Thy word; the fettered page
> From killing bondage free:
> Light up our way; lead forth this age
> In Love's large liberty.
> O Light of light! Within us dwell,
> Through us Thy radiance pour,
> That word and life Thy truths may tell,
> And praise Thee evermore.
>
> *Washington Gladden* [12]

SOME TOPICS FOR REFLECTION

1. How is it that words can have such power? Is it just through their relationship to personality? What is that relationship? In what way are words "spiritual"?

2. Relate words, in the full sense explained, to creation. In God. In us.

3. How is a *kingdom* a verbal, not a merely physical, reality?

4. How are "natural laws" related to God's Word?

5. Compare the Word as the Son and the Word as the Bible.

6. What exactly was it that the Roman centurion knew, and how did it relate to his faith in Jesus?

7. Explain the relationship between prayer and "speaking with" God.

8. "The 'rock' that Moses struck was Christ." What are we to make of this?

9. Do you feel threatened by the contents of this chapter?

10. Distinguish the Christian faith in the power of the Word of God from voodoo.

Notes

1. Plato, *Theaetetus,* trans. F. M. Cornford, in *Plato: The Collected Dialogues,* E. Hamilton and H. Cairns, eds. (Princeton, NJ: Princeton University Press, 1961), 190.
2. St. Augustine, *On the Trinity,* in *Basic Writings of St. Augustine,* Vol. 1, Whitney J. Oates, ed. (New York: Random House, 1948), bk. 10, chap. 6, 804.
3. William Penn, *The Peace of Europe, Etc.* (London: J. M. Dent, n.d.), 65.
4. Mary W. Calkins, ed., *Berkeley: Essay, Principles and Dialogues with Selections from Other Writings* (New York: Scribner's, 1929), 370.
5. Calkins, *Berkeley,* 373.
6. Dylan Thomas, "The Hand That Signed the Paper Felled a City," in *The Golden Treasury* (New York: New American Library), 455.

7. Fuller, *Spurgeon's Lectures to His Students,* 182.

8. Martin Buber, *I and Thou,* trans. Ronald G. Smith (New York: Collier Books, 1958), 83.

9. Consider, on this point, the studies of the physiologist Walter Cannon, referred to in *Psychology Today,* June 1983, pp. 71–72.

10. Mary Ann Lathbury, "Break Thou the Bread of Life," v. 1, hymn #192 in *The Broadman Hymnal* (Nashville, TN: The Broadman Press, 1940).

11. Lathbury, "Break Thou," v. 3.

12. Washington Gladden, "The Holy Scriptures," hymn #391 in *The Methodist Hymnal* (Chicago: The Methodist Publishing House, 1939).

7 Redemption Through the Word of God

> It is too small a thing that You should be My Servant to raise up the tribes of Jacob, and to restore the survivors of Israel; I will also make You a light of the nations so that My salvation may reach to the ends of the earth.

IS 49:6, NASB

> You are the light of the world.

MT 5:14, NASB

Becoming Children of Light Through the Word of God

To understand guidance we must in some good measure understand what the Word of God is, for divine guidance is basically God speaking. In the Way of Christ, as we have said, guidance is essentially one dimension of a certain kind of life as a whole—of the *eternal* kind of life, which is a life lived in conversational relationship with God (Jn 17:3).

Our studies of the Word of God are necessary that we might better understand what the eternal kind of life is and how we are, by the graciousness of God, to take part in it.

Lack of understanding of, and confidence in, the Word of God as a substantial reality, providing and pervading the eternal kind of life, flatly rules out the possibility of any great degree of practical competence and confidence in divine guidance itself.

But, to renew an earlier theme, God's guidance of us is not something given only for us and our purposes, nor is it primarily for our own prosperity, safety, or gratification. Those who receive the grace of God's saving companionship in the ambiance and environment of the Word are, by that very fact, also fitted to show mankind how to live.

In this sense these recipients are to be the light of the world. Their transformed nature automatically suits them to this task, which, therefore, is not something optional or tacked on externally as an afterthought. The light they radiate is not what they *do,* over and above what they *are.*

Individuals close at hand, as well as world events at large, demonstrate what great need there is for light on how to live. There is no informed disagreement about this. The popular media of newspaper, radio, and television, as well as scholarly research and publications, constantly update us on our burgeoning social and personal problems. These problems remain unsolved because of the confusion, ignorance, or perversity, both of our leaders and of most of the world's population, with regard to the fundamental causes of human happiness and misery.

Solutions to the problems of humanity—from incest to atomic warfare, from mental illness to poverty and pollution—are by no means easy or simple. But what we know of human nature seems clearly to indicate that light on how to live can be brought forward in a manner that will effectively meet the need only by those prepared to lead the way by example.

Only by showing how to live can we teach how to live. It is by our example—more precisely, by the kind of life that is in us and makes us exemplary as a God-indwelt people—that we lay the basis for redemptive communication of divine Word and Spirit to an ever larger circle of human beings. This is the pattern set forth in the New Testament book of Acts and at subsequent points of Christian history. In us, as in Jesus Christ himself, *the Life* is to be *the light* of men (Jn 1:4).

Collectively, the called-out people of God, the church, is empowered to stand forth to wandering humanity like the cloudy pillar by day and the pillar of fire by night that guided the Israelites through the desert (Ex 13). When faced with starvation, crime, economic disasters and difficulties, disease, loneliness, alienation, and war, the church should be, because it *can* be, the certified authority on living to which the world looks for answers. The resources of God's government are at the church's disposal.

However dimly, we sense this and say this when we say, "Christ is the answer!" Although you might not have actually thought of these problems as "questions," they do pose the precise issues of life, which he alone can resolve.

Individually, the disciple and friend of Jesus who has learned to work shoulder to shoulder with his or her Lord stands in this world as a point of contact between heaven and earth, a kind of "Jacob's ladder" by which the angels of God may ascend from and descend into human life (Jn 1:51; Gn 28:12). Thus the disciple stands as an envoy or "receiver" by which the Kingdom of God is itself conveyed into every quarter of human affairs (Lk 10:1–11).

This, as Hannah Hurnard has so beautifully described it, is the role of the intercessor:

> An intercessor means one who is in such vital contact with God and with his fellow men that he is like a live wire closing the gap between the saving power of God and the sinful men who have been cut off from that power. An intercessor is the contacting link between the source of power (the life of the Lord Jesus Christ) and the objects needing that power and life.[1]

But what is *the process* by which we can be fully transformed into children of Light—"blameless and innocent, children of God above reproach in the midst of a crooked and perverse generation, among whom you appear as lights in the world, holding fast the word of life" (Phil 2:15–16, NASB)? How are we to understand the ongoing process—obviously involving divine guidance—by which our present life is to be redeemed, shaped, and conformed to the likeness of that of the Son (Rom 8:29)? And what is the role of the Word of God in this process?

These are the questions to be dealt with now. When they are answered, we shall be in position to deal in a fully practical manner in the last two chapters with divine guidance in the Way of Christ.

An ADDITIONAL Birth by the Word of God

> Let this mind be in you, which was also in Christ Jesus. (Phil 2:5)
>
> For you have been called . . . to follow in His steps, who committed no sin, nor was any deceit found in His mouth; and while being reviled, He did not revile in return; while suffering, He uttered no threats, but kept entrusting Himself to Him who judges righteously. (1 Pt 2:21–23, NASB)

In the light of our previous chapter on the Word of God, we now can give a clear and thorough answer to the question about the process of redemption, one that goes beyond mere figures of speech and poetic language. *It is through the action of the Word of God on us, throughout us, and with us that we come to have the mind of Christ and thus to live fully in the Kingdom of God.*

We now hold clearly before us what we have learned about the Word of God: that it is a creative and sustaining substance, an active power, not limited by space and time and physical constraints. It organizes and guides that on which it is directed by God and by persons in union with God. It is what lies at the foundation of all the kinds of life and being there are.

Life, in its various levels and types, is *power to act and respond in specific kinds of relations.* A cabbage has certain powers of action and response and a corresponding level of "life." There is a big difference between a cabbage that is alive and one that is dead, though the dead one still exists. The same is true of a kitten.

But even though alive, a cabbage has no response to a ball of string, which is precisely owing to the *kind* of life that is in it. Though alive as a cabbage, it is dead to the realm of play. Similarly, a kitten playing with the string has no response to numbers and poetry and in this sense is dead to the realms of arithmetic and literature. The live cabbage, though dead to one realm (that of play) is yet alive in another—that of the soil and the sun and the rain. And the same can be said of the kitten.

Human beings once were alive to God. They were created to be responsive to and interactive with him. Adam and Eve lived in a conversational relationship, daily renewed, with their Creator. Their mistrust and disobedience toward God cut them off from the realm of the spirit. Thus they became dead in relation to it, much as the kitten is dead to arithmetic. As God said, "In the day that you eat thereof you will certainly die" (Gn 2:17). And they did.

Biologically they continued to live, of course. But they ceased to be responsive and interactive in relation to God's kingly cosmic rule. It was necessary for God to confer an additional level of life on them and their children through "a birth from above" in order for them once again to live unto God, to be able to respond toward and act within the realm of the Spirit.

Human beings born "of water" (Jn 3:5)—that is, of semen and of the fluid in the birth sac that bursts as they move out of the womb—are alive in "the flesh," in the biological and psychological realm of nature. But they remain "dead in trespasses and sins" (Eph 2:1) in relation to God. Therefore they "have no hope and are without God in the world" (Eph 2:12). They *can,* however, be born a second time, born "from above" (Jn 3:3, JB). This is *not* to be "born again," in the sense that something is *repeated* or a new start from the same place is provided. Instead, it is a matter of an *additional* birth whereby we become aware of and enter into the spiritual Kingdom of God. Imagine an otherwise "normal" kitten that suddenly begins to appreciate and compose poetry, and that will give an impression of the huge transition involved in this additional birth.

This additional birth is one brought about by the Word and the Spirit and is spiritual in its effects. "That which is born of the flesh is flesh; and that which is born of the Spirit is spirit" (Jn 3:6).

The Teacher Who Did Not Know

A respected spiritual leader of the Jews was very impressed with what he had seen of Jesus and approached him with the words: "Rabbi, we know that you are a teacher come from God; for no one can do these things that you do, unless God is with him" (Jn 3:2, RSV). Thus he complimented Jesus. And at the same time he complimented himself on being an insider who had the good sense to recognize God at work.

Jesus' reply to him was, in fact, a stinging rebuke, though gently delivered in such a way as to be palatable and helpful. In effect, Jesus told him he had not the slightest idea of what he was talking about. Nicodemus came claiming to be able to recognize, to "see" God at work. Jesus said, "Unless a man is born from above, he cannot see the kingdom of God" (v. 3, JB), he cannot recognize God's workings. Like all seeing, spiritual seeing also requires the appropriate faculties and equipment.

But Jesus' simple observation immediately tripped up Nicodemus, revealing the true limits of his understanding. He could only think of the usual sort of birth, so he gropingly inquired, "How can a grown man have *that* again?" Then Jesus explained that unless one has had the birth "of water" and an additional birth of Spirit, he or she cannot participate in God's governance, his "Kingdom."

Those born of the Spirit manifest a different kind of life. Recall, now, that *a life* is *a definite range of activities and responses.* The spiritually born exhibit a life deriving from an invisible spiritual realm and its powers. In natural terms one cannot explain what is happening with them, "where they come from, or where they go" (v. 8). But just as with the invisible wind and its effects, we recognize the presence of God's Kingdom in people by its effects in and around them.

Birth Through the Word

We have already seen that the words of Jesus are Spirit and in what sense the Spirit is also Word. Now we find that the additional birth that brings one to life in the realm of God is attributed both to the Spirit (Jn 3:5–8) and to the Word.

In 1 Peter 1:23, those who are alive to God are described as being "born again, not of the seed which is perishable, but imperishable, that is, through the living and abiding word of God" (NASB). And James 1:18 tells us that "of his own will begat he us with the word of truth."

This testimony of James and Peter was based on their observations of the effects that the Word of God through Christ had had on them and of the effects that God's Word through them and the early church had had on others. It is a simple matter of fact that Paul so expressed:

"Faith is awakened by the message, and the message that awakens it comes through the Word of Christ" (Rom 10:17, NEB).

As the Word of God in creation brought forth light and matter and life, so the gospel of Christ comes to us while we are biologically alive but dead to God. This gospel both empowers and calls forth a response by its own power, enabling us to see and to enter the Kingdom of God as participants. It opens the door of the heart and enters the mind. From there it is able progressively to transform the whole personality.

Thus, "the sower sows the Word" of the Kingdom (Mk 4:14). When this message takes root in the heart and mind, a new life has entered our personality, which increasingly becomes *our* life as we learn to "walk in the Spirit" (Gal 4:25) and "sow to the Spirit" (Gal 6:8).

Redemption in this respect is but a further aspect of creation, a "new creation." This new creation is the only thing that matters in a person's relation to God, as Paul says (Gal. 6:15). Without it there is no relation to God as something in which one *lives*. And from this creation there arise all further developments of God's rule in the human soul.

Once again we draw on the wisdom of Spurgeon:

> Even so we have *felt* the Spirit of God operating upon our hearts, we have known and perceived the power which He wields over human spirits, and we know Him by frequent, conscious, personal contact. By the sensitiveness of our spirit we are as much made conscious of the presence of the Spirit of God as we are made cognizant of the existence of souls, or as we are certified of the existence of matter by its action upon our senses. We have been raised from the dull sphere of mere mind and matter into the heavenly radiance of the spirit-world; and now, as spiritual men, we discern spiritual things, we feel the forces which are paramount in the spirit-realm, and we know that there is a Holy Ghost, for we feel Him operating upon our spirits.[2]

The Engrafted Word of God

The image of a *graft* is used by James, the Lord's brother, to portray the relationship of the additional life in the Spirit to our natural fleshly life. Graft is now more commonly understood as a kind of political corruption in which someone taps into the flow of public wealth to enrich themselves. This, however, is but a figure of speech drawn from the original usage of the term.

Grafting is a horticultural practice commonly done with various kinds of fruit trees and plants. If you go to a plant nursery in the spring, you will find small fruit trees ready to be planted in your yard or orchard. Often they will bear tags reading "Santa Rosa Plum on Namgard," for example, or "Elberta on Wild Peach." If you look to the base of the tree, you will discover a swelling that encompasses the trunk and looks as if the trunk had been broken and healed over.

This swelling is where the top of a little sapling with a vigorous root—usually some wild variety of the same genetic type—has been cut off and a branch from a more desirable variety of fruit tree has been carefully attached, so that the life of the more vigorous root will flow into and through the new branch. The superior energies of the wild but useless root are transformed, by passing through the substance of the imposed branch, to produce delicious and abundant fruit foreign in quantity and quality to its source in the root.

This practice of the orchard keeper was familiar to the writers of Scripture. Paul uses it to explain the relationship of the Gentiles to the Jewish nation (Rom 11:17) so that the Gentile church might understand its dependence on the Jews. James, after indicating that we are *begotten* with the Word of truth, admonishes those who therefore have the additional life to "do away with all the impurities and bad habits that are still left in you, and humbly receive the engrafted word, which is able to save your souls" (see Jas 1:21).

This figure of speech signifies that, after the coming of our "additional" life, our natural powers are not left to run their own way under or alongside the new life but are to be channeled through and subordinated to that life "from above." All energies are redirected to spiritual ends, appointed to higher purposes, though they remain, in themselves, normal human powers.

The uniqueness of each individual personality remains in the beauty and goodness of its natural life. But a holy radiance rests on it and shines throughout it because it is now the temple of God, the area over which the larger and higher power of God plays.

"Washed" in the Word of God

We see, then, how an additional and spiritual life comes through the Word of God and how that Word then possesses and redirects the energies of the natural life to promote the ends of God's Kingdom.

A different description of the function of the Word of God in our redemption is seen in Ephesians 5:25–27. Here, speaking of the church, the apostle says that Christ "gave himself for it; that he might sanctify and cleanse it with the washing of water by the word, that he might present it to himself a glorious church, not having spot, or wrinkle, or any such thing; but that it should be holy and without blemish."

Here the Word is pictured as *washing away* the impurities and clutter that have permeated human personality during its life away from God. These impurities and distractions, which do not automatically disappear at the additional birth, limit and attack both individual spiritual growth and the role intended for Christ's corporate followers as the light of the world.

By his sacrificial death and triumphant resurrection, Jesus Christ finished welding his immediate followers into a totally new kind of social unit: the redemptive community, the living temple of the living God (Eph 2:21–22). This community in turn provided an environment within which God's Word would be present with such richness and power that the church *could* stand forth on the world scene as beyond all reasonable reproach. In this way the church was to fulfill the calling to be the light of the world, the haven and guide of all humanity on the earth.

Just think for a moment what happens when we wash a shirt that is dirty. The water and cleansing agent move through the fibers of the shirt and carry out the dirt lodged within them. Our minds and hearts when we come to God are like the dirty shirt, cluttered with false beliefs and attitudes, with deadly feelings, and with misguided plans and hopes and fears.

The Word of God, primarily the gospel of his Kingdom and of the life and death of Jesus on our behalf, enters our minds and brings new life through faith. As we open our entire lives to this new power, and as those sent by God minister the Word to us, the Word moves into every part of our personalities, just like the water and soap in the fibers of the shirt. It pushes out and replaces all that is false and opposed to God's purposes in creating us and putting us in our unique place on earth.

We are transformed by the renewing of our minds and thus are "able to discern the will of God, and to know what is good, acceptable, and perfect" (Rom 12:2, NEB). *The mind thus transformed by the "washing" is the one for which divine guidance becomes a completely obvious and practical matter.*

The Amazing Extent of the "Dirt"

And what a multitude of things there are to be washed from the mind! Only the powerful and living Word of God is capable of this task. For example, we usually think that if we are mean enough to people they will be good. We hope to control people by threatening them and punishing them. And yet this was not the way of Jesus. He let others punish him and said, "And I, if I be lifted up from the earth [on the cross], will *draw* all men unto me" (Jn 12:32).

We also are apt to believe that we must serve ourselves or no one else will. But Jesus knew that anyone who would save his or her life must lose it (Lk 9:24–25).

We are pretty well convinced that we gain by grabbing and holding, but he taught us: "Give, and it shall be given unto you" (Lk 6:38). An untold number of other false ideas and attitudes corrupt our minds and lives and must be "washed out" by the entry of his word. "The entrance of thy words giveth light" (Ps 119:130).

Even for most of those who already profess to follow Christ, much inward change is still needed. When trouble comes—for example, when we have car trouble or get crosswise of someone in our family or at work—how long does it take us to get around to bringing it to God in prayer?

When we observe an auto accident or some violent behavior or hear an ambulance coming down the street, do we *think* to hold those concerned up to God in prayer? When we go to meet with a person for any reason, do we go in a spirit of prayer that we would be prepared to minister to them, or they to us, in all ways possible and necessary?

When we are alone, do we constantly recognize that God is present with us? Does our mind spontaneously return to God when not intensely occupied, as the needle of the compass turns to the North Pole when removed from nearer magnetic sources? These questions make us sadly aware of how solidly our mind is trained in false ways.

Today, with all our knowledge, with all our technology and our sophisticated research, we find our world in the same basic situation as that described by Isaiah many centuries before Christ: "We hope for light, but behold, darkness; for brightness, but we walk in gloom. We grope along the wall like blind men, we grope like those who have no eyes; we stumble at midday as in the twilight, like dead men in the ghostly underworld" (Is 59:9–10, NEB). We walk in darkness because our minds—indeed our very brains—need to have the false thoughts and habits "washed" out of them. They so badly need to be washed that we rarely understand what life would be like if they *were* cleaned, and many do not even sense the need for cleaning.

A recent report from a mental health clinic told how the removal of coffee from the waiting rooms transformed patients' behavior. Before, when coffee was available, there was constant bickering and even violence among patients as well as between patients and staff.

After coffee was removed and the stimulation of caffeine withdrawn, there were only two or three unpleasant scenes per week. Like the caffeine, the poisonous thoughts, beliefs, fears, lusts, and attitudes that inhabit our minds compel human beings to destructive behaviors that they themselves do not understand and whose source they do not recognize.

Recall what a word is: a word is fundamentally a thought expressed. The *literal* truth is that Christ through his Word removes the old routines in the heart and mind—the old routines of thought, feeling, action, imagination, conceptualization, belief, inference—and in their place he puts something else: his thoughts, his ways of seeing and interpreting things, his words. He washes out the mind, and in the place of confusion and falsehood—or hatred, suspicion, and fear, to speak of emotions—he places clarity, truth, love, confidence, and hopefulness.

So, where there was fear, there is now hope; where there was suspicion, there is now confidence; where there was hate, there is now love; and all this is accomplished through a new understanding of God conveyed into us by the Word.

Vessels of wrath now become vessels of patience and kindness. Where there was covetousness and lust, there is now generosity and consideration. Where there was manipulation and possessiveness, there is now trust toward God and encouragement toward liberty and individuality. We now have the *character* to which divine guidance is natural.

Like the wild Gadarene of Mark 5, the legion of torments is gone, and now in our life we sit and we walk with Jesus, "clothed, and in our right mind" (v. 15).

Union with Christ

We have been thus far dealing with the Word of God as it comes to, on, and throughout us. But in the progress of God's redemptive work, *communication* advances into *communion*, and communion into *union*. When the progression is complete we can truly say: "Not I, but Christ liveth in me" (Gal 2:20) and "For me to live is Christ" (Phil 1:21).

In communication there is a certain distance, even a possible opposition. But we can still communicate with those with whom we are at war. God communicates with us even while we are his enemies, dead to him in trespasses and sins. When communication rises to the level of communion, there is still distinctness, but also a profound sharing of the thoughts and feelings and objectives that make up our lives. Each recognizes the thought or feeling as his or hers but knows with joy the other to be feeling or thinking in the same way.

When communion advances into union, however, the sense of "mine and thine" may often be absent. There is only an "ours," and although "mine" does mean mine, it no longer thereby also means "not thine." This condition of union is realized in a marriage that indeed is one. And it is for this reason that marriage can serve as a picture of the relation between Christ and his church and between the soul and its God.

It is this union beyond communion that Paul speaks of in describing the redeemed as having the mind of Christ (1 Cor 2:16), as well as in exhorting us to have the mind of Christ (Phil 2:5). It is this same union that Jesus prays for among the faithful: "That they may be one, just as We are one; I in them, and Thou in Me, that they may be perfected in unity, that the world may know that Thou didst send Me, and didst love them, even as Thou didst love Me!" (Jn 17:22–23, NASB).

To realize the good Christ offers to us in the redeemed life, we must at some point begin to appreciate the *literal* character of the Scriptures that speak of Christ being "in" us. Jesus Christ imparts himself to his church. In what may have been his first attempt to make this plain, he told his followers: "Truly, truly, I say to you, unless you eat the flesh of the Son of Man and drink His blood, you have no life in yourselves. He who eats My flesh and drinks My blood has eternal life; and I will raise him up on the last day. For My flesh is true food, and My blood is true drink" (Jn 6:53–55, NASB).

Those who heard these words took deep offense, for they did not understand that when he spoke of his flesh and blood he was speaking in the most concrete terms of himself. As he immediately explained, his literal flesh, when taken apart from his spiritual reality, the personal, would do them absolutely no good at all (v. 63). In this same verse he describes his *words* as Spirit and as Life.

Through his words he literally imparted himself while he lived and taught among the people of his day. And, on the foundation of his words to his followers, the powerful events of Calvary, of the resurrection presence, and of Pentecost brought forth a communion and then a union later expressed by the Apostle Paul as the great mystery of the ages, "Christ in you, the hope of glory" (Col 1:27).

Christ's Faith as My Faith

The faith by which Jesus Christ lived, his faith in God and his Kingdom, is expressed in the gospel he himself preached. That gospel is the good news that the Kingdom rule of God is available to mankind here and now. His followers did not have this faith within themselves, and they long regarded it only as *his* faith. Even after they came to have faith *in him,* they did not share his faith.

Once in the midst of the Sea of Galilee, their boat was almost beaten under by the waves while Jesus slept calmly. His disciples awoke him, crying, "Lord, save us: we perish!" (Mt 8:25). He then reproachfully said, "Why are you such cowards? . . . How little faith you have!" (v. 26, NEB).

Now they obviously had great faith in him. They called on him, counting on him to save them. They had great faith in him, but they did not have *his great faith in God.* It was because they did not have *his faith* that he spoke of how little faith they had.

The contrast and relationship between having faith *in* Christ and having the faith *of* Christ is brought out by the wording of Galatians 2:16 and 20, as this passage is translated in the King James version: "Knowing that a man is not justified by the works of the law, but by the faith *of* Jesus Christ, even we have believed *in* Jesus Christ that we might be justified by the faith *of* Christ, and not by the works of the law" (v. 16, italics added).

Further discussion of the relation of the works of the law to the believer culminates in Paul's great declaration of union, of identification, with Christ: "I am crucified with Christ: nevertheless I live; yet not I, but Christ liveth in me: and the life which I now live in the flesh I live by the faith *of* the Son of God, who loved me, and gave himself for me" (v. 20, italics added).

My suggestion is that Paul here presents faith *in* Christ—such as the apostles certainly had on the occasion of the storm at sea and at other times—as that that leads to having the faith *of* Christ. This faith in Christ leads to the believer actually having the *same* faith in God that Jesus himself had.

Most modern translations, it is to be admitted, translate the *of's* from the above passages as *in's.* Thus, the New American Standard Bible: "Knowing that a man is not justified by the works of the Law but through faith *in* Christ Jesus, even we have believed *in* Christ Jesus, that we may be justified by faith *in* Christ, and not by the works of the Law" (v. 16, italics added); and, likewise: "The life which I now live in the flesh I live by faith *in* the Son of God" (v. 20, italics added).

In this latter reading, the work of redemption and the power of the new life is brought about by *my* faith *in* the person of Christ. But in the reading the older translation gives, by contrast, it is Christ's faith *within* me that is my life, my redemption from the power of sin and darkness. I believe that the entire message of the Bible throws its weight behind this older reading.

A similar point is to be made with reference to 2 Corinthians 5:14. Here Paul is attempting to explain his behavior as an "ambassador for Christ" (v. 20). In so doing he remarks: "The love of Christ [*agape Christo*] constrains us" (v. 14). In this case, the New American Standard Bible may be in support of our line of argument in its rendition of this passage as follows: "The love of Christ controls us." Not mere love *for* Christ, which is in me and directed toward him, but the love *of* Christ, which is in me—mine *and yet* his in the union of our lives— and directed toward God and the world of people for whom Christ lived and died and lives again.

It is true that the grammatical forms involved here can be read as the "objective genitive," permitting the translation of these passages *without* the sense of "of," which is found in the older translation and that I support.

But, on the other hand, these forms do not *require* that reading, whereas the entire biblical picture of the redeemed life does require the other reading. And there is also, after all, the equally legitimate grammatical alternative of the "subjective genetive," which would render the passage in a manner supportive of the view just taken.

However, it is the overall view of the redeemed life that Paul and John and the apostles teach, as a life in union with Christ, that is definitive. This view is what forces us to take the "of" reading seriously and not degrade it into a mere "in" or "for."

In a manner all to commonly realized by individual Christians today, the notions "faith *in* Christ" and "love *for* Christ" leave Christ *outside* the personality of the believer. One wonders if the modern translations are not being governed by the need to turn our practice into the norm of faith. These "exterior" notions of Christ's faith and love will never be strong enough to yield a "not I, but Christ liveth in me!" They can never provide the unity of the branches with the vine in which the life that is in the branch is literally that that flows to it through the Vine and is the very life of the Vine to which it attaches (Jn 15:1–4).

Such exterior notions cannot provide that mutual "abiding in" (Jn 15:5) that causes us "branches" to bring forth much "fruit" and without which we can do nothing (v. 5). It is as such abiding "branches" that we "were reconciled to God through the death of His Son, and much more, having been reconciled, we shall be *saved by His life*" (Rom 5:10, NASB, italics added).

Our "additional life," though it is *our* life, is also him living in us: his thoughts, his faith, his love *literally* imparted to us, shared with us, by his Word and Spirit.

Paul on Salvation

The lifeblood of Paul's teachings about salvation is drained off when we fail to take literally his words about union and identification with Christ. His writings may then be handily subjected to elaborate "plans of salvation" or made into a "Roman road" of doctrinal assents by which we supposedly gain God's approval *merely* for believing what every demon believes to be true about Jesus and his work.

James S. Stewart's book, *A Man in Christ*, deals with this tendency in interpreting Paul and forcefully corrects it:

> Beyond the reproduction in the believer's spiritual life of his Lord's death and burial lies the glorious fact of *union with Christ in His resurrection*. "Like as Christ was raised up from the dead by the glory of the Father, even so we also should walk in newness of life" (Rom 6:4). Everything that Paul associates with salvation—joy, and peace, and power, and progress, and moral victory—is gathered up in the one word he uses so constantly, "life." Only those who through Christ have entered into a vital relationship to God are really "alive."
>
> . . . But what Paul now saw with piercing clearness was that this life into possession of which souls entered by conversion was *noth-*

ing else than the life of Christ Himself. He shared His very being with them.[3]

Stewart points out how Paul speaks of "Christ, who is our life" (Col 3:4) and of "the life of Jesus" being "made manifest in our body" (2 Cor 4:10). He points to Paul's contrast of "the law of sin and death" with "the law of the Spirit" that "brings the life which is in Christ Jesus" (Rom 8:2). And Stewart emphasizes, as has been stressed above, that "this life which flows from Christ into man is something totally different from anything experienced on the merely natural plane. It is different, not only in degree, but also in kind. It is *kainotes zoas* (Rom 6:4), a new quality of life, a supernatural quality."[4] This is what is meant by Paul when he says that if anyone is *in* Christ he is a new creation (2 Cor 5:17).

It is this identity between the "additional" life of the regenerate, or "restarted," individual and the person and life of Christ himself that turns believers into "a colony of heaven" (as Moffatt translates Phil 3:20) and enables them to fulfill the function of being the light of the world, showing the world what it is really like to be alive.

Reckon, Acknowledge, Your Aliveness to God

The person who has been brought into the additional life by the creative action of the Word of God now lives between two distinct realms of life and power: that of the natural or fleshly, and that of the supernatural or spiritual. Even while dead in trespasses and sin and unable to interact constructively with God, one is still capable of sensing the vacuum in the natural life apart from God and of following up on the many earthly "rumors" about God and where he is to be found.

Once the new life begins to enter the soul, however, *we* then have the responsibility and opportunity to ever more fully focus our whole being on it and wholly orient ourselves toward it. This is *our* part, and God will not do it for us.

We see how this happens by looking in Romans 7. Here Paul speaks of a time when he found the impulses of his personality, solidified through lifelong training in the ways of sin, continuing to move in their old patterns and not in conformity with the new life that had entered his soul when he encountered Christ. In this condition, he said, "I fail to carry out the things I want to do, and I find myself doing the very things I hate" (v. 15, JB).

It is like a boat traveling in the water. The boat does not immediately shift to the direction the pilot wants at the very moment he moves the rudder. And it may even continue moving forward for some time while the engine is in full reverse. The pilot must learn how to direct the ship or boat partly in terms of powers that move independently of his will and do not as such represent *his* intentions.

Deciding Who You Will Be

So Paul *chooses* to identify with his new life. He *acknowledges, reckons, affirms* his union with that in him that cleaves to the good: "When I act against my own will, that means I have a self that acknowledges that the Law is good, and so the thing behaving in that way is not my self but sin living in me. The fact is, I know of nothing good living in me—living, that is, in my unspiritual self—for though the will to do what is good is in me, the performance is not, with the result that instead of doing the good things I want to do, I carry out the sinful things I do not want. When I act against my will, then, it is not my true self doing it, but sin which lives in me" (Rom 7:16–20, JB). Or as the King James version simply says: "It is no more I that do it, but sin that dwelleth in me" (v. 20).

The "not I but sin" of this passage must be taken in conjunction with the "not I, but Christ" of Galatians 2:20. Of course people might say such things and only be seeking to excuse themselves from responsibility for a condition of sinfulness, as in the case of Romans 7, or from responsibility for sinful actions, as in the case of Galatians 2.

But not Paul. Paul—and he speaks for the hosts of men and women who have come to life in Christ throughout the ages—is beyond the point of excusing or accusing. He has accepted the full measure of his guilt. He is now concerned with how to enter into the new life to its fullest.

Entering this new life requires that *we* take a stand in the new energy from on high as to *who we are,* that we identify with the Christ life in us and against the sin still present in our members, that we settle in our will the question of who we intend to be. This is what it means to "reckon" ourselves "to be dead indeed unto sin, but alive unto God through Jesus Christ our Lord" (Rom 6:11).

As men and women of the additional birth, we stand at the intersection of the merely natural (fleshly) and the spiritual. Saint Thomas Aquinas coined a word to express just this state: *aevum,* as distinct from *tempus* and *aeternitas. Aevum* is the mean between eternity and time, sharing in them both. *Aevum* is two lives, two streams of awareness and power, mingling together in the individual who must choose which will be him or her.

Our identification with the one life or the other is not a fact to be discovered by subtle examinations of theological treatises or of our soul life and states of mind. It is a set of the will. *Will* I be the motions of sin in my bodily members? Or *will* I be the resurrection life of Christ that has entered into me through the impact of God's Word?

If we choose the latter, it is still with "fear and trembling" that we work out our own salvation, knowing that it is God himself who is at work in us "both to will and to do of his good pleasure" (Phil 2:12–13). It *is* I. Yet it is *not I,* but Christ. Beyond mere communication and communion we move toward union with him and have the opportunity of progressively unifying all aspects of our personalities with him so that, literally, "to me, to live is Christ, and to die is gain" (Phil 1:21).

The Written Word in the Progress of Redemption

Once the life of Christ has entered into us, there are many things we may do to increase the extent and depth of our identification and union with him. But the proper use of the *written* Word is most central to our cooperative efforts with God toward our full conformity with Christ.

Of course the written Word may come to us in many ways. It may come through sermon, art, casual conversation, dramatic performance, literature, or song. All of these are important.

For many centuries, the contents of the Bible were present to the people of Europe through the architecture and artistry of their great cathedrals and churches. Indeed, even today Christians who have read the Bible and know its contents well often are powerfully affected on first seeing the content of the Bible made physical in magnificent stone and rich and sweeping stained-glass windows such as are found in the cathedral at Chartres in France.

But although all of these means are good and helpful, those who wish to grow in grace are best advised by far to make a close and constant companion of *the book*—the Bible. This does not mean that it should be worshiped. Its uniquely sacred character is something that does not need to be exaggerated or even insisted on, because it is self-authenticating to any earnest and open-minded user. For just as openness to and hunger for God leads naturally to the Bible, if it is available, so the eager use of the Bible leads naturally and tangibly to the mind of God and to the person of Christ.

The written Word of God is an expression of God's mind as surely, though in a different manner, as are creation and the living Word, Jesus. As we read and study the Bible intelligently, humbly, and openly, we come evermore to share God's mind.

In a manner already explained, this use of the Bible is not superstitious or magical, precisely because there is a natural connection between a proper use of the Bible and its ideal result: union with Christ. The Bible expresses the mind of God, since through its pages God himself speaks to us. Thus we, in understanding the Bible, come to share his thoughts and attitudes and are even quickened by the Word to have his life. The Scripture is a *communication* that establishes *communion* and opens the way to *union,* all in a manner perfectly understandable once we begin to have the experience of it.

We will be spiritually safe in our use of the Bible if we follow a simple rule: *read in a repentant manner.* That is, read with readiness to surrender all we are, all of our plans, opinions, possessions, positions. Study as intelligently as possible, with all available means, but never merely to find the truth and still less merely to prove anything. Subordinate your desire to find the truth, and your desire to have others do the truth, to your desire to *do it yourself!*

Those who wish to hear the Word and know the truth often are not prompted by their desire to *do* it. The light such people find frequently proves to be their own snare and condemnation.

"Praying" the Scriptures

Therefore the Scriptures should only be read in an attitude of prayer, trusting to the inward working of the Holy Spirit to make their truths a living reality within us. (William Law)[5]

There is a simple technique or routine that all believers, no matter how trained or untrained, can follow with assurance that the very bread of life will be spread for them on the pages of the Scriptures. It is a practice very similar to one encouraged by Madame Guyon in her little book, *Short and Very Easy Way of Prayer,* first published in 1688 in Lyons, France. This book is still available today, having been recently republished, with some modifications, under the title *Experiencing the Depths of Jesus Christ.*[6] You will find it very useful to read the first four chapters of it as a supplement to what I am about to say.

When we come to the Scriptures as a part of our conscious strategy to cooperate with God for full redemption of our life, we must desire that his will in all things revealed should be true for us. Next, we begin with those parts of the Scripture with which we have some familiarity, such as the Twenty-third Psalm, the Lord's Prayer, the Sermon on the Mount, 1 Corinthians 13, or Romans 8.

You may think that this is not a "big" beginning. But keep in mind that your aim is not to become a "scholar" or to impress others with your knowledge of the Bible, which is quite a dreadful trap for so many fellowships aiming to be "biblical." Such an aim will only cultivate pride and lay a foundation for the petty, quarrelsome spirit so regrettably, yet commonly, observed in those outwardly identified as the most "serious" students of the Scriptures.

If you remember these words of Thomas à Kempis, it will help you:

Of what use is it to discourse learnedly on the Trinity, if you lack humility and therefore displease the Trinity? Lofty words do not make a man just or holy; but a good life makes him dear to God. I would far rather feel contrition than be able to define it. If you knew the whole Bible by heart, and all the teachings of the philosophers, how would this help you without the grace and love of God?[7]

Your aim must be only to nourish your soul on God's word to you. Hence, go to those parts you already know, and count on your later growth and study to lead you to other parts that will be useful.

In addition, do not try to read a great deal. As Madame Guyon wisely counsels: "If you read quickly, it will benefit you little. You will be like a bee that merely skims the surface of a flower. Instead, in this new way of reading with prayer, you must become as the bee who penetrates into the depths of the flower. You plunge deeply within to remove its deepest nectar."[8] You may have been told that it is good to read the Bible through every year and that you can ensure this by reading so many verses per day from the Old and New Testaments. If you do this you may enjoy the reputation of one who reads the Bible through each year and you may congratulate yourself on your accomplishment. But will you thereby become more like Christ and more filled with the life of God?

It is a proven fact that many who read the Bible in this way, like taking medicine or exercising on a schedule, do not advance spiritually. Better in one year to have ten good verses transferred *into the substance of our lives* than to have every word of the Bible flash before our eyes. Remember as always that "the letter killeth, but the spirit giveth life" (2 Cor 3:6). We read to open ourselves to the Spirit.

Come to your chosen passages as to the places where you will have a holy meeting with God. Read a small part of the passage selected and dwell on each of its parts, praying for the assistance of God's Spirit in bringing *fully* before your mind and into your life the realities expressed. Always ask What is my life like because this is true? and How shall I speak and act because of this? You may wish to turn the passage into a prayer of praise or of request.

Perhaps you are reading the great "God is love" passage from 1 John 4. You find it written that "there is no fear in love; but perfect love casts out fear, because fear involves punishment, and the one who fears is not perfected in love" (v. 18, NASB).

You dwell on the ways in which love—from God to us and from us to him and between people on earth—pushes fear out of all relationships. You think of the fearless child surrounded by loving parents, of how loving neighbors give us confidence and assuage our anxieties. You contemplate how assurance of God's love given to us through the death of his Son suggests that we will never get beyond his care. You then seek divine help in comprehending this and in realizing what your fear-free life might be like. Then lift your heart in joyful praise as you realize how things are for you, living in God's Kingdom. God's Word now speaking in you, not just *at* you, creates the faith that appropriates the fact *for you*.

Or perhaps you read "The Lord is my shepherd; I shall not want" (Ps 23:1). First, here is *information,* which we may not automatically transfer to ourselves. We may say, "This was true for David, the psalmist." But as we dwell prayerfully on the information there arises a *yearning* that it might be so for *us*. We can express it thusly: "I wish the Lord were my shepherd; that the great God would have for me that care and attention the shepherd has for his sheep!" And as we meditate on the psalm, *affirmation* may arise, as it has for so many people: "It must be so! I will have it to be so!" then perhaps *invocation:* "Lord, make it so for me." And then we may feel *appropriation*—the settled conviction that it *is* so, a statement of fact about you.

Do not hurry. Don't dabble in spirituality. Give time for each stage to play itself out fully in your heart. Remember, this is not something you are doing by yourself. *Watch* and pray.

Now practice the same type of process with those great passages from Romans 8, beginning with verse 28, for example—"All things work together for good to them that love God, to them who are the called according to his purpose"—and culminating in the declaration of triumph that no matter what befalls us "we are more than conquerors through him that loved us" (v. 37).

The general train of development again is:

1. *Information* with *longing* for it to be so;
2. *Affirmation* that it *must* be so;
3. *Invocation* to God to make it so; and finally,
4. *Appropriation* by God's grace of its being so.

This last stage must not be forced or, especially, faked. The ability for it will be given, as you watch for God to move in your life.

When there is the inner agreement of our minds with the truth expressed in the passages, we have these parts of the mind of Christ in us as *our own*, for these great truths conveyed from Scripture were the very things Jesus believed. These truths constituted the faith, hope, and love in which he lived. And as they become ours, his mind becomes our mind. We are outfitted then to function as true co-laborers with God, as brothers, sisters, and friends of Jesus in the present and coming Kingdom of God. We are then in position to know and understand in its fullness the *guidance* God gives to his children.

Some Topics for Reflection

1. "Redemption" is understood in this chapter to cover people and their lives as a whole. Redemption is not *merely* a matter of forgiveness of sins to guarantee heaven when we die. Do you regard this view of redemption as biblical? Does it make sense in your theological background? In what way is a *redeemed life* automatically the light of the world?

2. What is life—in a cabbage, in a kitten? Characterize the "life from above" in terms of its presence in day-to-day human existence.

3. "Grafting" and "washing" are two metaphors relating to the "additional life" of the Christian. Explain the meaning of each in this context and illustrate each in practical contexts.

4. Did the discussion of communication, communion, and union make sense to you in terms of human experiences you have had or know about? In terms of your experience of Jesus?

5. What is the difference between "the faith *of* Christ" and "faith *in* Christ"? What difference does the difference make? Which is "saving" faith? Saving of what?

6. What does it mean to "*reckon* ourselves to be dead unto sin"? What will be the results of *not* doing this reckoning?

7. Our identification with the sin life or the Christ life in us "is not a *fact* to be *discovered* by subtle examinations of theological treatises or of our soul-life and states of mind. It is a set of the will." What does this mean? Do you agree?

8. Experiment several times with "praying the Scriptures," and summarize the results of the exercise. Share them with a friend.

Notes

1. Hannah Hurnard, *God's Transmitters* (Wheaton, IL: Tyndale House, 1981), 12.

2. Fuller, *Spurgeon's Lectures to His Students*, 172.

3. James S. Stewart, *A Man in Christ* (London: Hodder & Stoughton, 1935), 192f.

4. Stewart, *Man in Christ*, 193.

5. Dave Hunt, ed., *The Power of the Spirit* (Ft. Washington, PA: Christian Literature Crusade, 1971), 62.

6. Madame Guyon, *Experiencing the Depth of Jesus Christ* (Goleta, CA: Christian Books, 1975).

7. Thomas à Kempis, *The Imitation of Christ*, trans. Leo Sherley-Price (London: Penguin Books, 1952), 27.

8. Guyon, *Experiencing the Depth*, 16.

8 *Recognizing the Voice of God*

The shepherd in charge of the sheep . . . calls his own sheep by name, and leads them out. . . . He goes ahead and the sheep follow, because they know his voice. . . . I am the good shepherd; I know my own sheep and my sheep know me. . . . My own sheep listen to my voice; I know them and they follow me.

JN 10:2–4, 14, 27, NEB

The doctrine of the inner light is not sufficiently taught. To the individual believer, who is, by the very fact of relationship to Christ, indwelt by the Holy Spirit of God, there is granted the direct impression of the Spirit of God on the Spirit of man, imparting the knowledge of His will in matters of the smallest and greatest importance. This has to be sought and waited for.

G. CAMPBELL MORGAN[1]

When a word or thought comes to us—whether by our own thinking, the inner voice, or some special experience or from the Bible or circumstances—*how* do we know whether or not it is a word from God to guide us? What is it about it that indicates a divine source?

We can, of course, know that the word is from God if it is the plain statement or meaning of the Bible *and* is construed in such a way that it is consistent with biblical teaching as a whole, soundly interpreted.

Thus everyone can know at all times that God directs them not to worship an idol or be covetous.

But beyond this the only answer to our question is "*By experience.*" Even a word-for-word quotation from the Bible can be put to a use that makes it a message from the Self or from Satan. Hence the well-known dangers of "proof texting," of taking biblical passages out of context to serve one or another preconceived purpose.

A single statement directly from the Bible—and these are so often invoked for personal guidance—may be *used* contrary to the purposes of God, contrary to any meaning that he may have in mind for us. That is why it is only the Bible *as a whole* that can be treated as the written Word of God.

And in any case we certainly must go beyond, though never *around*, the words of the Bible to find a divinely guided life. For, as we have already seen, the teachings of the Bible, no matter how thoroughly studied and firmly believed, can never by themselves constitute our personal walk with God. They have to be applied to us as individuals and to our individualized circumstance, or they remain no part of our lives.

"Recognition" in Nature

It is a remarkable fact that sheep or other domesticated animals or pets quite unerringly recognize the voice of their master or mistress *by experience*. When they first hear their master's voice, they do not recognize who is speaking, but they very quickly learn to do so. They do not need a voice meter or other device to analyze the sound scientifically; they recognize it immediately.

An edition of "Videolog," a regular program on the Los Angeles public television station KCET, recently told the story of Charlie Frank and his elephant Neeta. Charlie raised Neeta from birth and trained her as a circus performer. On retirement he gave her to the San Diego Zoo. Charlie and Neeta had not seen each other for fifteen years when "Videolog" filmed their reunion. Charlie called to Neeta across a large area of about one hundred yards. She came to him immediately and performed her old routines on command. Her past experience gave her the power of recognition.

Similarly, we human beings learn from experience alone how to recognize the color red, with its various shades and characteristics, and to distinguish it from green or yellow. Again, a musician learns by experience to distinguish a minor from a major key simply by listening. No psychologist or philosopher has even the beginnings of an explanation of *how* we do this, but we do it nevertheless.

Comparison of humans with animals on this point is a prophetic theme. Isaiah marvels that "an ox knows its owner, and a donkey its master's manger. But Israel does not know, my people do not understand" (1:3, NASB). Jeremiah renews the complaint with reference to nondomesticated creatures: "Even the stork in the sky knows her seasons; and the turtledove and the swift and the thrush observe the time of their migration. But my people do not know the ordinance of the Lord" (8:7, NASB).

By contrast, the light that shines on every human being that comes into the world, according to John 1:9, vainly strikes the blinded eyes of fallen humanity. The word that has gone out to the very ends of the earth, according to Psalm 19:4, falls on deaf ears. But those who have been given the "additional" birth, through the specifically redemptive message of Christ that has entered their lives, can learn by experience to hear the speaking of God, recognize it, and confidently interact with it.

The simple statements quoted at the beginning of this chapter from the Gospel of John, chapter ten, are not merely a record of words Jesus spoke. They are also an expression of John's own experience with Christ, his Lord and friend. The emphasis given in the opening of John's first Epistle to seeing, hearing, and touching the Word of Life (vv. 1, 3) is quite startling. But it was in the presence of the visible, touchable Jesus that John learned to recognize when God was speaking.

In the course of later experience, he became so confident of the inner teacher that he could tell his children in the faith—precisely in a context in which he was warning against those trying to deceive them—that they had no need of anyone other than the inner teacher, the Holy Spirit: "The anointing which you received from Him abides in you, and you have no need for any one to teach you; but as His anointing teaches you about all things, and is true and is not a lie, and just as it has taught you, you abide in Him" (1 Jn 2:27, NASB).[2]

John therefore speaks to us with the authority of experience, just as Abraham did to his eldest servant in sending him into an unknown land for Isaac's wife (Gn 24), and just as Eli did to little Samuel (1 Sm 3).

We may mistakenly think that if *God* spoke to us we would automatically know, without having to learn, *who* it is that is speaking to us. But that is simply a mistake, and one of the most harmful of mistakes for those trying to understand divine guidance. It leaves us totally at the mercy of stray ideas we have picked up about what God's speaking is like.

Perhaps our lack of recognition of God's speaking is owing to our fallen and distorted condition, or perhaps the explanation lies in the very nature of *all* personal relations, for certainly you and I did not recognize on first hearing the voice of whoever it may be that is now most dear and intimate to us. Or perhaps we fail to recognize God's voice because of the very gentleness with which our heavenly Father speaks to us. But in any case it seems that at first we must be told *that* God is speaking to us and possibly even be helped to detect his voice. Only later do we come, without assistance, to confidently distinguish and recognize his voice as *his* voice. To repeat: this ability comes only with experience.

Certainly it is true that a little child is first spoken to, and knows that it is being spoken to, by a certain person and *then* learns to recognize the voice itself as belonging to that person. And, in general, as adults we can recognize a person's voice only after we are aware, by whatever means, that it is *that person* who has spoken to us on a number of occasions.

With assistance from those who understand the divine "voice" from their own experience, and given an openness and will to learn on our part, we can come to know the voice of God without great difficulty.

We should understand that it is in the interest of evil, on the other hand, to make an inherent *mystery* of God's Word coming directly to the individual, for then the power of his specific directions for our lives is hindered or totally lost. Without qualified help working with our own ardent desire to learn and readiness to cooperate, guidance will most likely remain a riddle to us or at best a game of theological charades. This puzzlement is generally the condition of the church in the present day, I suspect, which, if so, explains why there is such great confusion and difficulty concerning what it is to really walk with God (Mi 6:8). This confusion, in turn, enables evil to step into the vacuum and carry us away.

The "Three Lights"

> God's impressions within and his word without are always corroborated by his providence around, and we should quietly wait until those three focus into one point. . . . If you do not know what you ought to do, stand still until you do. And when the time comes for action, circumstances, like glowworms, will sparkle along your path; and you will become so sure that you are right, when God's three witnesses concur, that you could not be surer though an angel beckoned you on. (F. B. Meyer).[3]

Many discussions of God's guidance include three points of reference, or "three lights," that we may consult in determining what God wants us to do.[4] These three lights are *circumstances, impressions of the Spirit,* and *passages from the Bible.* When these three point in the same direction, it is suggested, we may be sure that the direction is the one God intends for us.

If I could keep only one bit of writing on divine guidance outside of the Bible itself, it would be hard to pass over a few pages from F. B. Meyer's book entitled *The Secret of Guidance,* just quoted. Many other authors have very fine and helpful things to say on the subject, but Meyer draws the issues together in such a complete and yet simple fashion, and the spirit of his remarks—as is usual with him—is both so sane and so spiritual that he is certainly to be chosen over most who have written on this subject. According to Meyer:

> The circumstances of our daily life are to us an infallible indication of God's will, when they concur with the inward promptings of the spirit and with the Word of God. So long as they are stationary,

wait. When you must act, they will open, and a way will be made through oceans and rivers, wastes and rocks.[5]

It is possible to understand this precious advice in such a way that it completely resolves any problem about divine guidance. I believe that this will normally be the case for those who have *already* learned to recognize the inner voice of God. Probably none knew it more clearly than Meyer himself.

But for those who do not yet have a confident, working familiarity with the Voice, the three lights may speedily result in a swirl of confusion, and leave them hopelessly adrift or shipwrecked on the shoals of spiritual misadventures. These lights can be especially dangerous and disappointing for those without a deep experience of and commitment in the Way of Christ. Such people will certainly try to use them as a spiritual gimmick to get their own way, to secure their own prosperity and security.

The Problem of the Interdependence of the Three Lights

A large part of the *practical* problem in working with the "three lights" comes from the simple fact that they are *interdependent*. You cannot tell what the one "says" without already knowing what the others say.

First of all, it is commonly understood that the Scriptures depend on the Holy Spirit for their efficacy in guidance as well as redemption. A recent conference of evangelical scholars affirmed "that the Holy Spirit who inspired scripture acts through it today to work faith in its message" and also that "the Holy Spirit enables believers to appropriate and apply scripture to their lives." On the other hand this conference denied "that the natural man is able to discern spiritually the biblical message apart from the Holy Spirit."[6]

Many people commonly regarded as being in the evangelical tradition seem prepared to make even stronger statements on the role of the Holy Spirit in Bible study. Consider William Law:

> Without the present illumination of the Holy Spirit, the Word of God must remain a dead letter to every man, no matter how intelligent or well-educated he may be. . . . It is just as essential for the

Holy Spirit to reveal the truth of Scripture to the reader today as it was necessary for Him to inspire the writers thereof in their day. . . . Therefore to say that, because we now have all the writings of Scripture complete, we no longer need the miraculous inspiration of the Spirit among men as in former days, is a degree of blindness as great as any that can be charged upon the scribes and Pharisees. Nor can we possibly escape their same errors; for in denying the present inspiration of the Holy Spirit, we have made Scripture the province of the letter-learned scribe.[7]

But how are we to recognize or authenticate a thought movement or message as an intervention of the Holy Spirit, even in our studies of the Bible, except through the teachings of the Scriptures?

The biblical test of a spiritual impulse according to whether or not it confesses Jesus as Lord (1 Cor 12:3) or as Son of God (1 Jn 4:3) does not turn out to be helpful in practice, as, for example, when we are trying to decide whom to marry or which job to take. And testing of spiritual or mental impulses or messages cannot, in general, be done by invoking the teachings of Scripture, if Scripture itself, in turn, cannot be understood without spiritual assistance by means of those very impulses and "messages."

Finally, the mere open or closed "doors" of circumstances cannot function independently of the other two lights or of *some* additional factor, for one does not know merely by looking at these doors who is opening or closing them—God or Satan or human effort. Indeed, one often cannot tell whether they are open or closed until after one has acted. Hence one cannot use openness or closedness by itself to determine what to do.

No doubt those who think they can make the three-lights formula work will be very impatient with me for raising these difficulties. My experience suggests that people who, for whatever reason, do not really need help in the practical context of guidance may think that this formula can be made to work *as* a formula, which is how it is normally presented.

Those who do need help, on the other hand, frequently drive themselves to distraction trying to use this formula. Also, the formula is, *in retrospect,* often thought to have worked, after one has taken a certain alternative at the suggestion of the lights and all has turned out well. But once again, the confidence is present precisely when it is no longer needed.

I will restate the problem, hoping to be completely clear about it. Circumstances mean one thing only if the Bible says such and such, and the Bible says such and such only if the Spirit directs our understanding. But we know that it is a spiritual impulse that suggests that the Bible says such and such only if the suggestion that it says such and such is in line with what the Bible says.

And if the door is open, then the Spirit *must* be leading; and hence we also *must* be following the Bible, for we are "succeeding." And if, on the other hand, the door is closed, then we don't have to decide anyway because the door is closed.

But *is* it closed, or does it just look that way? What does the Bible or Spirit say? And if the door is closed and *we* can open it, *should* we open it? At this point someone is likely to tell us that God helps those who help themselves! But how would we know it is God who is helping us and not just ourselves or mindless circumstances? Such questions seem endless if all we have to go on are the three lights.

So it is simply not true that one can get a reading of what circumstances "say" and a *separate* one of what the Bible says and a further *separate* one of what the Spirit says. Consequently, there is no way that we can strengthen our reading of God's will from one of these sources by "checking" it against the other sources, as we well might get a more accurate reading of the time of day by consulting three clocks running independently of one another.

The Conditions of Responsible Judgment

And yet all who have much experience in the Way of Christ will know that it is *somehow* right, when searching for guidance, to look to circumstances, the Bible, and inner impulses of the Spirit. And all will know that these three lights *somehow* serve to correct one another.

Although they provide *no formula*, no *mechanism* for making decisions, these lights must not be simply abandoned. How are we to understand the role they play in divine guidance? The answer to this question comes in two parts.

First, the life in which divine guidance is actually functioning is *not* one that excludes our own judgment. Guidance from God does not exclude decision. We, or others who come under the influence of God's voice, still are the ones who make the decision. This is something that has already been discussed, and yet a new and very important aspect of it shall be considered in the final chapter. The three lights are simply *the factors we must consider in making a responsible judgment and decision* about what we are to do. To be responsible in judgment and action is to humbly and fully consider these factors.

Second, although none of the lights, nor all of them taken together, simply *give* us our guidance, each or all together may be, and usually are, the *occasion* of God's directive word coming to us. This is the way in which, as a matter of fact, guidance usually works.

The voice of God is not itself any one of the three lights, nor all of them together. But the inner teaching of which John speaks in his first epistle—the voice or Word of God coming to individuals, as repeatedly displayed in biblical events—*usually* comes to us in conjunction with responsible study and meditation on the Bible, with experience of the various kinds of movements of the Spirit in our hearts, and with intelligent alertness to circumstances that befall us.

Although there are exceptions to the rule, the divine directive does not usually come to us "out of the blue." This is important to us practically *because it enables us to do specific, concrete things that will help us as we seek to know the will of God.* The things we do—reflecting on the three lights—turn out to be the very things that go into exercising responsible judgment.

As we engage in this reflection, we also listen for the divine voice. But when God speaks and we recognize the voice as *his* voice, we do so because our familiarity with that voice enables us to recognize it. We do not recognize it because we are good at playing a guessing game about how the occasions through which it comes match up with one another.

Three Factors in the Voice

The voice of my beloved! Behold, he comes leaping upon the mountains, skipping upon the hills. (Song 2:8)

I sleep, but my heart wakes. It is the voice of my beloved. (Song 5:2)

To say that we learn to recognize the voice of God by experience is not, however, all that we can say or must say. There are certain factors that distinguish the voice of God, just as is the case with any human voice.

The most immediate factor in the human voice is one that is usually enough in itself to tell those familiar with it whose voice it is— namely, a certain *quality* of the sound produced. This quality is mainly a matter of which *tones* are produced and the manner in which they are modulated. "Quality" at the human level also includes the *style* of speech. For example, is it slow or fast, smooth or halting in its flow, indirect or to the point?

Besides quality, a certain *spirit* attaches to the human voice. A voice may be passionate or cold, whining or demanding, timid or confident, coaxing or commanding. "Spirit," of course, is no mere matter of *sounds,* but of attitudes or characters that become tangibly present in the voice.

And then, finally, there is the matter of *content,* or of information conveyed. Although this is rarely the *immediate* sign of who is speaking, it is in the end the most conclusive mark, for it reveals the history and conscious experience of the speaker. No matter if quality and spirit are totally different, a specific bit of information can conclusively identify a speaker in certain cases.

The three factors of quality, spirit, and content by no means exhaust the complexity of voice. Modern-day science and linguistics find in the voice vast fields for theoretical and practical study. From the philosophical point of view, there is yet much more to be said. Professor Don Ihde, of the State University of New York, has published a very helpful guide to a deeper examination of the phenomenon of voice in his *Listening and Voice.*[8] But enough has been said to allow us to turn to examination of the voice of God in our hearts.

The Weight of Authority

The question then is What are the factors of *that* voice that enable us to recognize it as *God* speaking? In this case too there is a distinctive quality with which we become familiar. But of course it is not the quality of a *sound*. According to our discussions in chapter 5, the voice of God will usually, but not always, take the form of certain thoughts or perceptions that enter our minds, and these are not manifest as sounds.

Rather, the quality of God's voice is more a matter of a certain weight or impact of the impression that its communications make on our consciousness. There is a certain steady, calm force with which communications that are from God impact our souls, inclining us to assent and even to conformity in action. The assent is frequently given, or the conformity conceded, before the *content* of the communication is fully grasped. So, at least, I find it.

We inwardly sense the immediate power of God's voice. And once we have experienced this power, we no longer wonder at the biblical phenomena of nature and spirits responding to this divine word. The unquestionable authority with which Jesus spoke to nature, humans, and demons was but a very clear manifestation of this quality of the Word of God.

Addressing the question of how one can distinguish the voice of God from one's own subconscious, E. Stanley Jones says,

> Perhaps the rough distinction is this: The voice of the subconscious argues with you, tries to convince you; but the inner voice of God does not argue, does not try to convince you. It just speaks, and it is self-authenticating. It has the feel of the voice of God within it.[9]

When Jesus spoke, his words had a weight of authority that opened up the understanding of the hearers and created faith in them. "He taught them as one having authority, and not as the scribes" (Mt 7:29).

The authority of the scribe or mere scholar comes from his "footnotes," his references to someone other than himself who is *supposed* to know. The Word of God, on the other hand, comes with a serene weight of authority in itself. People left the presence of Jesus with their heads and hearts full of thoughts and convictions that he had "authored" in them through the power of God's voice or Word with which Jesus spoke.

The immediate qualitative distinction of the voice of God is emphasized in John Wesley's first sermon on "The Witness of the Spirit" in which he poses the question, "But how may one who has the real witness in himself distinguish it from presumption?" He replies:

> How, I pray, do you distinguish day from night? How do you distinguish light from darkness; or the light of a star, or a glimmering taper, from the light of the noonday sun? Is there not an inherent, obvious, essential difference between the one and the other? And do you not immediately and directly perceive that difference, provided your senses are rightly disposed? In like manner, there is an inherent, essential difference between spiritual light and spiritual darkness; and between the light wherewith the Sun of righteousness shines upon our heart, and that glimmering light which arises only from "sparks of our own kindling": and this difference also is immediately and directly perceived, if our spiritual senses are rightly disposed.
>
> To require a more minute and philosophical account of the manner whereby we distinguish these, and of the *criteria*, or intrinsic marks, whereby we know the voice of God, is to make a demand which can never be answered: no, not by one who has the deepest knowledge of God.[10]

In my own experience, I first became aware of God's Word coming to me *by the effects* on me and others around me. My main work for God is that of a teacher. Insights occasionally have been "given" to me that, although perhaps of little significance in themselves, were experienced by me as literally staggering.

But then as I became aware, and began to trust, that it was God's word thus given, I immediately began to observe the qualitative difference that Wesley so faithfully emphasizes. And I began to find that certain others also understood, from their experience, exactly what this difference was.

Adela Rogers St. John remarks, perhaps somewhat overconfidently but yet to the point: "The first time you receive guidance you will know the difference. You can mistake rhinestones for diamonds, but you can never mistake a diamond for a rhinestone."[11]

The "Spirit" of God's Voice

The voice of God speaking in our souls also bears in it a characteristic *spirit*. It is a spirit of exalted peacefulness and confidence, of joy, of sweet reasonableness, and of will for the good. It is, in short, "the spirit of Jesus." By that we refer to the overall tone and internal dynamics of his personal life as a whole.

Those who saw him truly saw the Father, who shared the same "Spirit." And it is this Spirit that marks the voice of God in our hearts. Any word that bears an opposite spirit most surely is not the voice of God. Because his voice bears authority within itself, it does not need to be loud or hysterical.

Bob Mumford's statement about one of his experiences of guidance illustrates this point. The voice of God found him in Columbia, South America, and very distinctly said, "I want you to go back to school." His description of this experience brings out the quality and spirit of the voice:

> It couldn't have been any clearer if my wife had spoken the words right next to me. It was spoken straight and strong and right into my spirit. It wasn't a demanding, urgent voice. If it had been, I would immediately have suspected the source to be someone or something other than the Lord. The vocal impression was warm, but firm. I knew it was the Lord.[12]

The sweet calm spirit of God's voice carries over to the lives of those who speak with his voice: "The wisdom that is from above is first pure, then peaceable, gentle, and easy to be entreated, full of mercy and good fruits, without partiality, and without hypocrisy" (Jas 3:17). Would we but heed this statement we would never lack for sure knowledge of who speaks for God and who does not.

Content

And then, finally, there is a *content* that marks the voice of God. Perhaps we had better speak of *a dimension* of the content, because the specific content of an individualized word from God may not of itself be easily identifiable as being from God. But this much we can say: the content of a word that is truly from God will always conform to, and be consistent with, the truths about God's nature and Kingdom made clear in the Bible. Any content or claim that does not conform to *that* content is not a word from God. Period! As Charles Stanley comments, "God's Voice will never tell us to engage in any activity or relationship that is inconsistent with the Holy Scriptures."[13]

Evan Roberts, in college and studying for the ministry, was deeply moved by the sermons of Seth Joshua, who visited his college.

> Roberts could not concentrate on his studies after that and went to the principal of his college, and said, "I hear a voice that tells me I must go home and speak to the young people in my home church. Mr. Phillips, is that the voice of the devil or the voice of the Spirit?" Phillips answered, very wisely, "The devil never gives orders like that. You can have a week off."[14]

Although this response may seem a little glib, it was basically right. Subsequent events involving Roberts strongly confirmed that he was indeed directed by the Lord on this occasion.

The Principles Are What Counts

The conformity that a thought or perception or other experience must have in order to qualify as the voice of God is conformity to the principles, the fundamental truths, of Scripture. It is the *principles,* not the incidentals of Scripture, that count here. Study of the Scriptures makes it clear that there are certain things that are fundamental, absolute, and without exception. These elements show up with stunning clarity as we become familiar with the overall content of Scripture.

Reading in 1 Corinthians 11, on the other hand, we find ladies advised not to have short hair and men informed that long hair on them is shameful. Such things are clearly incidental.

More seriously, in Mark 10, the fine young man who came to Jesus was told by him to sell all that he had and give the proceeds to the poor. This too, contrary to what many have thought, is incidental to people generally. In the particular case of this young man, of course, Jesus' directive went right to the heart of his special problem with wealth. But it is not a principle to which all must conform. It is not a teaching emerging from the whole of Scripture, and it should not, without further consideration and guidance, be taken as God's word to you or anyone else.

However, when you read John the apostle and learn from him that "God is light, and in him is no darkness" (1 Jn 1:5), you are on to a principle: something that wells up from the whole Bible and the totality of the experience of God's people through history.

Also when we hear Jesus saying, "The first of all the commandments is, Hear, O Israel; the Lord our God is one Lord: and thou shalt love the Lord thy God with all thy heart, and with all thy soul, and with all thy mind, and with all thy strength; this is the first commandment. And the second is like, namely this, Thou shalt love thy neighbor as thyself" (Mk 12:29–31), we are in the presence of principles.

When we hear him say that "whosoever will save his life shall lose it; but whosoever shall lose his life for my sake and the gospel's, the same shall save it" (Mk 8:35), that too is a principle. When we hear him say, "Seek ye the kingdom of God; and all these things shall be added unto you" (Lk 12:31), this is a principle also. No specific guidance that is from God will ever contradict such principles. Such principles place an iron-clad restriction on what content can come with *God's* voice.

Principles of Scripture are most of all to be identified from the actions, spirit, and explicit statements of Jesus himself. When we take him in his wholeness as our model and the one to follow—and what else could it mean to *trust him?*—we will safely identify the content of the inner voice of God. "Those who follow me shall not walk in darkness, but shall have the light of life" (Jn 8:12).

In the awareness of this voice, we are set free to let our experience be open to the new and special things God wants to do in us and through us. We are free to develop the power and authority that come from the experience of dealing directly with God—free *and* safe within the pattern of Christ's life and teachings.

Beware the Spiritual Panacea!

But something should also be said about content of "voices" on the negative side. Any voice that promises total exemption from suffering and failure is most certainly not God's Word. In recent years, innumerable spokespersons for God have offered ways of using him and his Bible as guarantees of health, success, and wealth. The Bible is treated as a "how to" book, a manual for the successful life in the American way that, if followed, will assure that you will prosper financially, that you will not get cancer or even a cold, and that your church will never split or lack a successful pastor and program.

To the question from the old hymn,

> Shall I be carried to the skies,
> On flowery beds of ease;
> While others fought to win the prize,
> And sailed through bloody seas?[15]

these people shout, "Yes, most certainly!"

But if we will only consider those who stand throughout history as the best practitioners of the Way, we will find that they went through great difficulties, often living their entire lives and dying amidst them. The Word of God does not come just to lead us out of trouble—though that sometimes happens—or to make sure that we have it easy and that everything goes our way. When we hear a suggestion that it does, we will need to recall the interchange between Jesus and Peter: "I'm going to go up to Jerusalem and they are going to kill me," said Jesus. Peter, because he just *knew* it, replied, "Far be it from you, Lord. Such a thing shall not happen to you." Peter did not have *that* in mind for himself, and hence not for his Messiah, the star to which he had hitched his wagon. But Jesus said to him, "Get behind me, Satan, for you have no liking for the things of God, but for the things of man" (see Mt 16:21–23).

We must not be misled by wistful thinking. We are going to go through the mill of life like everyone else. We are different because we *also* have a higher, or "additional," life, a different quality of life, a spiritual life, an eternal life, not because we are spared the ordinary troubles that befall ordinary human beings. "The righteous suffer many things, but the Lord delivers them in every case" (Ps 34:19).

In summary, then, *what* we learn when we learn to recognize God's voice in our heart is a certain *weight or force,* a certain *spirit,* and a certain *content* of the thoughts that come as God's communications to us. These three things in combination mark the voice of God. To those well experienced in the Way of Christ, these benchmarks give great confidence and accuracy in living day to day as the friends of Christ and co-laborers with God in his Kingdom.

The Voice of Satan?

There are other spiritual "voices" too. It is by *contrast* with the voice of God, as we have just described it, that we come to know the voice of our adversary, Satan, when he speaks in our heart, as he certainly will once he sees he no longer holds us in his hand. Only if we learn to recognize this voice as well, can we avoid many silly attributions of events to Satan. ("The devil made me do it!") And only so can we correctly identify and firmly resist him and make him flee from us (1 Pt 5:9; Eph 6:11).

Satan will not come to us in the form of an oversized bat with bony wings, hissing like a snake. And very seldom will he assume any external manifestation at all. Instead, he will usually, like God, come to us through our thoughts and our perceptions. We must be alert to any marked contrast to the weight, spirit, and content of God's voice, for this may signify that we are under attack.

The temptations of Jesus in Matthew 4 illustrate this well. It does not take much imagination to realize that if some batlike creature suggested to Jesus that he turn the stones into bread, this would certainly have tended to curb his appetite. How then did "the tempter come to him?" (v. 3). Actually, there is no indication given in the Gospel passages.

I would only suggest that, as Jesus suffered extreme hunger, the stones about him reminded him of—perhaps began to *look* like—the loaves from his mother's oven. Perhaps he began to *smell* them and then to think how easily he could turn those stones into such loaves— with butter! But this is only my suggestion.

But then he also realized the *conflict* of this vision with the great truth that the Word of God is a substance, a meat (Jn 4:32). He refused to allow himself to be turned away from learning the sufficiency of that Word to his every need. Man lives by every word that issues from God's mouth (Dt 8:3). The voice of temptation was clearly opposed in spirit and content to God's Word, and Satan was recognized and successfully resisted both in this and in the other temptations that followed.

Likewise, all followers of Christ must be encouraged to believe that they can come to understand and distinguish the voice of God if they will but look within their minds for much the same kinds of distinctions within their thoughts and perceptions as they would find in the communications received from other human beings through spoken or written language: a distinctive quality, spirit, and content.

All of the guidance we are going to receive from God, no matter what the external or internal accompaniments may be, will *ultimately pass through the form of our own thoughts and perceptions.* We must learn to find in them the voice of that God in whom we live and move and have our being.

Infallibility?

But, someone may say, "When I am sure that God is speaking to me, and sure about what he says, *could I not still be mistaken,* even though I have much apparently successful experience at hearing and understanding his voice?" The answer is yes—of course you still *could* be wrong. God does not, by his conversational walk with us, intend to make us infallible. You also could be wrong about most of the beliefs on which you very successfully base your life. But you are usually correct. You always could be wrong in believing that your gas gauge is working, that your bank is reliable, that your food is not poisoned. Such is human life. And our walk with the Lord does not exempt us from the possibility of error, even in our experienced reading of what his voice is saying.

Infallibility, and especially infallibility in discerning the mind of God, simply does not fit the human condition and should not be desired, much less expected, from our relationship with God.

The Centrality of the Bible, Once Again

Personally, I find great comfort and encouragement in the face of my fallibility by close association with the Bible. We have repeatedly emphasized the centrality of the written Word in the functioning of divine guidance. It cannot be too much stressed that the permanent address at which the Word of God may be contacted is the Bible. More of God's speaking to me has come in conjunction with study and teaching of the Bible than with anything else. As F. B. Meyer says, "The [written] Word is the wire along which the voice of God will certainly come to you if the heart is hushed and the attention fixed."[16]

Reading in the lives of the saints seems to confirm this. From the many available illustrations we select a few words from John Bunyan:

> One day, as I was traveling into the country and musing on the wickedness and blasphemy of my heart, and considering the enmity that was in me to God, that scripture came into my mind: "Having made peace through the blood of His cross" (Col 1:20). By which I was made to see, both again and again, that God and my soul were friends by his blood; yea, I saw that the justice of God and my sinful soul could embrace and kiss each other, through his blood. This was a good day to me; I hope I shall never forget it.
>
> At another time, as I sat by the fire in my house and was musing on my wretchedness, the Lord made that *also* a precious word unto me: "Forasmuch then as the children are partakers of flesh and blood, he also himself likewise took part of the same; that through death he might destroy him that had the power of death, that is, the devil; and deliver them who through fear of death were all their life-

time subject to bondage" (Heb 2:14–15). I thought that the glory of these words was then so weighty on me, that I was both once and twice ready to swoon as I sat, yet not with grief and trouble, but with solid joy and peace.[17]

It is, once again, *by experience* that many have come to know that there is all the difference in the world between an experience of the Scriptures in which there is a Word of God that seizes me and that experience in which I am simply seizing the words on the page, however interesting this latter may be in the work of scholarship.

In the former case I find myself addressed, caught up in all the individuality of my concrete existence by something beyond me. The action is from God to me in a distinctively personal manner. This experience is the common testimony across wide ranges of Christian fellowship and history. I think it is this sense of being "seized" in the presence of the Scripture, an experience that is so widely shared, that gives the Bible its power to assure us in the face of our continuing fallibility.

Both in the experience of Scripture and of other things— circumstances, our own inner thoughts and impulses, the reading of history or biography—the Word frequently comes in a way that at least approximates the experience of an *audible* voice. When examined closely, the data of Christian experience reveal that encounters with this audible voice are much more common than is generally thought.

But the "audibility" of the voice is not anything essential to it, nor does it have any effect on the reliability of our experience of the voice. The essentials remain, once again, the distinctive quality, spirit, and content that we have learned through experience to associate with the personal presence of God.

Scholarship too, both biblical and otherwise, certainly is important to the individual and to the church as a whole. It is a part of our share in responsible living before God. But it can never stand in the place of experience of the living voice of God; neither can it remedy or remove our fallibility.

In general, no person is dependent on the expertise of biblical or other scholars for a saving and walking knowledge of God. Humble openness before the recorded Word of God is sufficient as the occasion of God's saving and guiding Word to us. Those who know all *about* the Word of God may yet never have *heard* it. And those who have heard it and recognize it readily may have little to say about it. But we need both those who know it and those who know about it, that the Word might come to have a freer course and more competent reception in the community of believers and in the world. Such a congregation of knowledge will make God's guidance of his people more effective in realizing his purposes.

Practical Consequences

Knowing the voice of God, the *practical understanding* of that voice in our minds and hearts, is *not* a luxury to the people of God, not something to be allocated to those who like special spiritual high points. Let us consider four aspects of the importance of this understanding to vibrant life in God's Kingdom.[18]

A. *Direct, daily Kingdom access for all believers:* First, without this direct communication with Christ, who is the head of the church, the rule of God will not be promoted through our lives as it should and could be. The understanding of the voice of God as here described gives substance to the relationship between Christ and his church. *He talks to it.* That is a major aspect of *what it means* for his Word to live in the church.

When we align ourselves with the Kingdom of Christ, when we come into the family of God, we are then an outpost of that Kingdom. If you wish, though these are crude metaphors, we have the telephone installed so that we can take the heavenly orders and participate in decisions as we do Kingdom business.

We have a computer terminal put in place so we can communicate and act and interact with God in his work. It is important that we have God's instructions and directions for what we do. And, to repeat a crucial point, it is not true that the Bible *alone,* or our subjective experiences *alone,* or circumstances given to be interpreted will give us the kind of guidance we need.

And it was never so intended. We must be spoken to by God, specifically and concretely guided in thought and action to the extent and by the instrumentalities he chooses. We have in this book tried to make literal sense of what that might amount to.

B. *Provision of confidence, comfort, and peace:* Second, we as individuals must have the confidence and peace that comes from knowing that we are indeed in communication with God himself.

Think of the benediction that contains the blessing of Moses on God's people in Numbers 6:24–26: "The Lord bless thee, and keep thee." What does this mean? And also: "The Lord make his face shine upon thee." What does that mean?

Have you ever watched someone who loves another—as a little child, for example, loves its father—when the father's face was *not* lifted to that child and shining on it? Have you perhaps been in that place yourself? Do you remember what it was like to experience your father or mother turning away from you in anger and *withdrawal,* when their face did not shine but instead scowled on you or ignored you? Communication was cut off. You were agonized by it until you learned to harden your heart against it. Communication and guidance are absolutely necessary for us to have the kind of confidence and peace appropriate to a child of God.

A little child lost his mother to death. He could not be adequately consoled and continued to be troubled, especially at night. He would come into the room where the father was and ask to sleep with the father. This little child would never rest until he knew not only that he was with his father, but that the father's face was turned toward him. He would ask in the dark, "Father, is your face turned toward me now?" And when at last assured of this, he was at peace and was able to go to sleep. How lonely life is! Oh, we can "get by" with a God who does not speak. Many at least think they do. But it is not much of a life, and certainly not the life intended for us by God, or the *abundance* of life that Jesus Christ came to make available.

We love to sing the song, "This Is My Father's World." But in its words, for all their loveliness, there is no personal element. The song of the bird and the music of the spheres and the rustling of the grass to which it refers makes up an impersonal arrangement, though certainly a glorious one.

There is all the difference in the world between having a fine general view that this is our Father's world—or even that an "arrangement" has been made for our eternal redemption—and having experiential confidence that the Father's face, whether in the dark of the night or the brightness of the day, is turned toward us, shining on us, and that the Father is speaking to us individually.

C. *Protection from mad religionism and legalism:* Third, it is important for us to know on a practiced, experiential basis how God speaks so that we may *protect* ourselves and others for whom we are concerned.

We all know, as previously discussed, what foolishness sometimes comes following the words, "God told me." Indeed, we all know not only what foolishness, but also sometimes what horror can follow those words. We need to know what the voice of God is like, how it comes, and what kinds of things it might say in order to protect ourselves, and those around us in the fellowship of the faithful, from people who are malicious or who are being carried away with voices contrary to God that they themselves may not understand.

It is of vital importance that we be able to recognize when people in positions of power and authority do not, for all their "authority," know what they are talking about or when they are "guided" by evil. For our own protection, as well as for the protection of those we love and for the prosperity of the visible church, we need to understand how God's voice works. Hence guidance must be taken out of the realm of superstition and put in terms that everyone who wants to understand can understand.

Cult leaders, without exception, can be clearly identified if what has been said above about the spirit and content of God's voice and God's leadership is understood. The tragedy of Jim Jones and Jonestown—which we now know began long before Jonestown, among the decent citizenry of various cities across the United States—could have been stopped dead in its tracks if but a few of the people he gathered around him had been in a position to see through his claims to speak for God.

But they themselves had no competence in dealing with the voice of God as a practical, experiential matter, and through mystification of that voice and by "spiritual" bullying, they were led to the slaughter.

Right this minute some lesser version of this type of deception is being played out in hundreds or thousands of settings throughout the earth. If those who try to put their "guidance" over on others knew that they would be examined by compassionate but strong individuals who have understanding of such matters, things would go much better for our churches generally and for the individuals in them, not to mention our communities at large.

But danger not only comes from the "wild side" of religion, it can also come from the respectable side. When, in the ninth chapter of John, Jesus healed a blind man on the Sabbath, the leaders of the people, proud of being Moses' disciples (v. 28), "knew" that Jesus could not possibly be of God because he did not observe their restrictions on working during the Sabbath (v. 16).

They *knew* that this man Jesus was a sinner because they "knew" the Bible. And they "knew" that the Bible said that you were not supposed to do the kinds of things he was doing on the Sabbath. Therefore, since this man Jesus did these kinds of things on the Sabbath, he was a sinner. Q.E.D.

These leaders had good, reliable general knowledge of how things were supposed to be. For his part, the man healed could only report: "Whether he [Jesus] is a sinner or not, I do not know: one thing I know, that, whereas I was blind, now I see" (v. 25). But *that* was not "in the Bible," in the law. They had *their* guidance, and they thought it was sufficient. But it was not sufficient, though it was very respectable, for it allowed them to condemn the power and works of love in Jesus himself. "We know that God spoke to Moses; as for this fellow, we don't know where he is coming from" (v. 29).

"We don't know!" That is perhaps the most damning statement they could possibly have made about themselves. They looked at what Jesus did and said, "We don't know what this person is doing. We don't know where he is coming from. We don't know that he is of God."

What they were really confessing was that they did not know who God is or what his works are. They, in their own way, shared Nicodemus's problem of not being able to see the Kingdom of God, though they too were sure they did. And many stand in that same place today. They could look at the greatest works of love and righteousness, and if those works did not conform to their legalistic ideas of what the Bible or the church teaches, for example, or their ideas of what their subjective experiences confirmed, they could condemn those works without batting an eye. "We *know* that this is wrong!" We all need to be saved from such "knowledge."

We really have no recourse, no place to stand in the face of the mad religionist, on the one hand, or the blind legalist, on the other, if we do not have firsthand knowledge of individualized guidance, held safely within a community of brothers and sisters in Christ who also have such knowledge of God's personal dealings with their own soul.[19]

D. *Realization of a biblical quality of life:* Fourth, and finally, experience and understanding of God's voice speaking to us can alone make the events of the Bible real to us and allow our faith in the truth of the Bible to rise beyond mere abstract conviction that it *must* be true. This is a theme we have already touched on a number of times, but it is so important that we must return to it once again.

Consider, for example, the events recorded in 1 Samuel 16:1–13. This is the story of the selection of David as king over Israel. (As with so much of the Bible, the passage is filled with "the Lord said to . . . ," in this case to Samuel.) "The Lord said unto Samuel, 'How long will you mourn for Saul, seeing I have rejected him from reigning over Israel? Fill your horn with oil, and go, I will send you to Jesse the Bethlehemite: for I have provided me a king among his sons.' And Samuel said, 'How can I go? If Saul hears of it, he will kill me.' And the Lord said, 'Take an heifer with you, and say, I am come to sacrifice to the Lord. And call Jesse to the sacrifice, and I will show you what you shall do: and you shall anoint unto me him whom I name'" (vv. 1–3).

When the sons of Jesse came before Samuel, the first was Eliab. Apparently Eliab was a fine-looking person, for Samuel said, "Surely the Lord's anointed is before him." But the Lord said to Samuel, in words that should always remain before us, "Look not on his countenance, or on the height of his stature; because I have refused him: for the Lord does not see as man sees; for man looks on the outward appearance, but the Lord looks on the heart" (v. 7).

Abinadab, Shammah, and all of Jesse's other sons besides David, who was not present, then passed before Samuel with the same result. Finally, David was called out of the fields, where he was keeping the sheep. And when he came before Samuel, "The Lord said, 'Arise, anoint him: for this is he.' Then Samuel took the horn of oil, and anointed him in the midst of his brethren: and the spirit of the Lord came upon David from that day forward" (vv. 12–13).

It is essential to the strength of our faith that we be in some measure capable of inwardly identifying with Samuel's experience as he conversed with the Lord in the midst of Jesse's family.

The Astonishing Case of David

David's own conversational interactions with God are documented at many points in the Bible, but at none more graphically than in 1 Chronicles 14. After he had assumed the throne of Israel, the Philistines came to war against him. David then "inquired of God" (v. 10) what he should do. This was probably done by standing before the ark of God. The ark had been used earlier in the history of Israel for such inquiry and had been recently relocated by David in an effort to place it in Jerusalem, which he had chosen as his capital city (see 1 Chr 13). "And David inquired of God, saying, 'Shall I go up against the Philistines? And will you deliver them into my hand?' And the Lord said unto him, 'Go up; for I will deliver them into your hand'" (v. 10).

And so it happened. The Philistines then regrouped and later set themselves in array in the same valley. "Therefore David inquired again of God; and God said unto him, 'Go not up after them; turn away from them, and come upon them over against the mulberry trees. And it shall be, when you shall hear a sound of going in the tops of the mulberry trees, that then you shall go out to battle; for God is gone forth before you to smite the host of the Philistines'" (vv. 14–15). And it occurred just as God said.

One of the most interesting things about these cases, and the many similar passages the Bible contains, is the specific information, the clear and detailed *cognitive content*, given in the movement of God on the minds of Samuel and David. What we have here are not mere "impressions," "impulses," or "feelings," which are so commonly thought to be what God uses in guiding us. Rather, we have a specific and full cognitive or "propositional" content concerning what is the case, what is to be done, and what will happen.

David and Samuel were not left to wonder about the meaning of their "impulses" to do this or that or their "feelings" about this or that. Nor did they have to "test them against" the Scriptures or circumstances. They were simply *told.* David did not have to speculate about the meaning of "the sound of going in the tops of the mulberry trees." He was *told.*

It is possible to talk about conscious guidance in terms of mysterious feelings, curious circumstances, and special scriptural nuances of meaning to the point where God's very character is called into question. He is not a mumbling trickster.

On the contrary, it is to be *expected,* given the revelation of God in Christ, that *if* there is something he would have us know, he will be both able and willing plainly to communicate it to us if we are but open and prepared by our experience to hear and obey. This is exactly what takes place in the lives of such biblical characters as David and Samuel and others.

The very "mechanism" of inspiration—through which "the prophecy came not in old time by the will of man: but holy men of God spake as they were moved by the Holy Ghost" (2 Pt 1:21) and through which "all scripture is given by inspiration [or inbreathing] of God" (2 Tm 3:16)—is, in its human side, nothing but thought and perception of that distinctive character that its subjects had come, through experience, to recognize as the voice of God in their own souls. The thoughts and perceptions were indeed *their* thoughts and perceptions. It could not be otherwise. But they bore within themselves the unmistakable stamp of divine quality, spirit, intent, and origination.

Thus Paul is able to distinguish between what the Lord said with Paul and what Paul said on his own (1 Cor 7:12). Yet when he composed his letters under divine inspiration, *he* did not stop thinking or set aside his perceptions and feelings and become an unconscious writer or mindless voice box. His thoughts and perceptions were his, *but also God's.* And Paul recognized these thoughts and perceptions to be also God's because of the distinctive character he knew so well and worked with in such utter confidence.

When we, by our experiences and deliberations, have learned to recognize the voice of God as it enters into the texture of *our* souls, the lives of biblical personalities become real to us and the life of God in them becomes something we can identify with. Our faith then rises to claim our portion in the unified reign of God in his people throughout history on earth and in heaven.

SOME TOPICS FOR REFLECTION

1. It is a fact of nature that sheep recognize and respond to the voice of the one who takes care of them (Jn 10:1–4). What do you make of how Jesus uses this fact to explain the interaction between his voice and his people? (vv. 14–27).

2. What are the "three lights" referred to in this chapter, and what problems arise because of their interdependence?

3. What are the "three factors in the voice" treated in this chapter? Do you regard any of them as more important than the others? Why?

4. God's voice, or Word, does not usually come to us *via* sound waves unless he is speaking to us *with* a human being, as earlier explained. Does the lack of an "audible" quality diminish the reliability of our experience of his voice?

5. "Any voice which promises total exemption from suffering and failure is most certainly *not* God's Word." What do you think of this claim? Are there any "spiritual panaceas" for life's problems? Don't say no too quickly.

6. What would be some indications that a communication that "comes to you" is from Satan? From self?

7. Do you agree with what this chapter says about infallibility and hearing from God? What are some practical implications of the position taken? Or of *your* view on this matter?

8. Ability at recognizing the "voice of God" serves as protection against cultic leaders on both the "wild side" and the "respectable side" of religion. Illustrate and discuss.

Notes

1. G. Campbell Morgan, *God's Perfect Will* (Grand Rapids, MI: Baker Book House, 1978), 157.
2. It is possible to understand the teaching of the sufficiency of the anointing in various ways, but no biblical Christian can *deny* this reality. Since the flood tide of European mysticism in the thirteenth and fourteenth centuries (see *Master Eckhart and the Rhineland Mystics,* by Jeanne Ancelet-Hustache [New York: Harper Torchbooks, n.d.] for a good introduction to this topic), this teaching has been nowhere more strongly defended than by the Quakers; their best presentation is in Propositions I, II, and III of *An Apology for the True Christian Divinity,* by Robert Barclay, 9th ed. (Philadelphia: Joseph Crukshank, 1775).

   I believe that, on the whole, a more correct view of the relationship between the Bible and the anointing is given in William Law, John Wesley, and Andrew Murray. For Murray, see especially *The Spirit of Christ* (London: James Nisbet, 1899; and other editions). For Wesley, see the various discourses on the Spirit, and especially on the witness of the Spirit, in *Sermons on Several Occasions* (New York: B. Waugh and T. Mason, 1836) and in other editions of his sermons. For Law, see *The Power of the Spirit* (Fort Washington, PA: Christian Literature Crusade, 1971) as well as his *Serious Call to a Devout and Holy Life* (New York: Paulist Press, 1978).
3. F. B. Meyer, *The Secret of Guidance* (Chicago: Moody Press, n.d.), 14–15.
4. In addition to Meyer, see also Bob Mumford, *Take Another Look at Guidance: Discerning the Will of God* (Plainfield, NJ: Logos International, 1971), chap. 7; and G. Campbell Morgan, *God's Perfect Will,* 155f.
5. Meyer, *Secret of Guidance,* 18.
6. Beth Spring, "What the Bible Means," *Christianity Today,* December 17, 1982, pp. 45–48.
7. Law, *Power of the Spirit,* 61.
8. Don Ihde, *Listening and Voice* (Athens: Ohio University Press, 1976).
9. Jones, *A Song of Ascents,* 190.
10. Wesley, *Sermons on Several Occasions,* vol. 1, 91–92.
11. Adela Rogers St. John, *Guideposts,* December 1968, p. 8.
12. Mumford, *Take Another Look at Guidance,* 85–86.
13. Charles Stanley, *How to Listen to God* (Nashville, TN: Thomas Nelson, 1985), 51.
14. J. Edwin Orr, "What Made the Welsh Revival 'Extraordinary,'" *The Forerunner* 2, no. 8 (1987):11.

15. Isaac Watts, "Am I a Soldier of the Cross?," hymn #176 in *The Broadman Hymnal* (Nashville, TN: The Broadman Press, 1940).

16. Meyer, *Secret of Guidance*, 31.

17. John Bunyan, *Grace Abounding to the Chief of Sinners* (Grand Rapids, MI: Baker Books, 1981), 46–47.

18. I recommend reading with this section chapters 1 and 2 of Charles Stanley's *How to Listen to God.*

19. The communal side of guidance is not studied in this book, but the reader is referred to chapter 12 of Richard Foster's *Celebration of Discipline* (New York: Harper & Row, 1978), 150–62.

9

Guidance and Beyond: A Life More Than Guidance

To deliver the soul from the sin which is its ruin and bestow on it the holiness which is its health and peace, is the end of all God's dealings with His children; and precisely because He cannot merely impose, but must enable us to attain it ourselves, if we are really to have the liberty of His children, the way He must take is long and arduous.

JOHN WOOD OMAN[1]

If you scream for insight and call loudly for understanding, if you pursue it like you would money, and search it out as you would hidden treasure, then the Lord will be awesome to you, and you will come into possession of the knowledge of God.

PRV 2:3⁻5

Do everything you can to make it through the narrow gate.

LK 13:24

Using Our Mind to Love God

In the foregoing chapters we have dealt with many aspects of divine guidance for the individual child of God. This discussion may frequently have seemed remote, scholarly, or "merely philosophical." It is an unavoidable fact, however, that *what we understand or do not understand, in any area of our lives, determines what we can or cannot believe and therefore governs our practice and action with an iron hand.* You cannot believe a blank, and the "blanks" in our understanding can only be filled in by careful instruction and hard thinking.

Contrary to what many in our culture will tell you, this does not cease to be true when we enter the realm of the religious life. There is now a book for sale called *The Lazy Man's Guide to Riches.* What a great idea! Misunderstandings of faith and grace now prevalent lead people to think that the Christian gospel is *The Lazy Person's Guide to Getting into Heaven When You Die* or perhaps *The Passive Person's Path to Paradise.* But it isn't.

Faith is not opposed to knowledge; it is opposed to sight. And grace is not opposed to effort; it is opposed to earning. Commitment is not sustained by confusion, but by insight. The person who is uninformed or confused inevitably will be unstable and vulnerable in action, thought, and feeling.

Misunderstandings, mental confusions, and mistaken beliefs about guidance—or more generally about God and communications between him and his creatures—make a strong walk with him impossible. This is also the case if we "don't want to think about it." I have seen repeatedly confirmed, in often tragic cases, the dire consequences of refusing to give deep, thoughtful consideration to the ways in which God chooses to deal with us and of relying on whatever whimsical ideas and preconceptions on these matters happen to be passing by. This attitude is very dangerous to our health and well-being.

Indeed, refusal to make the effort to understand God's dealings with humanity, to study the Bible and whatever else may help us to understand it, is *rebellion* against the *express will of God,* who commands us to love him with *all our mind* as well as with all our heart, soul, and strength (Mk 12:30; compare Prv 1–8).

We can therefore say on scriptural grounds that it is the direct and inclusive will of God that we *study* his ways of guiding and communicating with us. The conscious rejection of thoughtful and careful study is not faith and does not spring from faith but rather is the rejection of the God-appointed means to God-appointed ends.

But now we have made the study. We have endured the hardship of thinking carefully and in depth about divine guidance in our world and about the presentation of divine guidance given in the Scriptures. It is now time to bring our results to bear on the life that any serious disciple of Christ consciously undertakes from day to day. If the foregoing chapters have been successful, we are now in a position to bring those who are concerned to know God's will *for them* into a place of rest and assurance, where they can be confident that the Lord's face does indeed shine on them.

The question we will deal with in this final chapter is, then, essentially a "how to" question:

> How may we come to live confidently and in a sensible fashion with God as a conversational presence in our lives?

This question leads to subordinate questions such as:

> How far can we *count on* guidance being given?
> What does it mean when it is *not* given?
> What *then* are we to *do?*

What will our answers be?

The Framework Now Provided for Our Answers

We set out toward answers from a brief *summary of fundamental points* elaborated in the course of this book. Repetition is necessary in order to counteract the powerful habits and misconceptions about guidance that are buried deeply in standard religious behaviors and thought patterns.

Although God's communications, including those intended to guide our specific choices, come through experiences of many kinds, the content or *meaning* of his specific and individualized communications to us always finally takes the form of the "inner voice," a characteristic type of thought or perception. Without this voice, the accompanying events, appearances, or biblical passages remain objects of puzzlement, mystification, and conjecture.

God may of course guide us "mechanically," without *addressing* us and guiding us through our own understandings and choices. He can guide us as we guide our automobile, without speaking to it. But whenever he guides us in our conscious cooperation with him as our friend and collaborator, he does so by *speaking* to us, by giving to us thoughts and perceptions that bear within themselves the marks of their divine origination.

This "speaking" most commonly occurs in conjunction with study of and reflection on the Bible, the written Word of God, wherever the Bible is effectively available. Less commonly, though very often, the Word comes in conjunction with a human being who is speaking to us. But it *may* come in any way God chooses.

Our ability to recognize the voice of God in our souls and to distinguish it with practical certainty from all else there is acquired by effort and experimentation, both on God's part and ours. It does not come automatically by divine imposition and fiat.

Those who really want to live under God's guidance—and who, by proper teaching or other special provision made by God, become convinced that he will speak, and perhaps *is* speaking, to them—can proceed to learn through a course of experience what is the quality, spirit, and content of God's voice. They will then distinguish and understand the voice of God, not infallibly, but at least as clearly and with as much accuracy as they do the voice of any other person with whom they are on intimate terms.

We emphasize once again that this does not mean that they will always correctly understand what God says to them, or even that it will be easy for them to get the message straight.

One great cause of confusion about divine guidance is that people make infallibility a condition of guidance. It helps, I believe and hope, to understand that guidance is communication and that communication occurs constantly in contexts in which infallibility is completely out of the question.

Even infallibility of the speaker, as in the case in which it is God who is speaking, does not and need not guarantee infallibility of the hearer. But fortunately, as we all know, communication does reliably occur, and on a regular basis, when the speakers are not even close to being perfect. I well know my children's voices and would recognize them under a very wide range of circumstances. Generally, I understand what they say. But I would know it was they who were speaking even if I could not understand what they said. (This has actually happened on several occasions.)

Indeed, careful study of personal relationships shows that recognition of a certain voice is often the cue for one to *stop* listening, or even for one to distort the message in ways that are relevant to the specific nature of the relationship between the people involved. I am convinced that this often happens in the divine-human conversation, and it almost always happens when God speaks to those who are in covert rebellion against him.

We have seen that one of the deepest teachings of Jesus concerns the manner in which we hear. This lesson is so important that it is emphasized here again. Specifically, Jesus alerted his hearers to the fact that they might not be using their ears simply to hear, but for other purposes, such as to filter and manage the message the better to fit their own lives and purposes. "If any man have ears to hear, let him hear. And he said unto them, 'Take heed what you hear: with what measure you mete, it shall be measured to you; and unto you that hear shall more be given.' . . . And with many such parables spoke he the word unto them, as they were able to hear it" (Mk 4:23–24, 33).

Listening is an *active* process that may select or omit from, as well as reshape, the message intended by the one speaking. Listening, and all our ways of perceiving, are fundamental displays of our character, of our freedom, and of our bondages.

If we really do not want God's guidance over our lives, then, no matter what we may say, this fact will position us before God in such a manner "that seeing we may see, and not perceive; and hearing we may hear, and not understand; lest at any time we should be converted, and our sins should be forgiven" (Mk 4:12). If we do not want to be converted from our chosen and habitual ways, if we really want to run our own lives without interference from God, our very perceptual mechanisms will filter out his voice or twist it to our purposes.

The doleful reality is that very few human beings really do want God's guidance in their lives. This is shown by how rarely we look for this guidance when we are *not* in trouble or faced with a decision we do not know how to handle. Those who understand and warmly desire God's guidance will, by contrast, be as concerned to have it when they are not facing trouble or "big decisions" as when they are.

This is a test we should all apply to ourselves as we go in search of guidance, and the results may reveal that our failure to get guidance when we want it is due to the fact that we do not in general want God to guide us except when "we need it."

The usual situation is that many who want God's guidance when in trouble cannot find it. Or at least they have no assurance that they have found it. This is because, first and foremost, they do not want God's guidance. At heart they only want to get out of trouble or make the decisions that will be best for them. Indeed, I have spoken with many who think of divine guidance *only* as something to help them avoid trouble.

Our lack of desire for God's guidance merely for itself, just because we believe it is the best way to live, is also shown by a disregard of the plain directives in the Scriptures. Sanctification from sexual uncleanness (1 Thes 4:3) as well as evidence of a continuously thankful heart (1 Thes 5:18) are among the many specific things clearly set forth in God's general guidance to all persons. It is not wise to disregard these plain directives and *then* expect to be given special guidance when we want it.

But we do not mean to say that God absolutely will not, in his mercy, guide and communicate with those who have departed from the general guidance he has given. Contrary to the well-meaning words of the blind man whom Jesus healed (Jn 9:31), God does, on occasion, "hear sinners."

But this cannot be counted on or be part of a regular and intelligible *plan* for living in a conversational relationship with God. Those who reject the general counsels of Scripture are, in fact, planning not to be guided by God and thus cannot count on being able to *use* God's guidance on particular occasions to deliver them from their perplexities.

However, there are many who honestly desire God's guidance in its own right and because God knows it is best for us. As a part of their total plan for living in harmony with God, these individuals adopt the general counsels of Scripture as the framework within which they are to know his daily graces. These people will most assuredly receive God's specific, conscious guidance through the inner voice, to the extent that such guidance truly is appropriate in developing their individualized conformation to Jesus Christ.

There *is* a limit to which such guidance is appropriate, and we will return to this point in what follows. But it is generally true, as G. Campbell Morgan has written, that "wherever there are hearts waiting for the Voice of God, that Voice is to be heard."[2]

With this summation of what we have learned from our studies before us, we turn now to deal with our concluding practical questions.

Listening for God

Dr. James Dobson has given some of the best practical advice I have ever heard on how the person who really wants the will of God, and has a basically correct understanding of it, should proceed. Describing his own process, he says: "I get down on my knees and say, 'Lord, I need to know what you want me to do, and I am listening. Please speak to me through my friends, books, magazines I pick up and read, and through circumstances.'"[3]

The simplicity of this process should not mislead us. When we are in a proper functioning relationship with our Lord, this is exactly what we are to do. Then we are, as Dr. Dobson says, to *listen*. This means that we pay a special kind of attention both to what is going on within us and to our surrounding circumstances.

We are talking about practicalities now, and it might be a good thing, until it becomes a habit, to write down Dr. Dobson's simple prayer for guidance and put it somewhere (the bathroom mirror?) where we can see and use it often. In conjunction with this approach, we should *observe regular times for listening* with respect to the matters that especially concern us.

At this practical level, we again heed the words of F. B. Meyer:

> Be still each day for a short time, sitting before God in meditation, and ask the Holy Spirit to reveal to you the truth of Christ's indwelling. Ask God to be pleased to make known to *you* what is the riches of the glory of this mystery (Col 1:27).[4]

If we have this general habit, then, when alerted to the need for particular guidance, we will be able to listen for *it* with greater patience, confidence, and acuity.

What I find personally to work best is, after asking for guidance in the manner indicated, to devote the next hour or so to some kind of activity that neither obsesses my attention with other things nor allows me to be intensely focused on the matter in question. Housework, gardening, driving about on errands, or paying bills will do.

I have learned not to worry about whether or not asking for guidance is going to "work." I know that it does not *have* to work, but I am sure that it will work if God has something he really wants me to know or do. This is *because I am sure of how great and good he is.*

Often, by the end of an hour or so, there has stood forth within my consciousness an idea or thought with that peculiar character of quality and spirit and content that I have come to associate with God's voice. If so, I may then write it down for further study. I may also decide to discuss the matter with others, usually *without* informing them that "God has told me" or suchlike. Or I may decide to reconsider the matter by repeating the same process after some short period of time. Remember Gideon. Scientists also check their results by rerunning the experiment. We should be so humble.

If, on the other hand, nothing emerges by the end of the hour or so, I am not alarmed. I set myself to hold the matter before the Lord as I go about my business and confidently get on with my life. Of course I make it a point to keep listening. Very often within a day, something happens through which God's voice, as previously described, is heard.

If it is not, however, I generally cease specifically to seek guidance on the matter in question. I do not cease my general attitude of listening. But I am neither disappointed nor alarmed, nor even concerned, as a rule, and I shall explain why as we proceed further. (Let us be clear that we are not speaking here of prayer generally, where a different approach of greater persistence and tenacity is often called for.)

I have followed this simple method of living with divine guidance in many situations: in university teaching, research, and administration; in family and business affairs; in writing and conducting sessions in conferences and seminars. Doing so is the furthest thing from a legalism or formality for me, and God takes ample occasion to slip up on me with "words" I am not seeking in this way. Generally speaking, it is much more important to cultivate the quiet inward space of a constant listening than it is to always be pestering God for guidance.

From my own experience, then, and from what I have been able to learn from from the Scriptures and from others who live in a working relationship with his voice, I am led to the following conclusion: direction will always be made available to the mature disciple if without it serious harm would befall persons concerned or the cause of Christ.

If I am right, the obedient, listening heart, mature in the things of God, will in such a case find the voice plain and the message clear, after the fashion of those experiences of the friends of God recorded in the Bible. This is a claim that must be tested by experience, and anyone willing to meet the conditions, and learn from failures as well as successes, can put it to the test. In every congregation we need a group of people who are explicitly learning and teaching life with guidance in the presence of the group.

Guidance Is Not a Gimmick

As just indicated, God often speaks *without* our initiating any procedure of seeking his individualized word as just described. Further, we must not be misled by anyone into thinking that there is some surefire *method* for squeezing what we want to know out of God. A life surrendered to God, a humble openness to his direction even when it is contrary to our wants and assumptions, experience with the way his Word comes to us, and fervent but patient requests for guidance do not constitute a mechanism or gimmick for getting an answer from him.

Once again, and for the last time: *guidance is not a gimmick.* Talk of "method" is, strictly speaking, out of place here, although we may lay down general practical guidelines. After all, God is not something we "work up" for a result, even though certain ways of behaving in relation to him are more or less appropriate.

We must, above all, beware of trying to *force* guidance from God. This is especially true at those times when such an attempt is most likely—that is, when we are not in peaceful union with him.

King Saul Forcing "Guidance"

Saul, first king of Israel, poignantly illustrates the folly of such attempts to force guidance. He certainly did not have as his highest priority to wait on God and see his will done. To keep control over his armies in the face of the Philistines, Saul did not wait before sacrificing, as he ought to have, for Samuel the priest to arrive. He blundered ahead on his own, even though it was not his place and made peace offerings and burnt offerings (1 Sm 13:5–10).

When Samuel at last arrived, he asked Saul why he had done this. The reply goes to the very heart of Saul's character: "Because I saw that the people were scattered from me, and that you did not come within the days appointed, and that the Philistines gathered themselves together at Michmash; therefore said I, 'The Philistines will come down now upon me to Gilgal, and I have not made supplication unto the Lord'; I forced myself therefore, and offered a burnt offering" (vv. 11–12).

Samuel immediately announced that Saul would lose his kingdom (vv. 13–14), for he clearly saw that Saul was a man who would take things into his hands to get his own way and that he also would find a "good reason" for doing so. Samuel knew that God would not stand by such a man.

A little later Saul disobeyed again, and again found a "good reason," when he did not utterly destroy Amalek (1 Sm 15). He even pretended to Samuel to have obeyed (v. 13), and when his deceit was uncovered he again blamed his disobedience on "the people" (v. 24). Again Samuel announced that the kingdom would be taken from Saul (v. 26).

Finally, Saul came to his extremity, facing death. Samuel himself was dead by this time, and "when Saul inquired of the Lord, the Lord answered him not, neither by dreams, nor by Urim, nor by prophets" (1 Sm 28:6). Now, as was his way, Saul attempted to *force* the knowledge he sought. Even though he himself had banned witches from Israel, he sought out a witch and compelled her to call up the spirit of Samuel (vv. 7–11) to tell him what to do. Samuel arose "out of the earth" (v. 13) and said to Saul, "Why have you troubled me, to bring me up?" (v. 15).

Then Saul poured out his tale of woe: "The Philistines make war against me, and God is departed from me, and answers me no more, neither by prophets, nor by dreams; therefore I have called you, that you may *make known unto me what I shall do*" (v. 15, italics added).

How pitifully typical this is of the human view of God and his guidance! We treat him like a celestial aspirin to cure the headaches brought on by the steady, willful tendency of our lives away from and even against him, like a cosmic butler whose job it is to clean up our messes. Then we seek gimmicks and tricks suited only to idols to compel him to serve us!

Samuel then read Saul's sentence to him: "Why, then, are you asking me, seeing the Lord is departed from you and has become your adversary? . . . Tomorrow you and your sons will be with me. The Lord also shall deliver the host of Israel into the hands of the Philistines" (vv. 16–19). At these words Saul fell flat on the earth, weakened by hunger and terror. God refused to be used by Saul any longer.

Deciding "on Your Own"

Now we turn to what surely is one of the greatest problems in the devout person's attempts to understand guidance. Even if we are not in disobedience to God, even if our hearts are perfectly attuned to his will, there will be many times in which no particularized guidance will come from God concerning what we are to do. Let us take this as a given.

We must not automatically assume that if God does not guide us in a particular matter, we are therefore displeasing to him. *If* this is the cause, which of course remains possible and should always be considered, there are ways of finding it out. The cause will be something that can be discovered and clearly known if we but seek it out through honest examination of our lives, counsel with Christian friends and ministers, and asking the Lord to reveal the reason to us.

At this point it is crucial to remember that God will not play games of hide-and-seek with us. Here, as earlier emphasized, it is all-important that we believe that he is the kind of person revealed by Jesus.

Such a person will show us what the problem is, if there is a problem, provided we sincerely and with an open mind pray and seek to be shown. God is not frivolous, is not coy, will not tease or torture us. In our relationship with him, there is no mysterious "catch" to guidance, no riddle to solve, no incantation to "get just right"—not with the God and Father of our Lord Jesus Christ! We must make a point of *not* thinking of him in terms of human beings—relatives, supervisors, authorities, and others—who may have enjoyed tricking us about what we had to do.

But there are other reasons than his displeasure that can explain why a specific word may not be forthcoming to guide us in a particular case. One major reason is this: *in general, it is the will of God that we ourselves should have a great part in determining our path through life.*

This does not mean that he is not with us—far from it. God both *develops* and, for our good, *tests* our character by leaving us to decide. He calls us to responsible citizenship in his Kingdom by, in effect or in reality, saying as often as possible: "MY WILL FOR YOU IN THIS CASE IS FOR *YOU* TO DECIDE ON YOUR OWN!"

In his profound chapter on "The Will of God," John Wood Oman gives us this excellent statement on the point:

> The practical effect of reconciliation to God is thus to find ourselves in an order of life which is our succor, so far beyond our own contriving and for ends so far above our own conceiving, that we have no concern except to serve in it. Practically, as well as theoretically, we, thereby, attain such a perfect unity of morality and religion that we can only be absolutely dependent upon God as we are

absolutely independent in our own souls, and only absolutely independent in our own souls as we are absolutely dependent on God. A saved soul, in other words, is a soul true to itself because, with its mind on God's will of love and not on itself, it stands in God's world unbribable and undismayed, having freedom as it has piety and piety as it is free.[5]

It is thus that there rings out from the Apostle Paul and the saints through the ages the full meaning of that robust and powerful saying: "I live! Yet not I, but Christ liveth in me!" (Gal 2:20). By this truth, individual human personality is not obliterated but is given its fullest expression. *In Christ we are called to count!* From him I learn to live *my* life as he would live it *if* he were me.

We are dealing here with the essence of human personality as God has ordained it. Children cannot develop into responsible, competent human beings if they are always told what to do. Personality and character are, in their very essence, inner directed. This inner directedness is perfected in redemption. This is Oman's point. Moreover, children's characters cannot be known, even to themselves, until they are turned loose to do what they want. It is precisely what children want, and how they handle those wants, that both manifests and makes them the people they are.

What we want, what we think, what we decide to do when the voice of God does not come—or, also, when we have so immersed ourselves in him that his voice within us is not held in distinction from our own thoughts and perceptions—shows *who we are*, either God's mature children, friends, and co-workers, or something less.

There is also, after all, a neurotic, faithless, and irresponsible seeking of God's will: a kind of spiritual hypochondria, always taking its own spiritual temperature, far more concerned with being righteous than with loving God and others and doing and enjoying what is good. There is such a thing as being righteous overmuch (Eccl 7:16). We may insist on God telling us what to do because we live in fear or are obsessed with *being right* as a strategy for *being safe*. But we may also do so because we do not really have a hearty faith in his gracious goodwill toward us.

If so, we need to grow up to Christlikeness, and nothing short of this will solve our problem. Certainly more guidance will not!

We may in our heart of hearts suspect that God is mean and tyrannical and therefore be afraid to make a move without dictation from him. We may even have the idea that if we can get God to tell us what to do, we will no longer be responsible for our decisions. So far from honoring God, such an attitude is blasphemous, idolatrous, and certain to prevent us from ever entering into that conversational relationship with God wherein sensible guidance is given as is appropriate, clearly revealed and reliably understood. How much would you have to do with a person who harbored such low opinions about you?

Often we just do not think through the things we say about God. A well-known minister of some decades ago, Bud Robinson, was called by a parishioner whose husband had recently died. The lady informed the pastor that God had told her to give the husband's suits to him. Would he please come over, she asked, to see if the suits fit? Pastor Robinson very sensibly replied: "If God told you to give them to me, they'll fit." How refreshing to hear from someone who actually believed in a competent God!

The "Perfect" Will of God

The children of God cannot be groveling robots or obsequious cringing sycophants and also be *the children of God!* Such creatures could never bear the family resemblance. A son or daughter is not the father's toady, and toadying is no part of either humility or worship before the God and Father of Jesus Christ. To suppose so is to live within a morbid and anti-Christian view of who God is. "The humility that cringes in order that reproof may be escaped or favor obtained is as unchristian as it is profoundly immoral."[6]

In this context we need to say something about being in the *perfect* will of God. If our lives conform to the general counsels of God for his people, as given to us in the written Word as a whole, then we are perfectly in God's general as well as moral will. If, in addition, we have received and obeyed specific guidance by a specific word of God to us concerning a particular matter, then we are *perfectly* in God's *specific* will for us, relevant to that matter.

But now suppose no such specific word has come to us concerning some matter of great importance to our lives. (Should we enter this school or that? Live here or there? Change employment? and so on.) Does this means that in the matter at hand we *cannot* be in God's perfect will, or that we can be so only by chance, following some anxiety-ridden guessing game about "what God wants me to do"?

Most assuredly it does not! We must resolutely resist the tendency automatically to blame the absence of guidance on our own wrongness. And we must equally deny that the absence of guidance means that we must be somewhat off the track and living in something less than God's perfect will.

If we are living in sincere devotion to the fulfillment of God's purposes in us, we can be sure that the God who stood forth in Jesus Christ will not mumble or tease or trick us regarding any specific matter he wants done. We cannot too often reemphasize this point, because the tendency to think otherwise is obviously so strong and ever present.

Think of it this way: no decent parents would obfuscate their intent for their children. A general principle for interpreting the behavior of God toward us is provided in Jesus' words: "If ye then, being evil, know how to give good gifts unto your children: how much more shall your heavenly Father give the Holy Spirit to them than ask him?" (Lk 11:13). How much more shall your heavenly Father give clear instructions to them that sincerely ask him, in those cases where he has any to give?

And where he has none to give, we may be sure that is because it is best so. Then whatever lies within his moral will and is undertaken in faith *is his perfect will.* It is no less perfect merely because it was not precisely dictated by him. Indeed, it is perhaps more perfect just because he saw no need for precise dictation. He expects and trusts us to choose and goes with us in our choice.

Several different courses of action may, then, *each* be his perfect will in a given circumstance. We should *assume* that this is so in all cases in which we are walking in his general will, are experienced in hearing his voice, and, on seeking, find no specific direction given.

In these cases there are various things that would equally please God, though he directs none of them in particular to be done. All are "perfectly" in his will, because there is none better than the other, as far as he is concerned, and all are good. He would not have you to do other than you are doing. (Of course being in his perfect will also does not mean you are quite flawless yet!)

In his book earlier referred to, *Decision Making and the Will of God,* Garry Friesen has done a masterful job of critiquing the view that God *always* has *one* particular thing for you to do in a given case and that correct decision making depends on your finding out what that thing is. If you miss it, you will only be in God's "permissive" will at best, and a second-class citizen in the Kingdom of God. Against this extremely harmful view, Friesen remarks:

> The *major point* is this: God does not have an ideal, detailed life-plan uniquely designed for each believer that must be discovered in order to make correct decisions. The concept of an "individual will of God" cannot be established by reason, experience, biblical example or biblical teaching.[7]

So the *perfect* will of God may allow, for a particular person, a number of different alternatives. For most people, for example, a number of different choices in selecting a mate (or none at all), various vocations, educational institutions, or places of residence may all equally be God's perfect will, none being in themselves "better" or preferred by God in relation to the ultimate outcome desired by him.

The sincere seeker should assume that this is so and move forward with faith in God if no specific guidance comes on the matter concerned after a reasonable period of time. All of this is consistent with there *some-times* being only one choice that would perfectly fit God's will for us. Our choices must be approached on a case-by-case basis, just as life is lived one day at a time, trusting God.

Just as character is revealed only when we are permitted or required to do as we want, so also are the degree and maturity of our faith manifested only in cases in which no specific command is given. It is not the great and mature faith that merely does what it is told. Rather, the mature faith—in the language of William Carey, going out as a pioneer missionary to India—is one that "attempts great things for God, and expects great things from God."

Such a faith moves to the work to be done, to the life to be lived, confident in the good-hearted companionship of the Father, Son, and Holy Spirit. Human initiative in the redeemed is not canceled, but is heightened, exponentialized, by immersion in the flow of God's life.

The mature vision of God, with extensive experience in his ways, excludes obsessive anxiety about doing the right thing. For the most part, of course, it simply *knows* what is right. But its confidence is, finally, not in guidance, but in the Lord who is with us.

Caught in Cosmic Conflict

But there exists not only those cases in which we do not have guidance because our Father wishes us to decide. There are also cases in which we come face-to-face with the powers of darkness that inhabit our universe. How many people have fallen under some affliction and have cast about desperately to find out what *they* did wrong? But often they did nothing wrong. Or whatever wrong they may have done was not what was responsible for their problem.

We live in a universe in which there is a battle going on. As we live in that universe and share in God's creativity, both of creation and redemption, there are moments when we stand alone. Jesus knew what such aloneness was like. You will remember how he spoke in Luke 22:53 of the time when *his* hour would come—the hour of darkness, the hour of the powers of evil. In that hour he cried out, "My God, my God, why hast thou forsaken me?" (Mt 27:46).

You and I are going to face these hours, even though in some sense, I believe, we will never be *utterly* forsaken and alone. As that magnificent saint John Wesley said at his death: "Best of all, God is with us!" But divine guidance, no matter how well we know it, will not spare us the times of grief and pain, as it did not spare Jesus. Our confidence remains that such sufferings too "work together for good" for those who love God and are called according to his purposes (Rom 8:28). In this belief we rest and refuse to harass ourselves with doubt and blame.

Similarly, we shall not doubt when we are given guidance, and are sure of it, but it does not come to pass. Other persons and events may be involved. And these people may not know, or may not do, the will of God. And God may not override them. Such a world as this is the crucible of soul making in which we still are always certain of inevitable triumph "more than conquerors." The will of God made plain to us is sometimes not fulfilled because of the choices of other people. We must not, because this is so, lose confidence in God's guidance.

Greater Than Guidance

There is something even greater than always knowing what is the right thing to do and always being guided by the present hand of God. Paul brought this out very clearly in 1 Corinthians 13 when he spoke of knowledge, of prophecy, and of many other great things we might find desirable. But he said that all of these are only partial and incomplete goods. The three greatest things—truly inseparable from one another, when properly understood—are faith, hope, and love.

In the hour of darkness, even these three remained with Christ: *faith, hope, and love.* The great height of our development as disciples of Christ is not that we shall always have guidance, but that we shall be trained under the hand of God in such a way that we are able to *stand even without guidance,* at our appointed time and place, in faith, hope, and love. "And having done all, to stand!" (Eph 6:13).

We can be assured, at a certain point in our progression toward spiritual maturity, simply that "he that sent me is with me: the Father has not left me alone; for I do always those things that please him" (Jn 8:29). It should be the hope and *plan* of every disciple of Christ to come, by gracious assistance, to this place of rest in God's companionship and service.

We will then, as Brother Lawrence advises, "not always scrupulously confine ourselves to certain rules, or particular forms of devotion, but act with a general confidence in God, with love and humility."[8]

We will simply "stand fast in the liberty wherewith Christ hath made us free" (Gal 5:1), not using this liberty as an opportunity for the flesh. Our freedom will instead be the arena within which we "by love serve one another" (Gal 5:13) just because "he that sent me is with me." The branch then abides in the vine. The branch and the vine share a common life and together produce abundant fruit unto God (Jn 15:1–8).

Never Beyond "Risk"

It is absolutely essential to the nature of personal maturation that we venture and be placed at risk. *Only risk produces character.* This truth is not withdrawn, but rather is intensified when it comes to our walk with God. It is clear, therefore, that we must disagree with certain very wise people, such as A. T. Pierson, who regard God's guidance as precluding risk:

> One great law for all who would be truly led by God's pillar of cloud and fire, is to take no step at the bidding of self-will or without the clear moving of the heavenly guide. Though the direction be new and the way seem beset with difficulty, there is never any risk provided we are only led of God. Each new advance needs separate and special authority from Him, and yesterday's guidance is not sufficient for today.[9]

This is a beautiful and helpful statement, except for what it seems to be saying about risk. We have to disagree with it, therefore, as a completely general account of living with God's guidance in our lives. Much of the deplorable immaturity to be found in the lives of Christians is because they adopt the general attitude expressed in this statement as the *whole* truth about divine guidance.

Once having done so, they then try to *use* guidance as a device for securing a life without risk. When this doesn't work, as it certainly will not, they then begin attacking themselves, someone else, or even God as a failure. Such a response partly explains why God remains humanity's greatest disappointment. Who does not have their own grievance against him?

With Guidance and Beyond . . . Life and Rest

We return once again to the themes that emerged in earlier parts of this book and have, because of their importance, been touched on again and again. The key concept underlying all of these themes is this:

> Divine guidance will never make sense except when set within a larger life of the right kind.

To try to locate divine guidance within human existence in its alienation from God is to return to idolatry, in which God is *for our use*. To try to solve all of the problems of life by divine guidance is to hide from life and from the dignity of the human role in creation intended by God. As John Boyken remarks, "God does not exist to solve our problems."[10] We exist to stand up with him and count for something in his world.

So we must finally move *beyond* the question of guidance in a life greater than our own—that of the Kingdom of God. Our concern for guidance must be overwhelmed by and lost in our worship and adoration of God and in our delight with his creation and his redemptive provision.

Our aim in such a life is to identify all that we are and do with God's purposes in creating us and our world. Thus, we learn how to do all things to the glory of God (1 Cor 10:31; Col 3:17). That is, we come in all things to think and act so that his goodness and greatness and beauty will be as obvious as possible, not just to ourselves, but to all those around us.

Guidance will always be an essential part of this life, to the extent and in the manner God deems suitable. And guidance will come without threat to the full participation of the redeemed self, as a unique individual, in the work of God. For those who come to this point, their life will be *theirs*—irreducibly, preciously so—and yet God's, and through them will flow God's life, which is yet theirs. This is the life beyond, and yet inclusive of, guidance. It is the life that has its rise in the "additional" birth and culminates in the everlasting glorious society of heaven.

With this life in view, John Wesley answered an intelligent and serious man who said to him: "I hear that you preach to a great number of people every night and morning. Pray what would you do with them? Whither would you lead them? What religion do you preach?

What is it good for?" Honest and searching questions, which no minister should allow out of his mind.

Wesley replied:

> I do preach to as many as desire to hear, every night and morning. You ask, what I would do with them: I would make them virtuous and happy, easy in themselves and useful to others. Whither would I lead them? To heaven; to God the Judge, the lover of all, and to Jesus the mediator of the New Covenant. What religion do I preach? The religion of love; the law of kindness brought to light by the gospel. What is this good for? To make all who receive it enjoy God and themselves: to make them all like God; lovers of all; contented in their lives; and crying out at their death, in calm assurance, "O grave, where is thy victory! Thanks be unto God, who giveth me the victory, through my Lord Jesus Christ.[11]

While I was teaching at a pastor's conference recently, one pastor asked me what was the human issue, irrespective of church life or religion, that Jesus came to answer. This is the question facing the Christian movement today. The answer is that Jesus came to respond to the universal human need to know how to live well. He came to show us how, through reliance on him, we can best live in the universe as it really is.

That is why he said, "I have come to give you life, in its most abundant form" (Jn 10:10). Putting our faith into worldwide competition at this level is the only way we can give it a chance to prove its power over life.

A Formula for Living with Guidance

Within such a life as Wesley described to his inquisitor, divine guidance—free of mystification, gimmickry, hysteria, self-righteousness, self-exaltation, self-obsession, and dogmatism—is to be reliably and safely sought and found. On the presupposition of such a life, we can lay down something close to a "formula" for *living with divine guidance*.

But note that it is *not* a formula for "getting guidance out of God" on matters that may concern us. Any such "formula" is ruled out by the very nature of God and of our relationship to him. This should now be clear. It is, I repeat, a formula for *living with* guidance in a life surrendered and quickened to maturity by God.

The first two steps in the formula may be described as foundational because they provide only the basis for individualized guidance but do not exclusively and specifically concern it.

Foundational Steps

1. We have entered into the "additional" life by the additional birth, and so far as lies in our understanding and conscious will, we plan and make provision to do what we know to be morally right and what we know to be explicitly commanded by God. This commitment includes the intention to find out what may be morally right or commanded by God, and hence to grow in our knowledge.

2. We seek the fullness of the new life in Christ at the impulse of the Spirit of God in service to the good wherever it may appear, venturing beyond our merely natural powers in reliance on God's upholding. Thus we move from faith to more faith (Rom. 1:17) as we find him faithful. Above all, we venture in the proclamation of the gospel of Jesus Christ and his Kingdom, as presented in the New Testament Gospels.

Guidance-Specific Steps

3. We meditate constantly on God's principles for life as set forth in the Scriptures, always striving to penetrate more deeply into their meaning and into their applicability for our lives.

"This book of the law shall not depart out of your mouth; but you shall meditate therein day and night, that you may observe to do according to all that is written therein: for, then you will make your way prosperous, and then you will have good success" (Jos 1:8; see Ps 1:1–3).

4. We are alert and attentive to what is happening in our lives and in our minds and hearts. It is there that God's communications come and identify themselves, whatever the external occasion may be. Of the

prodigal son it was said that he came *to himself* (Lk 15:17), and then he found the truth and repentance that saved him from his plight.

When God came to Adam after he had sinned, he did not ask, "Adam, where is God?" but "Adam, where are *you?*" (Gn 3:9). We must purposefully, humbly, and intelligently cultivate the ability to listen and see what is happening in our own souls and to recognize therein the movements of God, as earlier discussed.

5. We pray, speak to God constantly and specifically, about the matters that concern us. This is essential to our part of our conversation with God. You would not continue to speak to someone who did not talk with you; and you could not carry on a coherent conversation with someone who spoke to you rarely and on odd occasions only. The same is, in general, true of God.

Nothing is too insignificant or hopeless to communicate with God about. Share all things with God by lifting them to him in prayer, and ask for God's guidance, even—or perhaps especially—in those things you think you already understand.

6. Using some such regular plan as described above, *listen,* carefully and deliberately, for God. When God does speak to you, pay attention and receive his communication with thanks. It is a good habit to write down such things, at least until you become so adept at the conversational relationship that you no longer need to. If it is an insight into truth that is given, meditate on it until you have thoroughly assimilated it. If it concerns action, carry it out in a suitable manner. God does not speak to us to amuse or entertain us, but to make some difference.

7. In those cases in which God does *not* speak to you on the matter concerned:

   a. *Seek guidance on guidance.* Ask God to inform you, in whatever way he chooses, if there is some hindrance *in you.* Be quiet and listen in the "inner forum" of your mind for any indication that you are blocking guidance. But do not endlessly pursue this. In prayer, set a specific length of time for this inquiry about guidance itself—normally no more than three days. Believe that if there is a problem, God will make it clear to you. Share the robust confidence of Abraham Lincoln, who is reported to have said: "I am satisfied that, when the Almighty wants me to do, or not to do, a particular thing, He finds a way of letting me know it."

b. Counsel with at least two people whose relationship with God you respect, preferably *not* your "spiritual buddies." This may be done in a group setting if it does not concern an inherently private matter.

c. If you find a reason why guidance could not come, correct it. Whatever it is. Mercilessly. Just do it.

d. If you cannot find such a reason, then act on *what seems best to you* after itemized consideration of the details of the alternatives. If certain alternatives seem equally desirable, then select one as you wish. This will rarely be necessary, but your confidence, remember, is in the Lord who goes with you, who is with his trusting children even if they blunder and flounder. You will here not know God in his guidance, but you will know him in his faithfulness. "His compassions fail not. They are new every morning: great is thy faithfulness" (Lam 3:22–23). These words were written by the prophet Jeremiah in a time of utter failure, when the guiding hand of God was totally hidden from Israel and his punishing hand raised against them.

If we proceed in this way in quest of guidance, we will come to know God's guidance as a familiar personal fact that we can both comfortably live with and effectively introduce others into. We will know what to do when God speaks, of course. But we will also know what to do when he does not speak. We will know how to find and remove any hindrance if there is one, and how to move firmly but restfully onward, in loving peacefulness, when there is none. For God then is only inviting us to move forward to greater maturity, relying on his faithfulness alone. We will know, in short, how to live in our world with divine guidance.

Some Topics for Reflection

1. What is your response to the idea that hard study and thinking about basic issues of faith is *commanded* by God, as loving him with our minds?

2. In summary, what do you take to be the three most important points to understand about divine guidance?

3. What would be some signs that indicate that, whatever I may say, I really do not want God's guidance to have free play in my life?

4. What is the difference, if any, between not planning to be guided by God, and planning not to be guided by God?

5. What is it like to listen for God to communicate to us, and what are some practical tips that will help us to do so successfully?

6. What is the effect of too much guidance on personality? How are guidance and *deciding "on your own"* interrelated?

7. How can we be in God's perfect will with respect to matters on which he has given us no specific guidance?

8. Is it right to expect that adequate guidance will put a person "beyond risk" in life? Is it desirable to live without risk? What is the *ultimate* safety we have in God?

9. What more is there to life in Christ than being guided by God?

Notes

1. John Wood Oman, *Grace and Personality* (Cambridge, England: Cambridge University Press, 1931), 237.
2. Morgan, *How to Live,* 76.
3. James Dobson, "The Will of God," broadcast on radio station KBRT, Costa Mesa, CA, on December 3, 1982. See also the excellent chapter "Interpretations of Impressions," in Dobson's *Emotions: Can You Trust Them?* (Ventura, CA: Regal Books, 1981).
4. Meyer, *Secret of Guidance,* 43.
5. Oman, *Grace and Personality,* 251.
6. W. R. Sorley, *The Moral Life* (Cambridge, England: Cambridge University Press, 1911), 138.
7. Friesen, *Decision Making and the Will of God,* 145.
8. Brother Lawrence, *Practice of the Presence of God,* 51.
9. Pierson, *George Mueller of Bristol,* 196.
10. John Boyken, "The Door Interview: John Boyken—Rethinking the Will of God," *The Door,* no. 123 (May-June 1992): 12–16.
11. Herbert Welch, ed., *Selections from the Writings of Reverend John Wesley* (New York: Eaton & Mains, 1901), 138.

Epilogue: The Way of the Burning Heart

Blessed are those who believe without seeing!

JN 20:29

Did not our heart burn within us, while he talked with us by the way, and while he opened to us the scriptures?

LK 24:32

In this book I have tried to make a life with divine guidance, in the Way of Jesus, accessible to anyone who would enter it. I have aimed to give a biblical and experiential understanding of the theory and practice of this Way. As I release these words into the hands and hearts of readers, I am painfully aware of the one great barrier that will hinder their efforts to make such a life their own.

This barrier is what Henry Churchill King many years ago called *"the seeming unreality of the spiritual life"*[1] and could equally well be termed "the overwhelming presence of the visible world."

The visible world daily bludgeons us with its things and events, which pinch and pull and hammer away at our body and the bodies of those we love and care about. Few people arise in the morning as hungry for God as they are for cornflakes or toast and eggs. Instead of shouting and shoving, the spiritual world whispers at us ever so gently and appears wraithlike at the edges and interstices of events and things in the "real" world of the visible.

God's spiritual invasions into human life seem, by their very gentleness, almost to invite us to explain them away even as they soberly remind us that to be obsessed and ruled by the visible is death, but to give one's self over to the spiritual is life and peace (Rom 8:6).

Progress toward becoming a spiritually competent person finds its greatest hindrance in the ease with which the movements of God toward us can be explained away. The movements go meekly, without much protest. Of course their day will come. But for now they will cooperate with the desires and inclinations that make up our character as we evermore become the kind of person we will forever be.

God wants to be wanted and to be sufficiently wanted that we are *ready*, predisposed, to find him present with us. And if, by contrast, we are ready and set to find ways of explaining away his gentle presence, he will rarely respond with fire from heaven. More likely, he will simply leave us alone. We shall have our self-satisfaction that we were not so "gullible" as to respond to his soft call.

The test of character that lies in the gentleness of God's approach is especially dangerous for those formed by ideas that dominate our "modern" world. We live in a culture that has for centuries cultivated the idea that the skeptical person is always smarter than the one who believes. No matter that you can be almost as stupid as a cabbage and still doubt. The fashion of the age has identified mental sharpness with a pose, not with genuine intellectual method and character.

Thus, only a very hardy individualist or social rebel, or one desperate for another life, stands any chance of discovering the substantiality of the spiritual. Today it is the skeptics who are the social conformists, though because of powerful intellectual propaganda they continue to enjoy thinking of themselves as wildly individualistic and unbearably bright.

Partly as a result of this social force toward skepticism, which remains very powerful when we step into Christian congregations and schools for ministers, very few people ever develop competence in the life of prayer, chiefly because they are *prepared* to explain away, as "coincidences," the answers that come from prayer. Often they see this stance as a sign of how intelligent they are. ("Ha! *I* am not so easily fooled as all that!") And in their pride they close off the entrance to a life of increasingly confident and powerful prayer. They grow no further, for they have proven "to their own satisfaction" that prayer is not answered.

Nearly all areas of life in which we could become spiritually competent—including divine guidance—confront us with the same type of challenge. These areas all require of us a choice to be a spiritual person, to live a spiritual life. We are required to "bet our life" that the visible world, although real, is not reality.

We cannot make spirituality "work" without a significant degree of confidence that the visible world is always at the disposal of the unseen world of God. Our own spiritual substance and competence then grows as we put what faith we have into practice and thereby learn to distinguish and count on the characteristic "differences" that begin to emerge as the presence of God in our life. This is how, through the gospel of Christ, God's "righteousness"—what it is about him that makes him absolutely good, *really* "okay"—is revealed from faith to faith (Rom 1:17).

The greatest of divides between human beings and human cultures is that between those who regard the visible world as what is of primary importance—possibly alone real, or at least the touchstone of reality—and those who do not. Today we live in a culture that overwhelmingly gives primary, if not exclusive, importance to the visible. This stance is incorporated in the power structures that permeate our world, presided over by the university system and government.[2]

But God and the human mind and heart are not visible. "No one has ever seen God," Jesus reminds us. And although you know more about your own mind and heart than you could ever say, little or none of what you know was learned by sense perception. God and the self accordingly meet in the invisible world because they *are* invisible by nature. They are not parts of the visible world, though both are related to it.

The second of the Ten Commandments tries to help us find God by forbidding us to think of him in visual terms (Ex 20:4). This commandment forbids the use of images as representations of the divine. The entire weight of the history of Israel—and then of its extension through Jesus and his people—presses toward the understanding of God as personal, invisible reality. This God invades history to call human beings to the choice of whether they individually will live in covenant relation with him, or put something else, always something visible, in the place of ultimate importance.

This is the challenge I face every day when I awaken. It walks with me through the events of each day. Will I, like Moses, "endure as seeing Him who is invisible"? This tension is for me what it is to live as one who is learning from Christ how to live in the Kingdom of God.

Right where I am, moment to moment, I sweat it out with our brother Paul: "My visible self may be perishing, but inwardly I am renewed day to day. . . , producing something far greater than my troubles, and eternal in its glory, while we disregard the seen and focus on the unseen" (2 Cor 4:16–18).

God is not insensitive to our problem of overcoming the power of the visible world. He invades the visible. The elaborate visible provisions dictated to Moses by God—the rituals and equipment of sacrifice, tabernacle, and so forth—provided a point of constant interaction *in* the visible world between the invisible God and the people he had selected to reconcile the world to himself. There was to be a continual sacrifice, morning and evening, at the door of the tent for meeting between God and the Israelites, "where I will meet with you, and speak to you." This is the form in which God chose to "dwell among the children of Israel and be their God" (Ex 29:42–46).

The "speaking" here was not something metaphorical, as the biblical records clearly indicate. There was an *audible* voice, usually with no visible presence. Although still "physical" in the manner of sounds, it was a step away from the visible and toward the unseen and spiritual world.

As for Moses himself, when he "went into the tent of meeting to speak with God, he heard the voice speaking to him from above the mercy seat that was on the ark of the testimony, from between the two cherubim, so God spoke to him" (Num 7:98, NASB).

We have seen that the audible voice unaccompanied by visible presence continued well into the events of the New Testament. No doubt it can occur today as well because God is still alive and well on planet Earth. But the tendency of life in Christ is progressively toward the "inward word" to the receptive heart. The aim is to move *entirely* into the hidden realm of spiritual reality, where God desires to be worshiped (Jn 4:24).

God's audible voice "from heaven" also came in the presence of Jesus. But, as Jesus himself explained—on one occasion where "some said it thundered, and others thought an angel spoke to him"—"it came, not because I needed it, but to help you" (Jn 12:28–30). Jesus constantly presses us toward a life with our "Father who is in secret" (Mt 6:6)—that is, toward an eternal kind of life in the incorruptible realm of God.

After Jesus' resurrection, he appeared to his disciples in visible form only on a very few occasions over a period of forty days. His main task as their teacher during these days was to accustom them to hearing him without seeing him. Thus it was "through the Holy Ghost" that he gave instructions to his apostles during this period (Acts 1:2).

He made himself visible to them just enough to give them confidence that it was he who was speaking in their hearts. This prepared them to continue their conversation with him after he no longer appeared to them visibly.

An instructive scene from these very important days of teaching is preserved in the last chapter of Luke's Gospel. Two of Jesus' heartbroken students were walking to Emmaus, a village about seven miles northwest of Jerusalem. He caught up with them in a visible form they did not recognize and heard their sad story about what had happened to "Jesus of Nazareth" and about how, it seemed, all hope was lost.

He responded by taking them through the Scriptures and showing them how what had happened to their Jesus was exactly what was to befall the Messiah Israel hoped for. Then, as they sat at supper with him, suddenly "their eyes were opened, and they knew him; and he vanished out of their sight" (v. 31).

But the recognition went far deeper than the visual, and *that* was the whole point. They asked each other, "Did not our heart burn within us on the road as he talked to us and explained the scriptures?" (v. 32).

What were they saying to each other? They were recalling that his words always affected their "heart," their inward life, in a peculiar way and that this had been going on for about three years. No one else had had *that* effect on them. So they were asking, "Why did we not recognize him from the way his words were impacting us?" The familiar "Jesus heartburn" had certainly been a subject of discussion among the disciples on many occasions.

Soon he would rendezvous with them one last time as a visible presence. There, in the beauty and silence of the Galilean mountains, he would explain to them that he had been given say over everything in heaven and on the earth. Because of this, they were now to go to every kind of people on earth and make them his students; surround them with the reality of the Father, Son, and Holy Spirit; and teach them how to do all of the things he had commanded.

You can well imagine the degree of enthusiasm with which these poor fellows rose to greet the assignment. But his final words to them were simply: "Look, I am with you every minute, until the job is done" (Mt 28:20).

He is with us, and he speaks with us, and we with him. He speaks with us in our heart, which burns from the characteristic impact of his word. His presence with us is, of course, much greater than his words to us. But this presence is turned into *companionship* only by the actual communications between us and him, which frequently are confirmed by external events as life moves along.

This companionship with Jesus is the form that Christian spirituality takes as practiced through the ages. Spiritual persons are not those who engage in certain "spiritual practices," but those who draw their life from a conversational relationship with God. Thus they do not live their lives merely in terms of the human order in the visible world. They have "a life beyond."

And now today, as his trusting apprentices in the Kingdom of the Heavens, we live on the Emmaus road, with an intermittently burning heart. His Word pours into our heart, energizing and directing our life in a way that cannot be accounted for in "natural" terms.

The presence of the physical world is then, if I will have it so, no longer a *barrier* between me and God. My visible surroundings become, instead, God's gift to me, in which I am privileged to see the rule of heaven realized through my friendship with Jesus. He makes it so in response to my expectation. There, in some joyous measure, creation is seen moving toward "the glorious liberty of the children of God" and all because my life counts for eternity as *I* live and walk with God.

> Now is the shining fabric of our day
> Torn open, flung apart, rent wide by love.
> Never again the tight, enclosing sky,
> The blue bowl or the star-illumined tent.
> We are laid open to infinity,
> For Easter love has burst His tomb and ours.
> Now *nothing* shelters us from *God's desire*—
> Not flesh, not sky, nor stars, not even sin.
> Now glory waits so He can enter in.
> Now does the dance begin.[3]

Notes

1. Henry Churchill King, *The Seeming Unreality of the Spiritual Life* (New York: Macmillan, 1908).
2. You will be tremendously strengthened in your understanding of this situation by a study of P. A. Sorokin, *The Crisis of Our Age* (New York: Dutton, 1941).
3. Elizabeth Rooney, "The Opening." I unfortunately cannot supply a bibliographical reference for this poem or locate the author.

Index

Aaron, 99, 113, 115, 137
Abraham: covenant, 93; fathering, 44; and Lazarus, 60–61; sacrifice of Isaac, 96; and Sodom, 94; vision, 37; and wife for Isaac, 112, 181
Adam, 156–57, 230
Adler, Mortimer J., 93–94
Aevum, 171
Alienation, from God, 39, 227
Aloneness, ix, 34–58, 224
Ananias, 28, 47, 95
Angels, 93–95, 114
Arrogance, humble, 28–30
Art, physical medium of, 72
Attenborough, Richard, 28
Augustine, St., 8, 38, 126
Authority, 141; and "being right," 31; centurion and, 123, 135, 136; protection from false, 200–202; religious, xiii; university, 71; in voice of God, 188–90. *See also* Leaders; Power

Bacon, Francis, 15
Baillie, John, 12
Balaam, 26, 95, 100
Balak, 100
Barnabas, 28, 44
Berkeley, George, 131
Bible, 106, 116, 171–73; affirmation, 175; appropriation, 175–76; as communication from God, 47, 98; deism, 110–11; and fallibility, 196–98; God addressing people (six ways), 93–105; God addressing people (stories), 91–105; as "how to" book, 193; inerrancy of, 148; information with

longing, 175; invocation, 175; it's-all-in-the-Bible view, 53–55; life realization of, 202–3; needing more than, 108–10; "praying," 173–76; principles, 53–54, 191–93; priority of voice in, 114; read in a repentant manner, 172; and recognizing God's voice, 178–79, 182–85, 191–93, 196–98, 202–3, 211; role of, 62; "roulette" with, 24, 54, 55; students of, 173; understanding, 26–28; and wanting/not wanting guidance, 213; and Word of God, 148–50, 196
Biofeedback, 130
Birth, additional, 156–61, 171, 180, 227, 229
"Born again," 157, 158
Boyken, John, 227
Browning, Elizabeth Barrett, 59
Buber, Martin, 144
Bunyan, John, 196–97

Caffeine, 163
Calvin, John, 3
Carey, William, 223–24
Carrier, Norma, 34–35
Casting lots, 55
Centurion, 123, 135–36
Character: in decision making, 219–21, 223; and gentleness of God's approach, 235; for guidance, 164. *See also* Maturity
Charismata, 141
Christ. *See* Jesus
Communication, 46–47; beyond, 164, 171; confidence/comfort/peace from,

199–200; continuous, 230; fallibility and, 195–98, 211; God with ordinary human beings (four negative responses), 64; multifaceted interaction with God, 14–15, 30; one-to-one with God, 10–13; Scripture as, 172; spatialization of God's, 71–74. *See also* Guidance; Voice of God

Communion, 164–65, 171, 172

Confessions (Augustine), 8

Control, superstition and, 145, 146

Cornelius, 47

Cosmic conflict, doubting and, 224–25

Creation: finitude/restrictions, 128, 129–30; invention, 129; redemption and, 159, 169; by words, 128–31

Cults, 81, 200

Dale, R. W., 43–44

Darkness, powers of, 224–25

"Dark night of the soul," 40, 43

"Dark" sayings, 113

Darnall, Jean, 84

David, 202–4

Decision: loneliness of, ix; "on your own," 218–24. *See also* Guidance

Decision Making and the Will of God (Friesen), 106, 223

Deism, Bible, 110–11

Demonism, 143

Dobson, James, 214

Does God Speak Today? (Pytches), 60

Dorcas, 141

Doubting, and cosmic conflict, 224–25

Dreams, 95–96, 114

Ecclesiastes, 134

Eli, 3, 96–97, 112, 181

Eliab, 202

Elijah, 25, 26–27, 28, 88

Elisha, 28, 77, 141

Eternal life, 153

Eve, 156–57

Evil: hour of, 224–25; and mystery of God's Word, 181–82. *See also* Satan

Experiencing the Depths of Jesus Christ (Guyon), 173

Extrasensory events, 77

Ezekiel, 93

Faith: "blind," 39–41, 45, 50; of centurion, 123, 136; Christ's and our, 165–68; mature, 223–24; to more faith, 229; as one of greatest things, 225; and study, 209

Foster, Richard, 40

Fox, George, 7–8

Francis de Sales, St., 83–84

Frank, Charlie, 179

Freedom, standing fast in, 225–26

Friendship: beyond words, 49; with God, 23

Friesen, Garry, 106, 223

"Futurology," 15

Gadarene, wild, 164

Gandhi, 28–29

Geegh, Mary, 60

George Mueller of Bristol (Pierson), 30–31

Gideon, 13, 29, 92, 95, 215

Gladden, Washington, 150

God: "abiding," 9–10, 27, 168; addressing us, 88, 91–119, 211; alienation from, 39, 227; communicating with ordinary human beings (four negative responses), 64; as failure, 226; far away, 69–70; friends with, 23; "getting through," 71–74; greatness/lowliness of, 64–65; invisibility of, 236–38; Kingdom of, 127, 135–36, 141, 166, 198, 227; listening to, 65–66, 212, 214–16, 230; mind of, 48–51; multifaceted interaction with, 14–15, 30; necessity of general understanding of, 62–64; one-to-one with, 10–13; and order in nature, 73–74, 131, 133; "perfect" will of, 221–24; personal, x, 10–13, 45, 50, 84; rule of, 122–50, 198–99; science and, 70–71, 74–76; and silence, 108;

as taskmaster, 22–24; temple of, 50–51; using our mind to love, 208–10; will of, xi–xii, 4, 15–16, 56, 106, 221–24. *See also* Guidance; Presence of God; Voice of God; Word of God

God Guides (Geegh), 60

Goodwin, Thomas, 104

Graft, 159–60

Greatness, meaning of, 64–65

Guidance, 67–68, 153–54, 176; appropriateness of, 214; and beyond, 208–31; character for, 164; checking, 84; circumstances and, 182–86; community reactions to, 90–91; Dobson's prayer for, 214; doubting, 224–25; forcing, 217–17; forms of, 87–119; formula for living with, 228–31; greater than, 225–26; on guidance, 230–31; impressions of the Spirit and, 182–86; infallibility of, 195–98, 211–12; it's-all-in-the-Bible, 53–55; life more than, 208–31; listening for, 214–16, 230; for mature personality, 52, 114–17, 231; mechanical, 46; message-a-minute, 51–53; and method, 217; mistaken claims, 60; not a gimmick, 216–17; paradox concerning, 13–14; with passages from Bible, 182–85; personal type of, 46–47; self-aggrandizement and, 67; by shared activity, 48–51; spectacular forms, 114–15, 117–18; three lights, 182–86; "traditional view" and, 106; waiting for, 230–31; wanting/not wanting, 213–14; whatever-comes, 55–56; beyond words, 118–19; by words, 47–48, 50. *See also* Voice of God; Word of God

Guideposts, 89

Guyon, Madame, 173, 174

Hagar, 44

Hallam, A. H., 70

Heart, burning, 238–39

Hermann, Wilhelm, 12

Holy Living (Taylor), 51

Hope, as one of greatest things, 225

Huggett, Joyce, 84

Humans: "being right," 31–32; coming to ourselves, 229–30; decision making "on your own," 218–24; God personal to, x, 10–13, 45, 50, 84; God's presence and events unaccountable to, 42–44, 45, 50, 93; Jesus' answer to need of, 228; saints and heroes as, 24–28, 132; still small voice and spirit of, 88, 91, 101–5; voice of God through, 97–101, 211. *See also* Character; Life; Maturity

Humility, 28–32, 221

Hurnard, Hannah, 155

Hymns: personal God in, 12–13; whatever-comes in, 55–56

Idolatry, 227, 236

Ihde, Don, 187

Intercessor, role of, 155

Isaac, 44, 96, 112, 181

Isaiah, 9, 95, 115, 163, 180

Ishmael, 44

Israelites: Balak vs., 100; and invisibility of God, 236–37; King David of, 202–3; kingdom of God taken away from, 139; King Saul of, 202, 217–18; Moses interceding for, 38, 56; voice of God heard by, 9, 93; war with Philistines, 203, 217, 218; war with Syria, 77; water needed by, 137. *See also* Moses

Jacob, 78, 95–96

James, 25, 116–17, 125, 158, 159–60

Jean, James, 74

Jeremiah, 3, 96, 100–101, 104, 180, 231

Jericho, 94–95

Jesse, 202–3

Jesus, 24, 55, 116, 132, 143; "abiding," 9–10, 27, 168; action vs. prayer by, 139–40; and aloneness, 224; answer to human need, 228; authority of words, 188–89; baptism, 93; being in, 23, 51, 165–68; blind man healed by, 213; and centurion, 123, 135–36; companionship with, 239; death and resurrection, 161; on divine helper, 44; gleeful, 138–39; and God giving guidance, 222; on hearing, 66, 212; "heartburn," 238–39; humanity of, 25, 26, 28, 132; and invisibility of God, 236, 238; John recognizing, 180–81; and Lazarus, 60–61; leading like, 83–84; and legalism, 146; and lowliness of God, 65; "manifesting," 9; and message-a-minute, 51–52; and mind of God, 50; and Nicodemus, 157–58, 201; and oneness, 102–3; personal appearance, 89–90; Peter and, 63, 132, 193–94; principles stated by, 192; refusing religious stunts, 61; after resurrection, 238–39; Sabbath healing, 201; "speak to the mountain," 141; temptations of, 194–95; union with, 164–65, 166, 167, 168, 171; and words, 125–26, 137, 149, 158, 165, 188–89; and worthy servant, xii

Jews, 139, 160. *See also* Israelites

Jezebel, 25

Job, 46, 117

Joel, 48

John, 116–17, 141; and principles, 192; and recognizing voice of God, 180–81, 186; Simon the Sorcerer and, 147

John of the Cross, St., 40

Johnston, Russ, 15, 103

Jones, E. Stanley, 16–17, 52, 65, 114, 188

Jones, Jim, 14, 81, 200

Joseph, 95, 96

Joshua, 94–95

Joshua, Seth, 191

Judas (Iscariot), 55

Judas (Thaddeus), 9, 89

KCET, 179

King, Henry Churchill, 234

Kingdom of God, 127, 135–36, 141, 166, 198, 227

Knowledge: vs. love, 32; and still small voice, 102–3; university as authority on, 71

Landorf, Joyce, 7

Laplace, 71

Lathbury, Mary Ann, 150

Latimer, Lucy, 1–2

Laubach, Frank, 69

Law, William, 3, 173, 183–84

Lawrence, Brother, 1, 225

Lazarus, 60–61

Leaders, 78–84; and chaos in church, 78–79; cultic or Christlike, 81; guidance for, 6–9; protection from false, 200–202; redemptive relationship, 80; sheepdogs or shepherds, 79–81. *See also* Authority

Legalism: protection from, 200–202; as superstition, 146–47

Life: acknowledging new, 169–70; additional level of, 156–61, 168–71, 180, 194, 227, 229; affirming new, 170; Bible realized in, 202–3; creativity and, 130; eternal, 153; formula for living with guidance, 228–31; as light, 154–55; "living stones," 78–79; more than guidance, 208–31; reckoning new, 169–71; spiritual vs. visible, 234–40. *See also* Maturity; Spirituality

Light: becoming children of, 153–55; creation of, 128

Lights, three, 182–86

Lincoln, Abraham, 230–31

Listening: to God, 65–66, 212, 214–16, 230. *See also* Voice of God

Listening and Voice (Ihde), 187

Lively, Virginia, 89–90

Living Bible (Taylor), 7

"Living stones," 78–79
Loneliness, ix, 34–58, 224
Lord's Prayer, 67–68
Lot, 94
Love: *agape*, 21, 98; Bible on, 174–75; as one of greatest things, 225; and service, xii; using our mind to love God, 208–10; way of "being with," 22

McFarlane, Robert C., 11–12
Magic, 143–48
Man in Christ (Stewart), 168–69
Manson, Charles, 81
Marriage, as union, 164–65
Marshall, Peter, 59–60
Mary, 95
Maturity: of faith, 223–24; guidance related to, 52, 114–17, 231; and risk, 226; spectacular and, 114–15. *See also* Character
Meditation, 229
Meyer, Frederick B., 16, 182–83, 196, 215
Micah, 101
Miracle, 52
Miriam, 113, 115
Moody, Dwight Lyman, 43–44
Morgan, G. Campbell, 68–69, 178, 214
Moses, 29, 48, 92, 113; Aaron and Miriam jealous of, 113, 115; benediction, 199; and burning bush, 28, 92, 93, 98–99; and external effects, 38; and invisibility of God, 237; meekness of, 30; not eloquent, 98–99, 100; and rock with water, 137–38; and whatever-comes, 56
Mumford, Bob, 117, 190
Murray, Andrew, 109

Napoleon, Emperor, 71, 134
Naturalism, 71, 127
Nature: "godless" course, 69–70; order in, 73–74, 131, 133; "recognition" in, 179–82; and superstition, 144, 145; unity in, 133
Nebuchadnezzar, 96
Neeta, 179
Newsweek, 5
Nicodemus, 157–58, 201
Nouwen, Henri, 80

Oehler, Gustave, 96
Oman, John Wood, 208, 219–20

Palsy, 135
Pascal, Blaise, 73
Paul, 204, 220; and abundance of revelations, 5; as ambassador for Christ, 167; Ananias and, 28, 47; angels addressing, 95, 111; and Christ in us, 51, 165, 166; on Damascus road, 47, 93; first missionary journey, 44; and God's purposeful order, 74; and graft, 160; and greater things than guidance, 225; identifying with new life, 169–70; and invisibility of God, 237; on knowledge vs. love, 32; and mind of Christ, 48, 102, 165; not eloquent, 99, 100; and personal God, 45; Sadducees and, 111; on salvation, 168–69; on Scripture, 149–50; and self-knowledge of man and God, 102; seven sons of Sceva and, 147; "thorn in the flesh," 108; and union with Christ, 165, 166, 167; vision, 95; and Word of God, 141, 158–59
Penn, William, 126
Peter: healing by, 141; and Jesus, 63, 132, 193–94; on rooftop, 28, 47, 95; and Simon the Sorcerer, 147; on Word of God, 158
Pharaoh, dream of, 96
Pharisees, 111
Philip, 25
Philistines, 203, 217, 218
Phillips, J. B., 101

Physics, and theology, 74–75
Pierson, A. T., 30–31, 226
Plato, 126
Power: given to human beings, 137–39; "willpower," 130; of words/Word of God, 123–26, 133–34, 140–41. *See also* Authority
Prayer, 107, 142, 216; and action, 139–41; and "being right," 31–32; Dobson's, 214; Lord's Prayer, 67–68; *Newsweek* on, 5; Scripture reading with, 173–76; seeking guidance, 214; seeking guidance on guidance, 230–31; skepticism and, 235–36
Prayer: Conversing with God (Rinker), 107
Presence of God, 34–58; "blind" faith and, 39–41, 45, 50; conversational manner of, 45; external effects, 37–38; humanly unaccountable effects with, 42–44, 45, 50; seeing, 78; sense of, 41–43, 45, 50. *See also* Guidance
Pride, vs. humble arrogance, 30
Pytches, David, 60

Quakers, 7, 126

Redemption, 132; and creation, 159; and recognizing voice of God, 180; through Word of God, 153–76
Religionism: protection from, 200–202. *See also* Legalism
Religious authority, abuses of, xiii
Rinker, Rosalind, 107
Risk, never beyond, 226
Roberts, Evan, 191
Roberts, Oral, 6
Robinson, Bud, 221

Sabbath observances, 201
Sadducees, 6, 111
St. John, Adela Rogers, 190
Salvation: Paul on, 168–69. *See also* Redemption
Samson, 95

Samuel: and Eli, 3, 96–97, 112, 181; and King David, 202–3; and King Saul, 202, 217–18; and voice of God, 3, 28, 91, 96–97, 112, 181, 202–4
Sanford, Agnes, 61–62
Sarah, 44
Sarfatt, Jack, 75
Satan, voice of, 194–95
Satanism, 143
Saul, King, 202, 217–18
Science, and theology, 70–71, 74–76
Secret of Guidance (Meyer), 182–83
Secularism, 71
Shoemaker, Samuel, 98
Short and Very Easy Way of Prayer (Guyon), 173
Signs: limits of, 61–62; spectacular, 114–15, 117–18; unaccountable to humans, 42–44, 45, 50, 93; unreality of, 117–18
Silence: God and, 108; that speaks, 118–19
Simon the Sorcerer, 147
Skepticism, 235–36
Sodom, 94
Son of God: as Word of God, 124, 131–33. *See also* Jesus
Spirituality: Christian, xiii, 239; skeptics vs., 235–36; visible life vs. life of, 234–40; words as forces of, 125–27
"Spiritual warfare," 141
Spurgeon, Charles Haddon, 82, 110, 137, 159
Stanley, Charles, 191
Roberts, Evan, 191
Stepford Wives, 20–21
Stewart, James S., 168–69
Strong, A. H., 74
Supernatural messenger/angel, God addressing people as, 93–95, 114
Superstition, 143–47, 200

Taylor, Jeremy, 51
Taylor, Ken, 7
Temple, William, x–xi

Ten Commandments, xii, 236–37
Tennyson, Alfred Lord, 70
Teresa, Mother, 39
Thaddeus, 9, 89
Thomas, Dylan, 134–35
Thomas à Kempis, 38, 173–74
Thomas Aquinas, St., 171
Thoughts: creative, 130, 131; God addressing us through, 103–4; recurrent, 103; vain, 103–4; as words, 126
Timothy, 149–50
Tomlin, Lily, 6
Tozer, A. W., 27
Transforming Friendship (Weatherhead), 49
Twain, Mark, 143–44

UFO syndrome, 5–6
Union, 164–65, 166, 167, 168, 171, 172
University, as knowledge authority, 71

Vanity of Thoughts (Goodwin), 104
"Videolog" program, 179
Visions, 37, 95–96, 97, 114
Voice of God, 9, 41, 88, 91–105, 187–94, 210; audible, 96–97, 197, 237–38; authority in, 188–90; content of, 187, 188, 191, 194, 203–4; experience in recognizing, 179–97, 211; and fallibility, 195–98, 211–12; human, 97–101, 211; phenomenon plus, 93; practical understanding of, 198–203; principles, 191–93; priority of, 112–14; quality of, 187, 188–90, 194; recognizing, 47, 178–205, 211–12; vs. Satan's voice, 194–95; vs. spectacular, 117–18; spirit of, 187, 190, 194; still

small, 88, 91, 101–5, 113, 122–23. *See also* Word of God
Voodoo, 143–44, 145

Weatherhead, Leslie, 49
Wesley, John, 189, 224, 227–28
Westminster Abbey, 35
Westminster Cathedral, 35
Wheeler, John A., 75
Wigner, Eugene, 75
Wilkerson, David, 6–7
Will: of God, xi–xii, 4, 15–16, 56, 106, 221–24; our, 56; "perfect" will of God, 221–24; "willpower," 130
Willard, J. I., 42
Witchcraft, 143
Word of God, 124, 126–27, 153, 156; "abiding," 9–10, 27, 168; action and prayer and, 139–41; becoming children of light through, 153–55; Bible and, 148–50, 196; birth through, 156–61; vs. dream, 96; engrafted, 159–61; faith and, 123; human voice and, 97, 100–101; power of, 133, 138, 140–41; redemption through, 153–76; and rule of God, 122–50; as Son of God, 124, 131–33; "washed" in, 161–64; written, 171–73. *See also* Bible; Jesus; Voice of God
Words, 139–41, 163; creation by, 128–31; guidance beyond, 118–19; guidance by, 47–48, 50; kingdom of, 127; power of, 123–26, 133–34, 140–41; as spiritual forces, 125–27. *See also* Word of God

Zacharias, 95

DATE DUE